lonely planet

D0877294

Nepali
PHRASEBOOK & DICTIONARY

Acknowledgments

Publisher Mina Patria
Product Editor Kate Mathews
Series Designer James Hardy
Language Writers Mary-Jo O'Rourke, Bimal Man Shrestha, Krishna Pradhan
Cover Image Researcher Naomi Parker

Thanks

Elizabeth Jones, Chris Love, Wayne Murphy, Eleanor Simpson, Angela Tinson, Branislava Vladisavljevic, Tony Wheeler

Published by Lonely Planet Global Limited
CRN 554153

6th Edition – September 2014
ISBN 978 1 74321 190 8
Text © Lonely Planet 2014
Cover Image Durbar Square, Bhaktapur, Nepal, Felix Hug/Getty ©
Printed in China 10 9 8 7 6 5 4

Contact lonelyplanet.com/contact

Although the authors and Lonely Planet try to make the information as accurate as possible, we accept no responsibility for any loss, injury or inconvenience sustained by anyone using this book.

Paper in this book is certified against the Forest Stewardship Council™ standards. FSC™ promotes environmentally responsible, socially beneficial and economically viable management of the world's forests.

MIX
Paper from
responsible sources
FSC™ C021741

acknowledgments

about the authors

This edition was written by Mary-Jo O'Rourke, the primary author, and Bimal Man Shrestha, the consulting author. Krishna Pradhan provided the Sustainable Travel section of this book. Mary-Jo is a linguist, writer and editor with a special interest in Nepal and its people, in particular its languages and food. She has travelled, lived and worked in Nepal a number of times since the 1980s, and has completed a Master of Arts in Newari Linguistics at La Trobe University in Melbourne. Bimal is a Newar from Kathmandu, who now lives in Melbourne. He's bilingual in Newari and Nepali and speaks several other languages including English and Japanese. Among many other jobs, he has worked as a tour guide and as an interpreter in various languages.

from the authors

The authors wish to thank family and friends around the world for their support. Many have contributed to lively discussions of particular words and usages. Our young daughter Bellana has also been cooperative and helpful in her own special way. Particular acknowledgement goes to Dr Rita Tuladhar for her expert help with the Health chapter, especially Women's Health. *Dhan·ya·bahd* Rita.

Thanks also to the whole Lonely Planet team, especially Sophie Putman for her painstaking editing, and also Karina Coates for understanding, Ben Handicott for help with fonts and script, and Yukiyoshi Kamimura for his care with the wonderful illustrations.

make the most of this phrasebook ...

Anyone can speak another language! It's all about confidence. Don't worry if you can't remember your school language lessons or if you've never learnt a language before. Even if you learn the very basics (on the inside covers of this book), your travel experience will be the better for it. You have nothing to lose and everything to gain when the locals hear you making an effort.

finding things in this book

For easy navigation, this book is divided into sections. The Pronunciation and Grammar chapters are the ones you'll thumb through time and again. The Getting Around and Accommodation chapters cover basic travel situations like catching transport and finding a bed. The Meeting People and Interests chapters give you conversational phrases and the ability to express opinions – so you can get to know people. Food has a section all of its own: gourmets and vegetarians are covered and local dishes feature. The Health and Emergencies chapters equip you with health and police phrases, just in case. The Sustainable Travel section, finally, completes this book. Use the comprehensive Index to find everything easily. Otherwise, check the traveller's Dictionary for the word you need.

being understood

Throughout this book you'll see coloured phrases on each page. They're phonetic guides to help you pronounce the language. Start with them to get a feel for how the language sounds. The Pronunciation chapter will explain more, but you can be confident that if you read the coloured phrase, you'll be understood.

communication tips

Body language, ways of doing things, sense of humour – all have a role to play in every culture. The boxes included throughout this phrasebook give you useful cultural and linguistic information that will help you communicate with the locals and enrich your travel experience.

CONTENTS

nepali

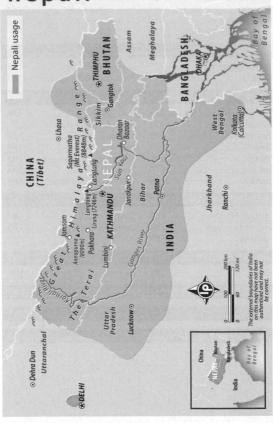

Nepali belongs to the Indo-European language family, and so is closely related to Hindi, and distantly related to various European languages, including English and French. It's been spoken (in older forms at least) since around 300 AD, when Hindu Indo-Aryans invaded the area from the south, displacing the Buddhist Kirantis.

When Nepal became a nation state in the 1760s, numerous small kingdoms were unified under one capital. There are still many ethnic groups throughout the country, each with its own culture and language. Some of these are the Kiranti, Newars, Tamang, Tharu and Tibetans (including the Sherpa), as well as the Nepali-speaking majority group. With over 100 indigenous languages, Nepali, the national language, acts as a unifying force in this heterogeneous nation of 23 million. It's also widely spoken in Sikkim, Darjeeling and other parts of India, as well as Tibet and Bhutan. In total, Nepali is spoken by some 35 million people and is a second language for about 50 per cent of the Nepalese population. Foreign-aid volunteers, researchers and other long-term foreign residents of Nepal are among the many non-native speakers.

Nepali has a number of dialects. This phrasebook uses the standard form, which is understood throughout most of the language area. It's written in the Devanagari script, a writing form also used for Hindi and the parent of both languages, Sanskrit. The Nepali alphabet has 67 characters and, unlike English, most of them have only one pronunciation. Likewise, most Nepali sounds have only one spelling. This almost one-to-one correspondence between sounds and letters means that spelling in Nepali is much more straightforward than in English.

This phrasebook includes the Devanagari script for every word, sentence and phrase (except in the Grammar chapter, where you've got enough to think about). The phonetic version is also provided in Roman script – we refer to it as the 'pronunciation guide' (you'll see it in colour next to the script). If you're having any difficulty with pronunciation, try pointing out the script to a local.

INTRODUCTION

There are some significant differences between everyday spoken Nepali and the more formal written language. However, the information in this book is presented in the informal spoken style, which is all you'll need. Nepali has a smaller vocabulary than English, which means that a word can be more general in meaning and may have several translations. For instance, *rahm·ro* (रामो) means 'good' but can also mean 'nice' or 'beautiful', depending on the context.

Since Nepal opened its doors to foreigners and tourism in 1951, it has become very popular with travellers from all over the world. Most Nepalese in urban and popular tourist areas speak some English, as it's a compulsory school subject. However, as you move away from the main tourist centres, it does get harder to find local people who speak more than rudimentary English, as many hill villages continue to lack even the most basic educational facilities. Besides, as a traveller you'll find that life in Nepal is easier and a lot more interesting if you try to learn a little of the language. Even if you're not fluent, being able to communicate on a basic level will help to narrow the cultural gap and thus deepen your experience.

All you need to make learning enjoyable are a few Nepalese companions to practise with – impossible to avoid in friendly Nepal. Simply gather a few phrases from this book and prepare yourself for some fascinating encounters. Good luck in your travels and na·ma·*ste* (नमस्ते), 'best wishes'!

ABBREVIATIONS USED IN THIS BOOK

adj	adjective	m	masculine
ani	animate	pl	plural
f	feminine	pol	polite
inani	inanimate	poss	possessive
inf	informal	sg	singular
lit	literal translation		

PRONUNCIATION

Nepali is fairly easy to pronounce because many of the vowel and consonant sounds of English are also found in Nepali.

In this book we provide both the Nepali script and the way you pronounce it – phonetic guides are in colour next to the phrases. We break up the Nepali words into syllables and where these are italicised, you should stress that part of the word as you say it.

VOWELS

Nepali has six vowels and two diphthongs (vowel combinations) – all but one of these (o) also occur as nasal vowels, making 15 vowels in total. The nasals are pronounced with the airstream coming out of the nose. Speakers of English can approximate this by putting a weak 'n' at the end of such a syllable. Nasals are indicated in the text by a tilde (~) over the vowel.

SOUND	DESCRIPTION
a/ã	as the 'u' in 'cup'
ah/ãh	as the 'a' in 'father'
i/ī	as the 'ee' in 'see', but shorter
u/ū	as the 'u' in 'put'
e/ē	as the 'e' in 'bet'
o	as the 'o' in 'hot'

Diphthongs (Vowel Combinations)

Diphthongs consist of two vowels pronounced together as a single syllable, such as the 'ou' in 'out'. As with single vowels, diphthongs may also be nasalised in Nepali.

SOUND	DESCRIPTION
ai/aī	as the 'ai' in 'aisle'
au/aū	as the 'ow' in 'vow', but shorter

CONSONANTS

Most Nepali consonants are pronounced the same as you would expect in English, but for easy reference all are listed below in English alphabetical order:

SOUND	DESCRIPTION
b	as the 'b' in 'bat'
c	as the 'ch' in 'chew'
d	as the 'd' in 'dog'
g	as the 'g' in 'get', always hard
h	more forcefully than in English, except in the middle of a word, where hardly pronounced at all
j	as the 'j' in 'jaw' (you may also hear it pronounced as the 'ds' in 'bands' or the 'z' in 'zebra')
k	as the 'k' in 'skin'
l	as the 'l' in 'last', always clear
m	as the 'm' in 'mother'
n	as the 'n' in 'now'
ng	as the 'ng' in 'finger'
ny	as the 'ny' in 'canyon'
p	as the 'p' in 'spot'
r	trilled slightly and clearer than the English 'r'
s	as the 's' in 'sit'
sh	as the 'sh' in 'ship' (you may also hear it pronounced as the English 's')
t	as the 't' in 'stop'
w	as the 'w' in 'word'
y	as the 'y' in 'yellow'

Occasionally, you'll come across doubled consonants in words. A doubled consonant means the sound is pronounced twice – this is important for the correct meaning to be conveyed:

ka·mal	lotus	*kam*·mal	blanket
chah·nu	sloping roof	*chahm*·nu	to choose

PRONUNCIATION

Aspirated Consonants

Aspirated consonants are pronounced much more forcefully than their unaspirated counterparts (listed above) and with a puff of air, like the 'th' in 'hothouse'.

Aspiration is indicated in the text by an h following the consonant, so th represents an aspirated t. Don't confuse this with the English sound 'th' (as in 'think' or 'then'), which doesn't occur at all in Nepali. There's one exception: sh is not an aspirated s but is pronounced as the 'sh' in 'ship'.

The aspirated consonants are listed below in English alphabetical order:

SOUND	DESCRIPTION
bh	as the 'b' in 'bus', pronounced with a puff of air
ch	as the 'ch' and following 'h' in 'punch hard'
dh	as the 'd' in 'duck', pronounced with a puff of air
gh	as the 'g' in 'go', pronounced with a puff of air
jh	as the 'j' in 'jump', pronounced with a puff of air
kh	as the 'k' in 'kill'
ph	as the 'p' in 'pit' (you may also hear it pronounced like an 'f' made with both lips)
th	as the 't' in 'time'

Aspiration is used to differentiate between the meaning of words in Nepali, so the difference in pronunciation is important:

kahm	work	khahm	envelope
tahl	lake/pond	thahl	plate
be·lah	time	*bhe*·lah	meeting

Retroflex Consonants

Retroflex sounds are made by curling your tongue up and back towards the roof of your mouth. In Nepali d and t – both unaspirated and aspirated – and n occur as retroflex sounds. These are the sounds that make the Nepali (and Indian) pronunciation so distinctive from English! They're not too difficult to get the hang of with a bit of practice – try saying the sound several times, moving your tongue a bit further back along the roof of your mouth each time.

Retroflex d and dh are sometimes also pronounced as a retroflex r which is a quick flap of the tongue against the roof of the mouth, like the 'd' sound in 'ladder' when said quickly. Retroflex consonants are indicated throughout the text by a dot beneath the letter.

As the following examples show, the pronunciation of retroflex consonants is important for the correct meaning to be conveyed:

top	cannon	ṭop	helmet
dho·kah	fraud	*dho*·kah	door/gate

STRESS

The position of the stressed syllable in Nepali words depends on whether the vowels are short or long, and whether the syllables end in vowels or consonants. As a rough guide, in two-syllable words the last syllable is normally the stressed one, while in words of three or more syllables it's normally the second-last syllable. The pronunciation guides show you the word stress: the emphasis in each word is indicated in italics.

ka·*lah*	art	din·*car*·yah	diary

THE NEPALESE ALPHABET

Nepali is written in the Devanagari script. Each character contains part of (or is on) a horizontal line, and characters are joined together into words by this line. The vowel a is inherent in the basic form of all consonants, so k would be pronounced ka instead. Different symbols are written before, after or below the consonant to indicate different vowel sounds (see page 16). The complete Nepali alphabet is listed below (in Nepali alphabetical order). Note that there's no differentiation between upper and lower case; also, some sounds have two written forms but are said the same way.

PRONUNCIATION

THE NEPALESE ALPHABET

Vowels

अ	आ	इ	ई	उ	ऊ	ऋ	ए	ऐ	ओ	औ
a	ah	i	i	u	u	ri	e	ai	o	au

Consonants

क	ख	ग	घ	ङ
k	kh	g	gh	ng

च	छ	ज	झ	ञ
c	ch	j	jh	ny

ट	ठ	ड	ढ	ण
t	th	d	dh	n

त	थ	द	ध	न
t	th	d	dh	n

प	फ	ब	भ	म
p	ph	b	bh	m

य	र	ल	व	
y	r	l	w	

श	ष	स	ह	
sh	s	s	h	

In the Devanagari script, nasal vowels are indicated by either a dot or half circle and dot above the letter, as shown below:

| here | ya·hāh | यहाँ |
| finger | aū·lah | औंला |

Vowels

Vowels, other than a, have two forms: a full one when written alone or at the beginning of a word, and an abbreviated form when attached to a consonant. The abbreviated form is written above, below or beside the consonant, as indicated below :

Vowel	ah	o	e	i	u
Symbol	ा	ो	`	ि/ी	ु/ू
Position	after	after	above	before/after	below

To illustrate, we've taken the first consonant k (क) as an example:

Script	Pronunciation
का	kah
को	ko
के	ke
कि / की	ki
कु / कू	ku

Note that the two different forms of i and u are pronounced identically.

This chapter contains basic information to help you make your own sentences. There are plenty of examples, including a pronunciation guide for each. This will increase your ability to communicate simply – just insert different vocabulary items into the basic sentences provided.

WORD ORDER

Nepali word order is usually subject-object-verb, rather than subject-verb-object, as it is in English:

Anita read the book.   a·*ni*·ta ki·*tahb lekh*·yo
                           (lit: Anita book read)

The Nepali verb comes at the end of the sentence, with any objects or locations before it. In spoken Nepali, information that's clear from context, or not relevant in a particular situation, will generally be left out. This includes subject pronouns, particularly 'I':

I'm a traveller.   *yah*·tri hũ
                           (lit: traveller am)

ARTICLES & DEMONSTRATIVES

In Nepali, there are no articles like the English 'the' or 'a/an'. Whether the speaker is referring to 'a market', 'the market' or 'market' is clear from context:

Where's the market?   ba·*jahr ka*·hãh cha?
                           (lit: market where is?)

To be specific, the demonstratives 'this', yo, or 'that', tyo, can be used:

I see the old building.   ma tyo pu·*rah*·no ghar
                           her·chu
                           (lit: I that old building see)

The plural forms 'these', yi, and 'those', ti, may be used in a similar way. In everyday speech, however, singular forms are often used even with plural subjects:

those people   tyo *mahn*·che·ha·ru
                        (lit: that people)

The demonstratives yo and tyo are also used as third-person pronouns to mean 'he', 'she' and 'it' (see Pronouns, page 19).

AFTER THE FACT

Keep in mind that Nepali has postpositions that come after the noun, instead of prepositions as in English.

The book is on the table.   ki·*tahb* ṭe·bul·mah cha
                             (lit: book table-on is)

For more, see page 33.

NOUNS

To make a noun plural, the ending -ha·ru is added, although in speech it's often left out when plurality is clear from context or unimportant.

friend   *sah*·thi
friends   *sah*·thi·ha·ru

Spoken Nepali is also sometimes grammatically simplified. In everyday speech, singular forms are often used with a plural meaning.

Where are the books?   ki·*tahb* ka·hāh cha?
                        (lit: book where is?)

instead of:

Where are the books?   ki·*tahb*·ha·ru ka·hāh chan?
                        (lit: books where are?)

Nepali nouns have no grammatical gender (such as masculine/feminine/neuter), but they can have different endings, depending on how they're used in a sentence (see Pronouns, pages 19 - 21).

GRAMMAR

PRONOUNS

Nepali pronouns have both formal and informal variations – you should use the formal ones, except with intimate friends, children and animals. Formal forms are used throughout this book, unless indicated otherwise.

Subject Pronouns

Like nouns, pronouns have no grammatical gender. There are three informal third-person singular pronouns commonly used, two of which (tyo/yo) can mean 'he', 'she' or 'it', and a third, *u*·ni, which can only mean 'he' or 'she'. Apart from *u*·ni, the pronouns are interchangeable and are often omitted in speech when they can be understood from context (for example, when they're the subject of the sentence (see page 17)).

SUBJECT PRONOUNS			
Singular		**Plural**	
I	ma	we	*hah*·mi(·ha·ru)
you (inf)	*ti*·mi	you (inf)	*ti*·mi·ha·ru
you (pol)	ta·*paī*	you (pol)	ta·*paī*·ha·ru
he/she (inf)	*u*·ni (ani)	they (inf)	*u*·ni·ha·ru (ani)
he/she/it (inf)	tyo/yo (inani)	they (inf)	ti/yi (inani)
he/she (pol)	*wa*·hāh	they (pol)	*wa*·hāh·ha·ru

Note that for 'we', the short form *hah*·mi is often used instead of the full form *hah*·mi·ha·ru. Remember also that *u*·ni and *u*·ni·ha·ru are used only for animate (living) objects. For inanimate (not living) objects, use tyo/yo (sg) and ti/yi (pl).

Pronouns (like nouns) take different endings according to their function in the sentence (whether they're the subject or object, or indicate possession or location). These endings generally translate as prepositions like 'to', 'of' and 'with' in English. For subjects of sentences without objects, however, the basic pronouns are used without any additional endings:

He/She sleeps.   *u*·ni *sut*·cha (inf)
                   (lit: he/she sleeps)

GRAMMAR

Where sentences do contain objects, the ending -le is generally added to the basic subject pronoun. This ending is a grammatical requirement but makes no difference to the meaning. There are some irregular forms to note. The first-person singular ma becomes *mai·le* and the third-person singular forms tyo and yo become tyas·le and yas·le:

I understand this.	*mai·le yo bujh·chu*
	(lit: I-le this understand)

When used with nouns, the ending -le translates as 'by', 'with', 'from', 'of' or 'in', according to context:

In the opinion of the	sar·*kahr*·ko *rah*·ya·le ...
government ...	(lit: government-ko opinion-le)

Sentences can contain two instances of -le – one attached to the subject pronoun and one attached to the instrument (in this example, 'the broom'):

He/She swept the floor	*wa*·hāh·le *ku*·co·le bhui la·*gah*·yo
with the broom.	(lit: he/she-le broom-le floor swept)

TYPICAL ENDINGS

A challenge for English speakers may be to remember to add the Nepali noun/pronoun endings -le (for subjects), -lai (for objects) and -ko (for possessives), which generally translate as prepositions – (such as 'by', 'to' and 'of') in English.

I cooked rice.	*mai·le bhaht pak·ah·ē*
	(lit: I-le rice cooked)
He/She gives me tea.	*wa·hāh·le ma·lai ci·yah di·nu·hun·cha*
	(lit: he/she-le I-lai tea gives)
This is Rita's book.	yo *ri·ta·ko ki·tahb* ho
	(lit: this Rita-ko book is)

However, don't worry if you find the endings hard to master – context will often make it clear.

Object Pronouns

Pronouns and nouns used as objects (whether direct or indirect objects) normally take the grammatical ending -lai, particularly if the object is a name or refers to a person:

I see Anita. ma a·*ni*·ta·lai *her*·chu
(lit: I Anita-lai see)

The ending -lai often translates as 'to' or 'for', as in the following example:

I give it to you. ma yo ta·*paī*·lai *din*·chu
(lit: I it you-lai give)

If an object is inanimate, -lai is usually left out.

He/She made a chair. *wa*·hāh mec ba·*nah*·yo
(lit: he/she chair made)

Sometimes, subject nouns and pronouns also take the ending -lai. These are really grammatical objects in Nepali, but translate as subjects in English:

I feel tired. *ma*·lai *tha*·kai *lahg*·yo
(lit: I-lai tired feel)

POSSESSIVES

The possessive ending for both nouns and pronouns is -ko, 'of'. Since several possessive pronouns are irregular, they're all listed below.

POSSESSIVES			
Singular		Plural	
my	*me*·ro	our	*hahm*·ro
your (inf)	*tim*·ro	your (inf)	*ti*·mi·ha·ru·ko
your (pol)	ta·*paī*·ko	your (pol)	ta·*paī*·ha·ru·ko
her/his (inf)	*u*·ni·ko	their (inf)	*u*·ni·ha·ru·ko
her/his/its (inf)	*tyas*·ko/ *yas*·ko		
her/his/its (pol)	*wa*·hāh·ko	their (pol)	*wa*·hāh·ha·ru·ko

GRAMMAR

This is our baby.	yo *hahm*·ro *bac*·cah ho
	(lit: this our baby is)
Where's the tiger's lair?	*bahgh*·ko ghar *ka*·hāh cha?
	(lit: tiger-ko lair where is?)

As in English, possessives come before the nouns they refer to.

my cat	*me*·ro bi·*rah*·lo
	(lit: my cat)
Ram's shirt	*rahm*·ko ka·*mij*
	(lit: Ram-ko shirt)

Possessive pronouns can also stand alone, in which case they translate as 'mine, ours, yours, his, hers, its, theirs'.

Is this hat yours?	yo *ţo*·pi ta·*paī*·ko ho?
	(lit: this hat yours is?)
This room is ours.	yo *ko*·ţhah *hahm*·ro ho
	(lit: this room ours is)

ADJECTIVES & DEMONSTRATIVES

As in English, Nepali adjectives precede the nouns they refer to:

expensive shop	ma·*hā*·go *pa*·sal
	(lit: expensive shop)
tall woman	*a*·glo *ai*·mai
	(lit: tall woman)

To compare two things, attach -bhan·dah, 'than', to the noun that would follow 'than' in English:

| Ram is bigger than Anita. | rahm a·*ni*·ta·bhan·dah *ţhu*·lo cha |
| | (lit: Ram Anita-than big is) |

To create a superlative, insert*sab*·bhan·dah 'than all' before the adjective:

Mt Everest is Nepal's	*sa*·gar·*mah*·thah ne·*pahl*·ko
highest mountain.	*sab*·bhan·dah *u*·co pa·*hahḍ* ho
	(lit: Mt-Everest Nepal-ko
	than-all high mountain is)

VERBS

Verb formation in Nepali is fairly straightforward, except with the verb 'to be' (see page 27). There are quite a few tenses, but you only really need to know the present and past tense forms and their negatives. Simple additions to these give you the continuous, future and imperative verb forms. Each section includes a list of tense endings, with an example, so you can easily look up the verb form you need at the time.

Nepali verbs are made up of two parts: the stem and the tense ending. The stem stays the same, while the ending changes according to person (first/second/third) and number (singular/plural). Infinitives (the dictionary form of a verb) end in -nu:

| to do | *gar*·nu | to eat | *khah*·nu | to go | *jah*·nu |

Negation

There's no single negative form in Nepali that corresponds to 'not' in English. Instead, the verb forms for each person and number take a different ending to form the negative. They do follow a pattern, however, and are not difficult to learn alongside the positive ones. For this reason, positive and negative forms are listed together in the following verb sections.

The Neutral Verb

In conversation, the Nepalese commonly use a versatile neutral verb form for present and, especially, future tenses. It's used mainly in short statements and questions, and pronouns are usually left out. This is the simplest verb form to use when you get stuck!

The ending -ne replaces the infinitive ending -nu to form this neutral verb, and its negative is simply formed with the prefix na-:

Let's go out.	*bah*·hi·ra *jah*·ne
	(lit: outside to-go)
Let's not go out.	*bah*·hi·ra na-*jah*·ne
	(lit: outside not-to-go)

Present Tense

The present tense is used for regular actions and corresponds to the present in English:

I work every day.　　ma *din*·hū kahm *gar*·chu
　　　　　　　　　　(lit: I daily work do)

As in English, it can also be used to indicate the future:

Next week we go to Nepal.　*au*·ne *hap*·tah *hah*·mi
　　　　　　　　　　　　　ne·*pahl jahn*·chaū
　　　　　　　　　　　　　(lit: next week we Nepal go)

Informal

To make the informal forms of the present tense, the following endings are added to the infinitive:

I do/don't	ma	*gar*·chu/*gar*·di·na
you (sg) do/don't	*ti*·mi	*gar*·chau/*gar*·dai·nau
he/she/it does/doesn't	*u*·ni/tyo/yo	*gar*·cha/*gar*·dai·na
we do/don't	*hah*·mi(·ha·ru)	*gar*·chaū/*gar*·dai·naū
you (pl) do/don't	*ti*·mi·ha·ru	*gar*·chau/*gar*·dai·nau
they do/don't	*u*·ni·ha·ru	*gar*·cha/*gar*·dai·nan

Polite

In the present tense, the polite verb forms all add the same endings to the infinitive: -hun·cha in the positive, and -hun·na in the negative:

you (sg) do/don't	ta·*paī*	
you (pl) do/don't	ta·*paī*·ha·ru	*gar*·nu·hun·cha/
he/she does/doesn't	*wa*·hāh	*gar*·nu·hun·na
they do/don't	*wa*·hāh·ha·ru	

Verbs whose stems end in a vowel keep the n – remember that ah is a vowel (see Pronunciation, page 11):

| to go | *jah*·nu | I go | ma *jahn*·chu |
| to come | *au*·nu | I come | ma *aun*·chu |

ESSENTIAL VERBS

to arrive	*pug·nu*	to leave	*choḍ·nu*
to ask	*sodh·nu*	to look/watch	*her·nu*
to be	*hu·nu*	to make	*ba·nau·nu*
to be able	*sak·nu*	to read	*paḍh·nu*
to call	*bo·lau·nu*	to remember	*sam·jha·nu*
to carry	*bok·nu*	to say	*bhan·nu*
to come	*au·nu*	to see	*dekh·nu*
to die	*mar·nu*	to speak	*bol·nu*
to do	*gar·nu*	to stay/sit/live	*bas·nu*
to drink	*pi·u·nu*	to stop	*rok·nu*
to eat	*khah·nu*	to take	*li·nu*
to forget	*bir·sa·nu*	to tell	*bhan·nu*
to give	*di·nu*	to understand	*bujh·nu*
to go	*jah·nu*	to want/need	*cah·ha·nu*
to hear/listen	*sun·nu*	to write	*lekh·nu*

Continuous Tense

The present continuous is common in spoken Nepali, and corresponds to the English present continuous – the '-ing' form. The continuous tense can be applied to the present, past and future tenses. It's formed by inserting -dai- between the verb stem and the ending. Like the simple present, it may also be used to indicate future (see page 27). The present continuous for the verb 'to eat', *khah·nu*, is listed below:

Informal

I am eating	ma	*khahn·dai·chu*
you (sg) are eating	*ti·mi*	*khahn·dai·chau*
he/she/it is eating	*u·ni/tyo/yo*	*khahn·dai·cha*
we are eating	*hah·mi(·ha·ru)*	*khahn·dai·chaũ*
you (pl) are eating	*ti·mi·ha·ru*	*khahn·dai·chau*
they are eating	*u·ni·ha·ru*	*khahn·dai·chan*

GRAMMAR

GRAMMAR

Polite

you (sg) are/aren't eating	ta·*paī*	*khahn*·dai·hu·nu·hun·cha
he/she is/isn't eating	*wa*·hāh	*khahn*·dai·hu·nu·hun·na
you (pl) are/aren't eating	ta·*paī*·ha·ru	*hahn*·dai·hu·nu·hun·cha
they are/aren't eating	*wa*·hāh·ha·ru	*khahn*·dai·hu·nu·hun·na

Past Tense

The past tense is used for completed past actions, and corresponds to the English past tense.

Informal

Below are the informal positive and negative forms for the verb 'to do', *gar*·nu:

I did/didn't	ma	*ga*·rē/*ga*·ri·nā
you (sg) did/didn't	*ti*·mi	*gar*·yau/*ga*·re·nau
he/she/it did/didn't	*u*·ni/tyo/yo	*gar*·yo/*ga*·re·na
we did/didn't	*hah*·mi(·ha·ru)	*gar*·yaū/*ga*·re·naū
you (pl) did/didn't	*ti*·mi·ha·ru	*gar*·yau/*ga*·re·nau
they did/didn't	*u*·ni·ha·ru	*ga*·rel/*ga*·re·nan

Polite

For the polite forms, attach -bha·yo (for positive past tense) and -bha·e·na (for negative past tense) after the infinitive:

you did/didn't (sg)	ta·*paī*	
you did/didn't (pl)	ta·*paī*·ha·ru	*gar*·nu·bha·yo/
he/she did/didn't	*wa*·hāh	*gar*·nu·bha·e·na
they did/didn't	*wa*·hāh·ha·ru	

When a past tense sentence contains an object, the subject always takes the ending -le (see page 20):

I did it.	*mai*·le yo *ga*·rē
	(lit: I-le it did)
I didn't do it.	*mai*·le yo *ga*·ri·nā
	(lit: I-le it didn't)

Future Tense

The simplest and most common future tense used in spoken Nepali is formed with a positive or negative verb in the present tense followed by *ho*·lah (the third-person singular future form of 'to be', see page 28):

I will go.	ma *jahn*·chu *ho*·lah
	(lit: I go will-be)
They will not go.	*wa*·hāh·ha·ru
	jah·nu·hun·na *ho*·lah
	(lit: they not-go will-be)

TO BE

The Nepali verb 'to be', *hu*·nu, is complex – it's explained below in full detail. There are three alternate present tense forms of *hu*·nu: cha, ho and *hun*·cha, each used in a different way. The most common forms cha and ho both translate as 'is' and they're sometimes interchangeable. Generally cha is used for location (indicating where) and ho for defining (indicating who and what):

My house is in Nepal.	*me*·ro ghar ne·*pahl*·mah cha
	(lit: my house Nepal-in is)
My mother is a doctor.	*me*·ro ah·mah ḍahk·ṭar ho
	(lit: my mother doctor is)

Although *hun*·cha also translates as 'is', it refers to general facts or events, unlike cha or ho:

This mango is sweet.	yo āhp *gu*·li·yo cha
	(lit: this mango sweet is)
Mangoes are sweet.	āhp *gu*·li·yo *hun*·cha
	(lit: mango sweet is)

GRAMMAR

Present Tense
Informal

Cha

I am/am not	ma	chu/*chai*·na
you (sg) are/are not	*ti*·mi	chau/*chai*·nau
he/she/it is/is not	*u*·ni/tyo/yo	cha/*chai*·na
we are/are not	*hah*·mi(·ha·ru)	chaũ/*chai*·naũ
you (pl) are/are not	*ti*·mi·ha·ru	chau/*chai*·nau
they are/are not	*u*·ni·ha·ru	chan/*chai*·nan

Ho

I am/am not	ma	hũ/*hoi*·na
you (sg) are/are not	*ti*·mi	hau/*hoi*·nau
he/she/it is/is not	*u*·ni/tyo/yo	ho/*hoi*·na
we are/are not	*hah*·mi(·ha·ru)	haũ/*hoi*·naũ
you (pl) are/are not	*ti*·mi·ha·ru	hau/*hoi*·nau
they are/are not	*u*·ni·ha·ru	hun/*hoi*·nan

GRAMMAR

Huncha

As well as the irregular present tense forms of cha and ho, *hu*·nu has a set of regular present tense forms, made from the stem hu· and the usual present tense endings (see page 23):

I am/am not	ma	*hun*·chu/*hun*·di·na
you are/are not (sg)	*ti*·mi	*hun*·chau/
		hun·dai·nau
he/she/it is/is not	*u*·ni/tyo/yo	*hun*·cha/*hun*·dai·na
we are/are not	*hah*·mi(·ha·ru)	*hun*·chaũ/
		hun·dai·naũ
you are/are not (pl)	*ti*·mi·ha·ru	*hun*·chau/
		hun·dai·nau
they are/are not	*u*·ni·ha·ru	*hun*·chan/
		hun·dai·nan

Polite

The polite versions are the same for cha, ho and *hun*·cha:

you (sg) are/are not	ta·*paī*	
you (pl) are/are not	ta·*paī*·ha·ru	*hu*·nu·hun·cha/
he/she is/is not	*wa*·hāh	*hu*·nu·hun·na
they are/are not	*wa*·hāh·ha·ru	

Past Tense
Cha & Ho

Informal

In the past tense, cha and ho are identical:

I was/was not	ma	*thi*·ēl/*thi*·e·nā
you (sg) were/were not	*ti*·mi	*thi*·yau/*thi*·e·nau
he/she/it was/was not	*u*·ni/tyo/yo	*thi*·yo/*thi*·e·na
we were/were not	*hah*·mi(·ha·ru)	*thi*·yaū/*thie*·naū
you (pl) were/were not	*ti*·mi·ha·ru	*thi*·yau/*thi*·e·nau
they were/were not	*u*·ni·ha·ru	*thi*·el/*thi*·e·nan

Polite

The positive and negative polite forms are as follows:

you (sg) were/were not	ta·*paī*	
you (pl) were/were not	ta·*paī*·ha·ru	*hu*·nu·hun·thyo/
he/she was/was not	*wa*·hāh	*hu*·nu·hun·na·thyo
they were/were not	*wa*·hāh·ha·ru	

Huncha
Informal

I was/was not	ma	*bha*·ēl/*bha*·i·nā
you (sg) were/were not	*ti*·mi	*bha*·yau/*bha*·e·nau
he/she/it was/was not	*u*·ni/tyo/yo	*bha*·yo/*bha*·e·na
we were/were not	*hah*·mi(·ha·ru)	*bha*·yaū/*bha*·e·naū
you (pl) were/were not	*ti*·mi·ha·ru	*bha*·yau/*bha*·e·nau
they were/were not	*u*·ni·ha·ru	*bha*·el/*bha*·e·nan

GRAMMAR

Polite

you (sg) were/were not	ta·*paī*	
you (pl) were/were not	ta·*paī*·ha·ru	*hu*·nu·bha·yo/
he/she was/was not	*wa*·hāh	*hu*·nu·bha·e·na
they were/were not	*wa*·hāh·ha·ru	

MORE OF THE OTHER

There are two words in Nepali meaning 'other': *ar*·ko 'the other of two' is generally used with singular nouns, while *a*·ru 'other, else, more' is used with plural nouns and objects that can't be counted:

I'll give you the other book.　　ma ta·*paī*·lai *ar*·ko
　　　　　　　　　　　　　　　　ki·*tahb* *din*·chu
　　　　　　　　　　　　　　　　(lit: I you-to other book give)

Please drink more tea.　　　　　*a*·ru ci·yah *piu*·nu·hos
　　　　　　　　　　　　　　　　(lit: more tea drink-hos)

TO HAVE

There's no verb equivalent to the English 'to have'. The idea of possession is expressed using a form of cha, 'to be', plus a possessive noun or pronoun:

He/She has five children.　　　*wa*·hāh·ko pahnc *ja*·nah
　　　　　　　　　　　　　　　　cho·rah·*cho*·ri chan
　　　　　　　　　　　　　　　　(lit: his/her five people
　　　　　　　　　　　　　　　　children are)

If the possession is portable, one of the 'with' postpositions, -sā·ga or -si·ta (see page 33), is added to the possessor:

Do you have some money?　　　ta·*paī*·sā·ga *pai*·sah cha?
　　　　　　　　　　　　　　　　(lit: you-with money is?)

I don't have a pen.　　　　　　*ma*·sā·ga *ka*·lam *chai*·na
　　　　　　　　　　　　　　　　(lit: I-with pen is-not)

MODALS

Nepali, particularly in its spoken form, almost always makes use of two or more verbs, including a modal (such as 'can', 'must' or 'should' in English) which comes after the main verb. The most common modals are (man) *lahg*·nu, 'to be felt/to seem', and (man) *par*·nu, 'to like/to be necessary'.

The present tense verb forms (*lahg*·cha and *par*·cha) are used for general situations and the past tense forms (*lahg*·yo and *par*·yo) are used for particular situations (as well as events that happened in the past), as reflected in the examples below:

Women like to dance.	*ai*·mai·ha·ru *nahc*·na (man) *lahg*·cha (lit: women to-dance feels)
Today I feel like eating spicy food.	*ah*·ja *ma*·lai *pi*·ro *khah*·nah *khah*·lai·na (man) *lahg*·yo (lit: today me spicy food to-eat felt)

Both verbs are also commonly used in a non-modal context – (man) *lahg*·nu 'to be felt' and (man) *par*·nu 'to fall':

I'm hungry.	*ma*·lai bhok *lahg*·yo (lit: me hunger felt)
Today it rains/will rain.	*ah*·ja *pah*·ni *par*·cha (lit: today rain falls)
Yesterday it rained.	*hi*·jo *pah*·ni *par*·yo (lit: yesterday rain fell)

Necessity

To express necessity, use the infinitive form of the main verb, plus a third-person singular form of the modal verb *par*·nu (see above).

It's necessary to walk there.	*tya*·hāh *hĩd*·nu·par·cha (lit: there walk-must)
It isn't necessary to come to this office.	yo kahr·*yah*·la·ya·*mah au*·nu·par·dai·na (lit: this office-to come-must-not)

The subject is usually omitted; if expressed, it takes -lai where there is no object and -le where there is an object.

I need to sleep.   ma·lai *sut*·nu·par·cha
                                 (lit: I-lai sleep-must)

I have to wash these clothes.   *mai*·le yo *lu*·gah *hu*·nu·par·cha
                                 (lit: I-le this clothing wash-must)

TO BE

The verb *hu·nu* 'to be' has a complex conjugation with three present-tense forms, each used differently. You may need to keep referring back to this section (page 27 - 30) for a while.

IMPERATIVE

The imperative form is used for giving orders or making requests. To make a polite imperative, add the suffix -hos to the infinitive ending -nu. To negate this, use the prefix na-:

Please eat.   *khah*·nu·hos
                                 (lit: to-eat-hos)

Please don't tell me.   ma·lai na·*bhan*·nu·hos
                                 (lit: I-to na-to-tell-hos)

Could you tell me where   ma·lai *bhan*·nu·hos, *me*·ro
my room is?   *ko*·thah *ka*·hāh cha?
                                 (lit: I-to tell-to-hos, my
                                 room where is)

QUESTIONS
'Yes/No' Questions

In Nepali, the simplest way to ask a question is to raise the tone of your voice at the end of the sentence. To answer a 'yes/no' question, repeat the main verb in the affirmative or negative:

Are you Nepalese?   ta·*paī* ne·*pah*·li
                                 hu·nu·hun·cha?
                                 (lit: you Nepali are?)

Yes (I am).   *hu*·nu·hun·cha
No (I'm not).   *hu*·nu·hun·na

GRAMMAR

Information Questions

Question words, which normally precede the verb, are used to form information questions:

How? (by what means)	*ka*·sa·ri?
How? (quality)	*kas*·to?
How much/many?	*ka*·ti?
What?	ke?
When?	*ka*·hi·le?
Where?	*ka*·hāh?
Which?	kun?
Who?	ko?
Whose?	*kas*·ko?
Why?	*ki*·na?

Where's the tiger?	bahgh *ka*·hāh cha?
	(lit: tiger where is?)
Whose book is this?	yo *kas*·ko ki·*tahb* ho?
	(lit: this whose book is?)

GRAMMAR

POSTPOSITIONS

In Nepali, 'prepositions' follow the noun they refer to and so are usually called postpositions.

about	*-ti*·ra	in front of	*-a*·*gah*·ḍi
after	*-pa*·chi	inside	*-bhi*·tra
at/in/on/to	-mah	near/close	*-na*·jik
behind	*-pa*·*chah*·ḍi	of	-ko
between	-bic	out(side)	*-bah*·hi·ra
by/with	-le	to	-lai
far	*-ṭah*·ḍhah	up	*-mah*·thi
for (the sake of)	-ko *lah*·gi	under	*-mu*·ni
from (time)	*-de*·khi	without	*-bi*·na
from (place)	*-bah*·ṭa	with/by	*-sā*·gal/*-si*·ta

I live near the market.	ma ba·*jahr*·na·jik *bas*·chu
	(lit: I market-near live)
What's in the bag?	*jho*·lah·mah ke cha?
	(lit: bag-in what is?)

Postpositions are also used with personal pronouns and, occasionally, adverbs:

Please come with me.	ma·sā·ga *au*·nu·hos
	(lit: I-with come-hos)
Please come in from outside.	bah·hi·ra·bah·ṭa *bhi*·tra *au*·nu·hos
	(lit: outside-from inside come-hos)

CONJUNCTIONS

Conjunctions in Nepali are used pretty much as they are in English. Here's a list of the most common ones:

and	ra	but	*ta*·ra
and then	*a*·ni	or	ki
because	*ki*·na·bha·ne	otherwise	*na*·tra

Is the water hot or cold?   *pah*·ni *tah*·to cha ki *ci*·so cha?
(lit: water hot is or cold is?)

MEETING PEOPLE

It's easy to strike up a conversation in Nepal and it will not only add to your understanding and enjoyment of the country, but also ensure your share of warm Nepalese *bya*·ba·hahr (ब्यवहार), 'hospitality'!

YOU SHOULD KNOW   थाहा हुनुपर्छ

Hello./Goodbye.	na·ma·*ste*	नमस्ते
Hello./Goodbye. (pol)	na·ma·*skahr*	नमस्कार
Pardon?	ha·*jur*?	हजुर ?
I'm sorry./Please forgive me.	mahph *gar*·nu·hos	माफ गर्नुहोस

There are several ways of saying 'yes' or 'no'. Generally, the main verb in the question is repeated in the affirmative or negative. This will often involve some form of the verb 'to be'; cha, ho or *hun*·cha (see Grammar, page 27):

YES & NO			
Yes		**No**	
ho	हो	*hoi*·na	होइन
cha	छ	*chai*·na	छैन
hun·cha	हुन्छ	*hun*·dai·na	हुन्दैन

A general word for 'yes' is ha·*jur* (हजुर) – see page 38.

In body language, nodding means 'yes' and a sideways shake of the head means 'no' as in a lot of countries. However, there's a kind of sideways tilt of the head, accompanied by a slight shrug of the shoulders, which the Nepalese often use to indicate agreement, during bargaining, for instance. Don't mistake this for a 'no'.

GREETINGS & GOODBYES   अभिवादनहरू

One key phrase to learn is the general Nepali greeting, na·ma·*ste* (नमस्ते). Literally meaning 'I bow to the god in you', this expression covers all sorts of situations, from 'hello' to 'goodbye'. It can be used at any time of the day, and the Nepalese consider it appropriate between all people.

A more polite form of the same greeting is na·ma·*skahr* (नमस्कार), but it's less commonly used. Both na·ma·*ste* and na·ma·*skahr* should be accompanied by holding your palms together in front of your face, as if in prayer.

How are you?
    ta·*paī*·lai *kas*·to cha?   तपाईंलाई कस्तो छ ?
    ah·rah·mai hu·nu·hun·*cha*? (pol)   आरामै हुनुहुन्छ ?
I'm fine. And you?
    ma·lai *san*·cai cha   मलाई सन्चै छ
    ani ta·*paī*·lai?   अनि तपाईंलाई ?
Goodnight.
    shu·bha·*rah*·tri   शुभरात्री

CIVILITIES   नम्रताहरू

The Nepali word for 'thank you', *dhan*·ya·bahd (धन्यबाद), is not used very often and is best kept to express thanks for particular favours – it would be inappropriate in shops and restaurants, for example. Similarly, the word for 'please', kri·*pa*·yah (कृपया), is very formal and reserved mainly for writing. Instead of 'please', the imperative verb suffix -hos (-होस्) is used in spoken Nepali (see Grammar, page 32).

You're welcome.
    swah·gat cha   स्वागत छ
Excuse me./Sorry. (pol)
    mahph *gar*·nu·hos   माफ गर्नुहोस्
May I?/Do you mind?
    ga·re·hun·cha?   गरेहुन्छ ?

MEETING PEOPLE

FORMS OF ADDRESS
नामहरू

In Nepal, people use kinship terms rather than first names. These kinship terms apply to non-relatives as well, and even strangers. For someone older than you (or someone you want to show respect to), use 'elder sister' for a woman or 'elder brother' for a man. If they're elderly, use 'grandmother' or 'grandfather'. For younger people and children, use 'younger sister' or 'younger brother'. Nepalese people will also use these terms towards you. Commonly used Nepali kinship terms include:

mother	*ah·*mah	आमा
father	*bu·*wah	बुवा
grandmother	*baj·*yai	बज्यै
grandfather	*bah·*je	बाजे
elder sister	*di·*di	दिदी
elder brother	dai	दाइ
elder brother's wife	*bhau·*jyu	भाउज्यू
elder sister's husband	*bhi·*nah·jyu	भिनाज्यू
younger sister	*ba·*hi·ni	बहिनी
younger brother	bhai	भाइ
little girl	*nah·*ni	नानी
little boy	*bah·*bu	बाबु

GET SHORTY

Instead of kinship terms, friends often use nicknames for each other, such as *pud·*ke, 'Shorty'!

When they do address someone by name, the Nepalese usually add the suffix -ji (or sometimes -jyu) to the name as a sign of respect or affection. It's good manners for travellers to do the same.

Ram, where are you going?
*rahm·*ji, ta·*paī ka·*hāh
*jah·*nu·hun·cha?
रामजी, तपाईं कहाँ
जानुहुन्छ ?

For other family terms, see Family (page 91).

MEETING PEOPLE

ATTRACTING SOMEONE'S ATTENTION
कोही बोलाउनु

To attract someone's attention, call yo, plus one of the kinship terms you'll find listed on page 37. Then say na·ma·ste and make your request. To beckon someone from a distance, wave your hand toward yourself, with the palm facing down and your fingers also pointing downwards.

Excuse me, sir/madam.
  yo, dai/di·di   यो दाइ/दिदी
Please come here.
  ya·hāh au·nu·hos   यहाँ आउनुहोस

For the proprietor of a shop, restaurant, hotel or any business, use 'proprietor', sah·hu·ji/sah·hu·ni (m/f), (साहुजी/साहुनी).

PLEASE EXPLAIN

A handy word that can be used in several different ways and for both men and women is ha·jur (हजुर). It literally means 'sir' but there's no exact equivalent in English. If someone calls out to you, respond with ha·jur?. You can also use it to express agreement or confirm what someone has just said to you, or add it to the answer of a simple 'yes/no' question, for politeness. But for the learner its greatest usefulness lies in the fact that if you didn't hear or understand something said to you, and want it repeated, you simply need to say ha·jur?.

BODY LANGUAGE   शरीरको सङ्केत

The Nepalese won't usually point out any mistakes to you directly (unless you ask) and are unlikely to be offended if you behave in a culturally inappropriate way. Just be sensitive to how the people around you are behaving.

Dressing conservatively, for example, means that Nepalese people will be much more at ease with you and so your contact with them will be even more friendly and effective. Ethnic Nepalese are very modest and will feel uncomfortable around travellers who are dressed revealingly. With the exception of some porters and labourers, the Nepalese don't wear shorts or short skirts, nor do men go without a shirt – not even in hot weather. It's still much more acceptable for women travellers to wear skirts than shorts or even long pants. If washing or bathing in public, be as discreet as possible and always keep at least some clothing on. Swimming costumes should be modest. Things are more relaxed for children, who can wear shorts and wash without clothing on.

Touching someone with your feet or legs is considered highly insulting in Nepal. If you accidentally do this, apologise by touching your hand to the person's arm or body and then touching your own head. It's also bad manners to step over someone's outstretched legs, and when you're sitting be sure to withdraw your own legs while someone is walking past you.

Open displays of affection between couples are distasteful to the Nepalese. Apart from the new custom of shaking hands, only close friends physically touch each other in public. But don't be surprised to see men and boys walking with arms around each other's shoulders or even holding hands, and women walking arm-in-arm. This kind of behaviour has no homosexual connotations as Nepal is generally not a gay-friendly society. If you're travelling with your children, it's accepted that you're affectionate with them.

MEETING PEOPLE

FIRST ENCOUNTERS   पहिलो भेट्‌हरू

In Nepal, civilities are a bit more formal than in Western countries and, as in many Asian cultures, the Nepalese way of going about things, including conversation, is often rather subtle and indirect. Get used to lots of small talk (and cups of *ci*-yah, चिया, 'tea') before the main reason for the contact can be stated openly. It's common to start chatting by asking where someone is going, or whether they have eaten (rather than how they are).

How are you?
　　ke cha? (inf)   के छ ?
Fine.
　　ṭhik cha   ठीक छ
What's your name?
　　ta-*paī*-ko nahm ke ho?   तपाईंको नाम के हो ?
My name is ...
　　me-ro nahm ... ho   मेरो नाम ... हो
Please introduce yourself.
　　ta-*paī*-ko *pa*-ri-ca-ya *gar*-nu-hos   तपाईंको परिचय गर्नुहोस
How are things?
　　hahl-kha-bar ke cha?   हालखबर के छ ?
OK./Not bad.
　　ṭhi-kai cha   ठीकै छ
Where are you going?
　　ta-*paī ka*-hāh   तपाईं कहाँ
　　jahm-dai-hu-nu-hun-cha?   जान्दैहुनुहुन्छ ?
Have you eaten?
　　khah-nah *khah*-nu *bha*-yo?   खाना खानु भयो ?
I hope we meet again!
　　phe-ri *bhe*-ṭaū-lah!   फेरी भेटौंला !

MAKING CONVERSATION गफ गर्नु

It's very easy to strike up conversation with the Nepalese – you'll be asked all sorts of questions about how you like Nepal, where you come from, your family, marital status, job and so on. If things get too personal, steer the conversation away by asking the other person about themselves or about Nepal and their region.

Do you live here?
    ta·*paī* ya·hāh *bas*·nu·hun·cha?   तपाई यहाँ बस्नुहुन्छ ?

What are you doing?
    ta·*paī* ke *gar*·dai·hu·nu·hun·cha?   तपाई के गर्दैहुनुहुन्छ ?

This is my friend.
    yo *me*·ro *sah*·thi ho   यो मेरो साथी हो

This is my partner/spouse.
    yo *me*·ro *ji*·ban *sah*·thi ho   यो मेरो जीवन साथी हो

What do you think (about ...)?
    (....*bah*·re) ta·*paī*·ko   (...बारे) तपाईको
    bi·*cahr* ke ho?   बिचार के हो ?

May I take a photo (of you)?
    (ta·*paī*·ko) *tas*·bir   (तपाईको) तस्बीर
    khic·nu·hun·cha?   खिच्नुहुन्छ ?

What's this called?
    yas·lai ke *bhan*·cha?   यस्लाई के भन्छ ?

How do you like Nepal?
    ta·*paī*·lai ne·*pahl*   तपाईलाई नेपाल
    kas·to *lahg*·yo?   कस्तो लाग्यो ?

We love it here.
    hah·mi·lai ya·hāh *ek*·dam   हामिलाई यहाँ एकदम
    man *par*·cha   मन पर्छ

It's great here.
    ya·hāh *ek*·dam *rahm*·ro cha   यहाँ एकदम राम्रो छ

I like Nepal.
    ma·lai ne·*pahl* man *par*·cha   मलाई नेपाल मन पर्छ

I like Nepal a lot.
    ma·lai ne·*pahl ek*·dam   मलाई नेपाल एकदम
    rahm·ro *lahg*·cha   राम्रो लाग्छ

MEETING PEOPLE

What a cute baby!
kas·to *rahm*·ro *bac*·cah!   कस्तो राम्रो बच्चा !

Are you waiting too?
ta·*paī* pa·ni *par*·kha·nu·hun·cha?   तपाई पनि पर्खनुहुन्छ ?

That's strange!
kas·to a·*nau*·tho!   कस्तो अनौठो !

That's funny! (amusing)
kas·to *hāh*·so·lahg·do!   कस्तो हाँसोलाग्दो !

How beautiful!
kas·to *rahm*·ro!   कस्तो राम्रो !

Are you here on holiday?
ta·*paī ya*·hāh *bi*·dah·mah   तपाई यहाँ बिदामा
ghum·na *au*·nu *bha*·ya·ko?   घुम्न आउनु भयको ?

I'm here ...   ma *ya*·hāh ... *ah*·ya·ko   म यहाँ ... आयको
  for a holiday   *bi*·dah·mah *ghum*·na   बिदामा घुम्न
  on business   *be*·pahr *gar*·na   बेपार गर्न
  to study   *padh*·na   पढ्न

How long are you here for?
ta·*paī ya*·hāh *ka*·ti   तपाई यहाँ कति
bas·nu·hun·cha?   बस्नुहुन्छ ?

I'm here for ... weeks/days.
ma *ya*·hāh ... *hap*·tah/din   म यहाँ ... हप्ता/दिन
bas·chu   बस्छु

We're here with our family.
hah·mi *ya*·hāh *pa*·ri·bahr·sā·ga   हामि यहाँ परिबारसँग
ah·yaū   आयौं

I'm here with my partner.
ma *ya*·hāh *ji*·ban *sah*·thi·sā·ga   म यहाँ जीबन साथीसँग
ah·ya·ko   आयको

No worries.
bhai·hahl cha, ni   भैहाल छ, नि

Get lost!
bhahg!   भाग !

Really?
sāh·cai? साँचै ?

Have a good rest.
rahm·ro·sā·ga *bas*·nu·hos राम्रोसँग बस्नुहोस

Have a good/safe trip home.
rahm·ro·sā·ga *jah*·nu·hos राम्रोसँग जानुहोस

What's to be done?
ke *gar*·ne? के गर्ने ?

It's OK.
ṭhik cha ठीक छ

It's important.
ma·*hat*·twa·pur·ṇa cha महत्त्वपूर्ण छ

It's not important.
ma·*hat*·twa·pur·ṇa *chai*·na महत्त्वपूर्ण छैन

It's possible.
sam·bhab cha सम्भब छ

It's not possible.
sam·bhab *chai*·na सम्भब छैन

CASUAL TALK

When constructing sentences in Nepali, remember information that's either clear from context or less important, such as 'I' or the plural ending -ha·ru, is often omitted in casual speech.

Look!
her·nu·hos! हेर्नुहोस !

Listen (to this)!
(yo) *sun*·nu·hos! (यो) सुन्नुहोस !

Are you ready?
ta·*paī* ta·*yahr* *hu*·nu·hun·cha? तपाई तयार हुनुहुन्छ ?

I'm ready.
ma ta·*yahr* chū म तयार छुँ

It's nothing./It doesn't matter.
ke·hi *hoi*·na केही होइन

MEETING PEOPLE

How much is it (this)?		
(yo) *ka*·ti ho?	(यो) कति हो ?
What's this/that?		
yo/tyo ke ho?	यो ∕त्यो के हो ?
What's the matter?		
ke *bha*·yo?	के भयो ?
You're right.		
ta·*paī*·le ṭhik *bhan*·nu *bha*·yo	तपाईले ठीक भन्नु भयो
It is/was enough.		
pug·cha/*pug*·yo	पुग्छ∕पुग्यो
... isn't it/aren't they?		
... ho ki *hoi*·na?	... हो कि होइन ?

OK.	ṭhik cha	ठीक छ
	hun·cha (pol)	हुन्छ
	has (very pol)	हस

NATIONALITIES   राष्ट्रियताहरू

You'll find that many country names in Nepali are similar to English, with all 't's and 'd's pronounced as retroflex (see Pronunciation, page 14).

Where are you from?		
ta·*paī* kun *desh*·bah·ṭa	तपाई कुन देशबाट
au·nu *bha*·ya·ko?	आउनु भयको ?

I'm/We're	*me*·ro/*hahm*·ro desh	मेरो∕हाम्रो देश
from ...	... ho	... हो
Africa	*a*·phri·kah	अफ्रिका
Australia	a·*stre*·li·yah	अष्ट्रेलीया
Belgium	*bel*·ji·yam	बेल्जीयम
Britain	be·*lah*·yat	बेलायत
Canada	*kyah*·nah·ḍah	क्यानाडा
China	cin	चीन
Egypt	*mis*·ra	मिस्र
England	*īg*·laīḍ	इँग्लैंड

Europe	*yu*·rop	युरोप
France	phrahns	फ्रान्स
Germany	*jar*·ma·ni	जर्मनी
Greece	yu·*nahn*	यूनान
Holland	ha·laīḍ	हलैंड
India	*bhah*·rat	भारत
Iran	i·*rahn*	ईरान
Ireland	*ah*·yar·laīḍ	आयरलैंड
Israel	i·ja·rail	इजराइल
Italy	i·*ṭa*·li	इटली
Japan	jah·*pahn*	जापान
Malaysia	mah·*le*·shi·yah	मालेशिया
Myanmar (Burma)	*bar*·mah	बर्मा
Nepal	ne·*pahl*	नेपाल
New Zealand	nyu *ji*·laīḍ	न्यू जिलैंड
Pakistan	*pah*·ki·stahn	पाकिस्तान
Russia	rus	रूस
Scotland	is·*kaṭ*·laīḍ	इस्कट्लैंड
Spain	spen	स्पेन
Sri Lanka	sri *lang*·kah	श्री लंका
Taiwan	cin ja·na·*bah*·di	चीन जनबादी
	ga·na·*tan*·tra	गणतन्त्र
Thailand	*thai*·laīḍ	थाइलैंड
Tibet	*ti*·bet	तिबेत
Turkey	*ṭar*·ki	टर्की
the USA	a·*me*·ri·kah	अमेरिका
Vietnam	*bhi*·yat·nahm	भियत्नाम
Wales	welj	वेल्ज

I live in/at the/a ...	ma ...·mah *bas*·chu	म ...मा बस्छु
city	*sha*·har	शहर
countryside	*sha*·har *bah*·hi·ra·ko	शहर बाहिरको
	bheg	भेग
mountains	pa·*hahḍ*	पहाड
seaside	sa·*mu*·dra·ko ki·*nahr*	समुद्रको किनार
suburbs of ...	...ko kāhṭh	...को काँठ
village	gaũ	गाउँ

CULTURAL DIFFERENCES   साँस्कृतिक अनेकताहरू

How do you do this in your country?
  ta·*paī*·ko *desh*·mah,   तपाईको देशमा,
  yo *ka*·sa·ri gar·ne?   यो कसरी गर्ने ?

Is this a local or national custom?
  yo *ca*·lan *sthah*·ni·ya ho   यो चलन स्थानीय हो
  ki *rah*·ṣṭri·ya ho?   कि राष्ट्रिय हो ?

local	*sthah*·ni·ya	स्थानीय
national	*rah*·ṣṭri·ya	राष्ट्रिय

I don't want to offend you.
  ma ta·*paī*·lai *cit*·ta du·*khau*·na   म तपाईलाई चित्त दुखाउन
  man *par*·dai·na   मन पर्दैन

I'm sorry, it's not the custom in my country.
  mahph *gar*·nu·hos, *me*·ro *desh*·mah   माफ गर्नुहोस, मेरो देशमा
  yo *hahm*·ro *ca*·lan *hoi*·na   यो हाम्रो चलन होइन

I'm not accustomed to this.
  yo *me*·ro *ca*·lan *hoi*·na   यो मेरो चलन होइन

I don't mind watching, but I'd prefer not to participate.
  ma *her*·chu, *ta*·ra bhahg *li*·na   म हेर्छु तर भाग लिन
  man *par*·dai·na   मन पर्दैन

I'll give it a go.
  ma *ko*·sis *gar*·chu   म कोसिस गर्छु

FIRE HAZARD

Fire is sacred in Nepal, to both Hindus and Buddhists. Never throw rubbish or anything else into one!

I'm sorry, it's against   mahph *gar*·nu·hos,   माफ गर्नुहोस,
my ...   yo *me*·ro ... *hoi*·na   यो मेरो ... होइन
  beliefs   bi·*shwahs*   बिश्वास
  culture   sā·*skri*·ti   संस्कृति
  religion/philosophy   *dhar*·ma   धर्म

AGE उमेर

In Nepal, it's not impolite to ask someone's age, particularly a child, an elderly person or someone younger than you. But many Nepalese do not know their exact age!

Remember to use the informal *ti*·mi for 'you' when talking to children.

How old are you?	ta·*paī*/*ti*·mi	तपाईं/तिमि
	ka·ti *bar*·sa	कति बर्ष
	bha·yo? (pol/inf)	भयो ?
I'm ... years old.	ma ... *bar*·sa *bha*·yo	म ... बर्ष भयो
18	a·*thah*·ra	अठार
35	*paī*·tis	पैंतीस

(See Numbers & Amounts, page 187, for your age.)

OCCUPATIONS कामहरू

The list below includes some typical Nepali occupations, as well as a few common Western occupations.

What's your occupation?
ta·*paī*·ko kahm ke ho? तपाईंको काम के हो ?
Where do you work?
ta·*paī* ka·*hāh* kahm तपाई कहाँ काम
gar·nu·hun·cha? गर्नुहुन्छ ?
How do you enjoy your work?
ta·*paī*·ko kahm *kas*·to *lahg*·cha? तपाईंको काम कस्तो लाग्छ ?
I enjoy/don't enjoy my work.
me·ro kahm ra·*mai*·lo मेरो काम रमाईलो
cha/*chai*·na छ/छैन

I'm a/an ...	ma ... hū	म ... हूँ
actor	a·bhi·*ne*·tah/	अभिनेता/
	a·bhi·*ne*·tri (m/f)	अभिनेत्री
architect	*vahs*·tu·kahr	वास्तुकार
artist	*ka*·lah·kahr	कलाकार
boatman/-woman	nau	नाउ

businessperson	*be*·pah·ri	बेपारी
chef/cook	*bhahn*·se	भान्से
cleaner	sa·phah *gar*·ne *mahn*·che	सफा गर्ने मान्छे
clerk	ba·hi·dahr	बहिदार
dancer	*nar*·ta·ki	नर्तकी
doctor	*ḍahk*·ṭar	डाक्टर
elephant driver	*mah*·hu·te	माहुते
engineer	in·ji·*ni*·yar	इन्जिनियर
factory worker	kah·ra·*khah*·nah·ko *maj*·dur	कारखानाको मजदुर
farmer	ki·*sahn*	किसान
fisherman/-woman	*mah*·jhi	माझी
gardener	*mah*·li	माली
gold-/silversmith	su·*nahr*	सुनार
guide	*bah*·ṭo de·*khau*·ne *mahn*·che	बाटो देखाउने मान्छे
housewife	*ghar*·bu·ḍhi	घरबूढी
journalist	*pa*·tra·kahr	पत्रकार
labourer	*maj*·dur	मजदुर
laundryman/-woman	*dho*·bi	धोबी
lawyer	*wa*·kil	वकील
manager	*hah*·kim	हाकिम
mechanic	*mi*·stri	मिस्त्री

musician	*sang*·git·kahr	सङ्गीतकार
nurse	nars	नर्स
office worker	kar·ma·*cah*·ri	कर्मचारी
painter	*ci*·tra·kahr	चित्रकार
police officer	pra·*ha*·ri	प्रहरी
porter	*bha*·ri·yah	भरिया
priest	pu·*jah*·ri	पुजारी
scientist	bai·*gyah*·nik	बैज्ञानिक
secretary	*sa*·cib	सचिब
soldier	si·*pah*·hi	सिपाही
student	bi·*dyahr*·thi	बिद्यार्थी
tailor	*su*·ci·kahr	सूचिकार
teacher	*shi*·chak	शिक्षक
tracker/hunter	shi·*kah*·ri	शिकारी
university lecturer	a·*dhyah*·pak	अध्यापक
waiter	*be*·rah	बेरा
writer	*le*·khak	लेखक

I'm retired.	ma a·wa·*kahsh* li·ē	म अवकाश लियें
I'm unemployed.	ma be·*kah*·ri chū	म बेकारी छुँ
What are you studying?	ta·*paī* ke *padh*·nu·hun·cha?	तपाई के पढ्नुहुन्छ ?

I'm studying ...	ma ... *padh*·dai·chu	म ... पढ्दैछु
arts/humanities	ka·*lah*	कला
business	*be*·pahr	बेपार
economics	ar·tha·*shahs*·tra	अर्थशास्त्र
engineering	in·ji·*ni*·yar	इन्जिनियर
English	ang·*gre*·ji	अङ्ग्रेजी
languages	*bhah*·sah·ha·ru	भाषाहरू
law	*kah*·nun	कानुन
medicine	*dahk*·ṭa·ri	डाक्टरी
Nepali	ne·*pah*·li *bhah*·sah	नेपालि भाषा
painting	*ci*·tra	चित्र
science	bi·*gyahn*	विज्ञान
teaching	*shi*·chaṇ	शिक्षण

FEELINGS

भावनाहरू

How do you feel?
ta·*paī*·lai *kas*·to cha?

तपाईंलाई कस्तो छ ?

Are you happy/sad?
ta·*paī khu*·si/*du*·khi
hu·nu·hun·cha?

तपाईं खुसी/दुःखी
हुनुहुन्छ ?

Do you feel ...?	ta·*paī*·lai ... *lahg*·yo?	तपाईंलाई ... लाग्यो ?
I feel/don't feel ...	*ma*·lai ... *lahg*·yo/ *lah*·ge·na	मलाई ... लाग्यो/ लागेन
afraid	ḍar	डर
angry	ris	रिस
cold	*jah*·ḍo	जाडो
depressed	u·*dahs*	उदास
drunk	*rak*·si	रक्सी
grateful	gun	गुन
happy	*khu*·si	खुसी
hot	*gar*·mi	गर्मी
hungry	bhok	भोक
lost	ha·*rau*·na	हराउन
OK/fine	ṭhik	ठीक
sad	*du*·khi	दुःखी
sick	bi·*rah*·mi	बिरामी
sleepy	*ni*·drah	निद्रा
sorry (condolence)	*da*·yah	दया
sorry (regret)	*du*·khit	दुःखित
thirsty	*tir*·khah	तिर्खा
tired	*tha*·kai	थकाइ
well	*san*·cai	सन्चै

BREAKING THE LANGUAGE BARRIER

भाषाको अवरोध गर्नु

Do you speak English?
ta·*paī* ang·*gre*·ji *bhah*·sah *bol*·nu·hun·cha?

तपाई अङ्ग्रेजी भाषा बोल्नुहुन्छ ?

Yes, I speak English.
ha·*jur*, ma ang·*gre*·ji *bhah*·sah *bol*·chu

हजुर, म अङ्ग्रेजी भाषा बोल्छु

No, I don't speak English.
ma ang·*gre*·ji *bhah*·sah *bol*·di·na

म अङ्ग्रेजी भाषा बोल्दीन

Does anyone here speak English?
ya·*hāh ko*·hi ang·*gre*·ji *bhah*·sah *bol*·na *sak*·nu·hun·cha?

यहाँ कोही अङ्ग्रेजी भाषा बोल्न सक्नुहुन्छ ?

I only speak a little (Nepali).
ma *a*·li *a*·li (ne·*pah*·li *bhah*·sah) *bol*·chu

म अलि अलि (नेपालि भाषा) बोल्छु

Do you understand?
ta·*paī bujh*·nu·hun·cha?

तपाई बुइनहुन्छ ?

I understand/understood.
ma *bujh*·chu/*mai*·le bu·jhē

म बुइछु/मैले बुइों

I don't understand.
mai·le bu·*jhi*·na

मैले बुझीन

Please speak more slowly.
bi·*stah*·rai *bol*·nu·hos

बिस्तारै बोल्नुहोस

Please say it again.
phe·ri *bhan*·nu·hos

फेरी भन्नुहोस

Please write that down.
tyo *ku*·rah lekh·*di*·nu·hos

त्यो कुरा लेखदिनुहोस

How do you say ...?
...lai ke *bhan*·cha?

...लाई के भन्छ ?

What does ... mean (in English)?
(ang·*gre*·ji *bhah*·sah·mah)
....lai ke *mah*·ne cha?

(अङ्ग्रेजी भाषामा) ...लाई के माने छ ?

I'm looking for it in this book.
ma yo ki·*tahb*·mah *her*·dai·chu

म यो किताबमा हेर्दैछु

Please wait a minute.
ek·chin *par*·kha·nu·hos एकछिन पर्खनुहोस

I know/don't know.
ma·lai *thah*·hah cha/*chai*·na मलाई थाहा छ/छैन

Do you speak ...?	ta·*paī* ... *bhah*·sah *bol*·nu·hun·cha?	तपाईं ... भाषा बोल्नुहुन्छ ?
I speak ...	ma ... *bhah*·sah *bol*·chu	म ... भाषा बोल्छु
Bengali	bā·*gah*·li	बँगालि
Chinese	cai·*nij*	चाइनिज
Dutch	ḍac	डच
English	ang·*gre*·ji	अङ्ग्रेजी
French	phrenc	फ्रेन्च
German	*jar*·man	जर्मन
Hindi	*hin*·di	हिन्दी
Indonesian	iṇ·ḍo·*ne*·si·yah·ko	ईण्डोनेसियाको
Japanese	ja·pa·*nij*	जापानिज
Nepali	ne·*pah*·li *bhah*·sah	नेपालि भाषा
Tibetan	ti·*be*·tan	तिबेतन

MEETING PEOPLE

GETTING AROUND

There are no trains in Nepal (except right on the Indian border) and much of the country can only be reached by walking or flying. In towns, rickshaws, tempos (three-wheeled auto-rickshaws) and taxis are cheap and readily available. Rickshaws are usually the cheapest form of transport, but you should always bargain over the cost of the journey beforehand.

For longer trips, you have the option of a bus, taxi, or chauffeur-driven car.

FINDING YOUR WAY
बाटो खोज्नु

The Nepalese are happy to help with directions and may even offer to escort you to your destination. It can be easy to get lost as you walk along the country's winding alleys and trails, but it's often the best way to see the country, and meet and interact with locals.

Where's the ...?	... *ka·*hāh cha?	... कहाँ छ ?
bus station	bas is·*te·*san	बस इस्टेसन
bus stop	bas bi·*sau·*ni	बस बिसौनी
road to ...	... *jah·*ne *bah·*ṭo	... जाने बाटो
What time does	... *ka·*ti ba·*je·*ti·*ra	... कति बजेतिर
the ... leave/arrive?	*choḍ·*chal/*pug·*cha?	छोड्छ/पुग्छ ?
aeroplane	*ha·*wai·ja·hahj	हवाईजहाज
boat	*ḍung·*gah	डुङ्गा
bus	bas	बस

How do I get to ...?
... ka·sa·ri jah·ne? ... कसरी जाने ?

Could you tell me where ... is?
ma·lai bhan·nu·hos, मलाई भन्नुहोस्,
... ka·hāh cha? ... कहाँ छ ?

Is this the way to ...?
yo bah·to ... jah·ne bah·to ho? यो बाटो ... जाने बाटो हो ?

Is it nearby?
na·jik cha? नजिक छ ?

Is it far from here?
ya·hāh·bah·ṭa ṭah·ḍhah cha? यहाँबाट टाढा छ ?

Is it difficult to get there?
jah·na gah·hro cha? जान गाह्रो छ ?

Can I walk there?
hī·ḍe·ra jah·na sa·kin·chu? हिंडेर जान सकिन्छु ?

It's near.
na·jik cha नजिक छ

Please show me (on the map).
(nak·sah·mah) ma·lai (नक्सामा) मलाई
de·khau·nu·hos देखाउनुहोस

Are there other means of getting there?
tya·hāh jah·ne ar·ko त्यहाँ जाने अर्को
u·pah·ya cha? उपाय छ ?

Thank you for showing us the way.
hah·mi·lai bah·to हामिलाई बाटो
de·khah·ya·ko·mah देखायोकोमा
dhan·ya·bahd धन्यबाद

What ... is this?   *yo kun ... ho?*   यो कुन ... हो ?
  city   *sha·har*   शहर
  place   *ṭhaū*   ठाउँ
  road   *bah·to*   बाटो
  village   *gaū*   गाउँ

DIRECTIONS

निर्देशन

Turn at the ...	... mod·nu·hos	... मोड्नुहोस
next corner	au·ne ku·nah	आउने कुना
street on the (right)	(dah·yāh) bah·to·mah	(दायाँ) बाटोमा

across	pah·ri	पारी
along	hun·dai	हुन्दै
behind	pa·chah·di	पछाडि
below	ta·la	तल
beside	cheu·mah	छेउमा
down	ta·la	तल
far	tah·dhah	टाढा
here	ya·hāh	यहाँ
in front of	a·gah·di	अगाडि
inside	bhi·tra	भित्र
left	bah·yāh	बायाँ
middle	bic	बीच

near	na·jik	नजिक
on	mah	मा
on top of	mah·thi	माथि
opposite	pah·ri	पारी
outside	bah·hi·ra	बाहिर
over	mah·thi	माथि
over there	u tya·hāh	उ त्यहाँ
right	dah·yāh	दायाँ
side	cheu	छेउ
there	tya·hāh	त्यहाँ
towards	ti·ra	तिर
up here/there	u mah·thi	उ माथि

north	ut·tar	उत्तर
south	da·chiṇ	दक्षिण
east	pur·ba	पूर्व
west	pash·cim	पश्चिम

GETTING AROUND

ADDRESSES   ठेगानाहरू

Addresses in Nepal are written in the Devanagari script and can be found on a metal plaque (usually blue) near the front door. The first line is a letter-number combination indicating the block, the second line is the suburb (if any), and the third line mentions the town plus the one-digit national zone number:

छ ४ - ९३८ - ३	Cha 4 - 938 - 3
नयाँ बजार	Naya Bazaar
काठमाडौं - ४	Kathmandu - 4

Unfortunately, block numbers aren't chronological and most streets don't have names, so trying to find someone's home can be quite a challenge. Most people are known by name in their neighbourhood, however, so ask around.

TEMPO, TAXI & RICKSHAW   टचाम्पु, टचाक्सी र रीक्सा

Tempos and taxis all have meters and are required to use them, but the drivers may refuse or ask to 'double the meter' at peak times, during rain and after dark, so bargain hard! Drivers are also notorious for being unable to change large bills (100 rupees or more) and not carrying any small change, so try to keep some with you.

Is this taxi available?
  tyahk·si khah·li ho?   टचाक्सी खाली हो ?
Please take me to ...
  ma·lai ....·mah lah·nu·hos   मलाई ...मा लानुहोस
How much is it to go to ...?
  ... jah·na·lai ka·ti   ... जानलाई कति
  pai·sah lahg·cha?   पैसा लाग्छ ?
How much is the fare?
  bhah·dah ka·ti par·cha?   भाडा कति पर्छ ?
For two people?
  du·i ja·nah·ko lah·gi?   दुइ जनाको लागि ?
Does that include the luggage?
  sah·mahn sa·met ga·re·ra?   सामान समेत गरेर ?

Instructions

निर्देशन

Go straight ahead.
  *si·*dhah *jah·*nu·hos
सिधा जानुहोस

Please drive slowly.
  bi·*stah·*rai *hāhk·*nu·hos
बिस्तारै हाँक्नुहोस

Please hurry.
  *chi·*ṭo *gar·*nu·hos
छिटो गर्नुहोस

Be careful!
  hos *gar·*nu·hos!
होस गर्नुहोस !

Stop!
  *rok·*nu·hos!
रोक्नुहोस !

Continue!
  *jahn·*dai *gar·*nu·hos!
जान्दै गर्नुहोस !

The next street to the left/right.
  *au·*ne *bah·*ṭo *bah·*yāh·mah/
  *dah·*yāh·mah
आउने बाटो बायाँमा /
दायाँमा

Please wait here.
  *ya·*hāh *par·*kha·nu·hos
यहाँ पर्खनुहोस

Stop at the corner.
  *ku·*nah·mah *rok·*nu·hos
कुनामा रोक्नुहोस

GETTING AROUND

BUYING TICKETS

टिकट किन्नु

Where do they sell (bus) tickets?
(bas)·ko ṭi·kaṭ ka·hāh bec·cha?   (बस)को टिकट कहाँ बेच्छ ?

I want to go to ...
ma ...·mah jahn·chu   म ...मा जान्छु

I'd like ...   *ma·lai ... di·nu·hos*   मलाई ... दिनुहोस
  a one-way ticket   *jah·ne ṭi·kaṭ*   जाने टिकट
  a return ticket   *jah·ne·au·ne ṭi·kaṭ*   जानेआउने टिकट
  two tickets   *du·i·wa·ṭah ṭi·kaṭ*   दुइवटा टिकट

What time does it ...?   *ka·ti ba·je ...?*   कति बजे ... ?
  arrive   *pug·ne*   पुग्ने
  leave   *jah·ne*   जाने
  return   *phar·ka·ne*   फर्कने

Do I need to book (a ticket)?
ma·lai (ṭi·kaṭ) sany·cit   मलाई (टिकट) सञ्चित
gar·nu·par·cha?   गर्नुपर्छ ?
I'd like to book a seat to ...
ma·lai ...·mah ek ṭhaū   मलाई ...मा एक ठाउँ
sany·cit gar·nu·par·yo   सञ्चित गर्नुपर्यो
The bus/flight is full.
bas/u·ḍahn bhar·yo   बस/उडान भर्यो
Can I have a stand-by ticket?
ma·lai is·ṭaiṇḍ·bai ṭi·kaṭ   मलाई इस्टैण्डबाइ टिकट
pain·cha?   पाइन्छ ?
How long does the trip take?
sa·phar ka·ti sa·ma·ya lin·cha?   सफर कति कमय लिन्छ ?

AIR
हवाई

Many tourist destinations in Nepal are only, or most easily, reached by air. Domestic flights should be booked at least a week in advance. It's essential to reconfirm your flight at least once beforehand, particularly if it's a busy time of year or a popular destination.

Is there a flight to ...?
...ko u·*ḍahn* cha? ...को उडान छ ?

When's the next flight to ...?
...ko ar·ko u·*ḍahn*
*ka·hi·le jahn·*cha? ...को अर्को उडान
कहिले जान्छ ?

How long does the flight take?
u·*ḍahn ka·*ti sa·ma·ya *lin·*cha? उडान कति कमय लिन्छ ?

What time do I have to check in
at the airport?
*bi·*mahn·sthal·mah *ka·*ti बिमानस्थलमा कति
*ba·*je·ti·ra cek in *gar·*nu·par·cha? बजेतिर चेक इन गर्नुपर्छ ?

Where's the landing strip?
*ha·*wai *grau·*na *ka·*hāh cha? हवाई ग्राउन कहाँ छ ?

Where's the baggage claim?
*mahl·*sah·mahn *li·*ne मालसामान लिने
ṭhaũ *ka·*hāh cha? ठाउँ कहाँ छ ?

My luggage hasn't arrived.
*me·*ro *mahl·*sah·mahn *pu·*ge·na मेरो मालसामान पुगेन

At Customs
भन्सारमा

I have nothing to declare.
*ma·*sā·ga ḍi·*klair gar·*nu·par·ne मसँग डिक्लैर गर्नुपर्ने
*ke·*hi *pa·*ni *chai·*na केही पनि छैन

I have something to declare.
*ma·*sā·ga ḍi·*klair gar·*nu·par·ne cha मसँग डिक्लैर गर्नुपर्ने छ

Do I have to declare this?
yo ḍi·*klair gar·*nu·par·cha? यो डिक्लैर गर्नुपर्छ ?

This is all my luggage.
*me·*ro *sa·*bai *mahl·*sah·mahn मेरो सबै मालसामान
*ya·*hāh cha यहाँ छ

GETTING AROUND

That's not mine.
  tyo *me*·ro *hoi*·na   त्यो मेरो होइन
I didn't know I had to declare it.
  ma·lai ḍi·*klair* gar·nu·par·cha   मलाई डिक्लैर गर्नुपर्छ
  bhan·ne *ku*·rah *thah*·hah *thi*·e·na   भन्ने कुरा थाहा थिएन

BUS   बस

Town buses are cheap but often crowded and slow, although
riding on the roof can be a good option for sightseeing and
watching your bags. It can be difficult to find the right bus and
get off at the right spot. Women may also experience unwanted
physical attention in the crush. Long-haul buses, especially
tourist ones, aren't so bad, although they do travel at hair-raising
speeds on narrow, winding roads.

When's the ... bus?	... bas *ka*·hi·le *jahn*·cha?	... बस कहिल जान्छे?
first	*pa*·hi·lah	पहिला
last	*an*·tim	अन्तिम
next	*ar*·ko	अर्को

How often do buses come?
  bas *ka*·ti *ak*·sar *aun*·cha?   बस कति अक्सर आउन्छ ?
Where do I get the bus for ...?
  ... *jah*·ne bas *ka*·hāh *li*·ne?   ... जाने बस कहाँ लिने ?
Which bus goes to ...?
  ...·mah kun bas *jahn*·cha?   ...मा कुन बस जान्छ ?
Does this bus stop at (Mugling)?
  yo bas (*mug*·ling)·mah *rok*·cha?   यो बस (मुग्लीङ)मा रोक्छ ?
Where does this bus go?
  yo bas *ka*·hāh *jahn*·cha?   यो बस कहाँ जान्छ ?
Is the bus full?
  bas *bhar*·yo?   बस भर्यो ?
Are there any stops?
  ka·tai *rok*·cha?   कतै रोक्छ ?

Will it be on time?
   sa·ma·ya·mah pug·cha?   समयमा पुग्छ ?
Is this seat taken?
   ya·hāh ko·hi mahn·che cha?   यहाँ कोही मान्छे छ ?
Please stop the bus when we get to ...
   ... ah·ye pa·chi bas   ... आये पछि बस
   ro·ki·di·nu·hos   रोकिदिनुहोस
The bus is delayed/cancelled.
   bas dhi·lo/rad·da bha·yo   बस ढिला/रद्द भयो
How long will the bus be delayed?
   bas ka·ti sa·ma·ya a·be·lah   बस कति समय अबेला
   hun·cha?   हुन्छ ?
Is it a direct route?
   si·dhah jahn·cha?   सिधा जान्छ ?
I want to get off at ...
   ma ...mah or·lin·chu   म ...मा ओर्लिन्छु
I want to get off here.
   ma ya·hāh or·lin·chu   म यहाँ ओर्लिन्छु

BOAT   डुङ्गा

Rowing boats can be hired, with or without boatmen, on Phewa
Lake in Pokhara and boats and canoes can be taken out on some
rivers, such as the Rapti River in the Royal Chitwan National
Park. There are also many rafting and kayaking trips available
through travel companies.

Where does the boat leave from?
   dung·gah ka·hāh·bah·ta chod·cha?   डुङ्गा कहाँबाट छोड्छ ?
What time does the boat arrive?
   dung·gah ka·ti ba·je·ti·ra pug·cha?   डुङ्गा कति बजेतिर पुग्छ ?
How much to hire a boat for (one day)?
   dung·gah (ek din)·ko lah·gi   डुङ्गा (एक दिन)को लागि
   bha·dah·mah ka·ti ho?   भाडामा कति हो ?
Is that with a boatman?
   mah·jhi·sā·ga ho?   माझीसँग हो ?

GETTING AROUND

CAR   मोटर

In Nepal, you're unlikely to drive a rental vehicle yourself: hiring a car, jeep or minibus typically means hiring a driver too. This is the most expensive type of road transport. However, the driver adds little to the overall cost and generally makes the trip easier and more enjoyable. The driver can also help to negotiate accommodation and other costs.

The hire charge is usually calculated by distance and whether the trip is one-way or return. It may or may not include the cost of petrol or the driver's expenses, so be sure to check. Insurance should also be checked out, and it may be worth asking to see the vehicle and meet the driver beforehand.

Where can I hire a car (and driver)?
mo·ṭar (ra ḍrai·bhar) ka·hāh   मोटर (र ड्रायभर) कहाँ
bha·ḍah·mah li·ne?   भाडामा लिने ?

How much is it daily/weekly?
din·ko/hap·tah·ko ka·ti ho?   दिनको/हप्ताको कति हो ?

How much is it to ...?
... ka·ti ho?   ... कति हो ?

Does that include insurance/mileage?
bi·mah/ṭah·ḍhah sa·met ho?   बिमा/टाढा समेत हो ?

I'll pay half now and half at the end of the trip.
ma ah·ḍhah pai·sah a·hi·le   म आधा पैसा अहिले
tir·chu ra bah·ki pai·sah sa·phar तिर्छु र बाकी पैसा सफर
pa·chi tir·chu   पछि तिर्छु

I'd like to meet the driver.
ma·lai ḍrai·bhar bheṭ·na   मलाई ड्रायभर भेट्न
man lahg·yo   मन लाग्यो

I'd like to see the vehicle.
ma·lai gah·ḍi her·na man lahg·yo मलाई गाडि हेर्न मन लाग्यो

Where's the next stop?
ar·ko ro·kai ka·hi·le aun·cha? अर्को रोकाइ कहिले आउन्छ ?

Please stop here/somewhere for a while.
ya·hāh/ka·tai ek·chin rok·nu·hos यहाँ/कतै एकछिन रोक्नुहोस

How long can we park here?
*gah·ḍi ya·hāh ka·ti
rok·nu·hun·cha?* गाडि यहाँ कति
रोक्नुहुन्छ ?

Does this road lead to ...?
yo bah·ṭo ...mah jahn·cha? यो बाटो ...मा जान्छ ?

BICYCLE साइकल

Bicycles are a cheap form of urban transport and often the most
convenient, as taxis can be difficult to find after dark. You can
also hire mountain bikes.

Is there a bike path?
sai·kal·ko bah·ṭo cha? साइकलको बाटो छ ?

Where can I hire a bicycle?
*sai·kal ka·hāh
bhah·dah·mah li·ne?* साइकल कहाँ
भाडामा लिने ?

Where can I find (second-hand)
bikes for sale?
(pu·rah·no) sai·kal ka·hāh kin·ne? (पुरानो) साइकल कहाँ किन्ने ?

How much is a bicycle per hour/day?
*sai·kal ghan·ṭah·ko/
din·ko ka·ti ho?* साइकल घण्टाको/
दिनको कति हो ?

I'd like to hire a bicycle for ...	*ma·lai ...ko lah·gi eu·ṭah sai·kal bhah·dah·mah cah·hi·yo*	मलाई ...को लागि एउटा साइकल भाडामा चाहियो
one day	ek din	एक दिन
two days	*du·i din*	दुइ दिन
one week	ek *hap·tah*	एक हप्ता

GETTING AROUND

Is it within cycling distance?
sai·kal·bah·ṭa jah·na sak·in·cha?   साइकलबाट जान सकिन्छ ?
I have a flat tyre.
me·ro cak·kah·mah pwahl bha·yo   मेरो चक्कामा प्वाल भयो

bicycle	*sai·kal*	साइकल
bicycle path	*sai·kal·ko bah·ṭo*	साइकलको बाटो
brakes	brek	ब्रेक
handlebars	*hen·ḍal*	हेन्डल
helmet	pha·*lah*·me *ṭo·*pi	फलामे टोपी
inner tube	ṭyub	ट्चुब
lights	*sai·kal bat·*ti	साइकल बत्ती
mountain bike	*maun·*ṭen baik	माउन्टेन बाइक
padlock	*tahl·*cah	ताल्चा
pump	pamp	पम्प
puncture	pwahl	प्वाल
racing bike	*re·*sing baik	रेसिङ बाइक
saddle	siṭ	सीट
wheel	*cak·*kah	चक्का

ACCOMMODATION

The Nepalese tourism sector has become more up-market in recent years, but there are still plenty of inexpensive places to stay. In Kathmandu, there's a huge choice of accommodation, ranging from five-star hotels to small guesthouses with picturesque roof gardens and tiny lodges with basic facilities and rock-bottom prices.

Outside Kathmandu, in towns and tourist centres, the range and prices are similar. Hotels and lodges are generally modestly priced, but standards differ so it's worth checking a few places in the same location. On trekking routes, accommodation can be particularly basic, especially in remote areas, although this is changing rapidly.

GO GREEN

Keep in mind that staying in a place that uses solar energy, kerosene or gas for cooking and hot water, instead of a wood stove, puts far less stress on the local forests.

FINDING ACCOMMODATION
डेरा खोज्नु

See Trekking, page 146, for words and phrases on Camping.

I'm looking for a/the ...	ma ... kho·je·ko	म ... खोजेको
camp site	shi·bir	शिबिर
guesthouse	pah·hu·nah ghar	पाहुना घर
hotel	ho·ṭel	होटेल
lodge	laj	लज
youth hostel	yuth hos·ṭel	युठ होस्टेल

Where's a ... hotel?	... ho·ṭel ka·hāh cha?	... होटेल कहाँ छ ?
cheap	sas·to	सस्तो
clean	sa·phah	सफा
good	rahm·ro	राम्रो
nearby	na·jik	नजिक

ACCOMMODATION

Where's the ... hotel?	... ho·ṭel ka·hāh cha?	... होटेल कहाँ छ ?
best	ek nam·bar	एक नम्बर
cheapest	sab·bhan·dah sas·to	सबभन्दा सस्तो

What's the address?
the·gah·nah ke ho?   ठेगाना के हो ?

Please write down the address.
the·gah·nah lekh·nu·hos   ठेगाना लेख्नुहोस

Also see Addresses, page 56.

BOOKING AHEAD   सञ्चित राख्नु

I'd like to book a room.
ma·lai ko·ṭhah sany·cit   मलाई कोठा सञ्चित
gar·nu·par·yo   गर्नुपर्यो

Do you have any rooms/
beds available?
ko·ṭhah/khaṭ pain·cha?   कोठा / खाट पाइन्छ ?

> **THEY MAY SAY ...**
> mahph gar·nu·hos, ho·ṭel bhar·yo
> Sorry, the hotel's full.

Do you have a room with ...?	... khaṭ·ko ko·ṭhah pain·cha?	... खाटको कोठा पाइन्छ ?
two beds	du·i·wa·ṭah	दुइवटा
a double bed	du·i·ja·nah·ko	दुइजनाको
a single bed	ek·ja·nah·ko	एकजनाको

How much for ...?	...ko ka·ti ho?	...को कति हो ?
one night	ek raht	एक रात
a week	ek hap·tah	एक हप्ता
two people	du·i ja·nah	दुइ जना

I'd like to share a dorm.
ma·lai chah·trah·bahs   मलाई छात्राबास
bāḥḍ·nu man lahg·yo   बाँड्नु मन लाग्यो

For (three) nights.
(tin) raht·ko lah·gi   (तीन) रातको लागि

I'll be arriving at ... o'clock.
   ma ... *ba*·je·ti·ra *pug*·chu
   म ... बजेतिर पुग्छु

My name's ...
   me·ro nahm ... ho
   मेरो नाम ... हो

Can I pay by credit card?
   kre·ḍiṭ *kahrḍ*·le *tir*·nu·hun·cha?
   केडिट कार्डले तिर्नुहुन्छ ?

CHECKING IN
चेक इन गर्नु

I have a (room) reservation.
   mai·le (*ko*·ṭhah) *sany*·cit ga·re·ko
   मैले (कोठा) सञ्चित गरेको

I/We want a   *ma*·lai/*hah*·mi·lai   मलाई/हामीलाई
room with (a) ...   ... *bha*·ya·ko *ko*·ṭhah   ... भयको कोठा
                     cah·hi·yo   चाहियो

bathroom   snahn *kak*·sha   स्नान कक्ष
hot water   *tah*·to *pah*·ni   तातो पानी
shower   snahn   स्नान
TV   *ṭe*·li·bhi·jan   टेलिभिजन
window   jhyahl   झ्याल

Can I see the room?
   ko·ṭhah *her*·na *sak*·in·cha?
   कोठा हेर्न सकिन्छ ?

Are there any other rooms?
   ar·ko *ko*·ṭhah *pain*·cha?
   अर्को कोठा पाइन्छ ?

Are there any cheaper rooms?
   ar·ko *ku*·nai *sas*·to *ko*·ṭhah cha?
   अर्को कुनै सस्तो कोठा छ ?

Where's the toilet?
   shau·*cah*·la·ya/*bahṭh*·rum
   ka·hãh cha?
   शैचालय/बाथरूम
   कहाँ छ ?

Is there hot water (all day)?
   (*din*·bha·ri) *tah*·to *pah*·ni
   aun·cha?
   (दिनभरि) तातो पानी
   आउन्छ ?

Is breakfast included?
   bi·*hah*·na·ko *khah*·nah sa·met ho?
   बिहानको खाना समेत हो ?

The room's fine. I'll take it.
   ko·ṭhah ṭhik cha, ma *lin*·chu
   कोठा ठीक छ, म लिन्छु

ACCOMMODATION

ACCOMMODATION

REQUESTS & QUERIES

अनुरोध र प्रश्न

I have a request.
eu·tah a·nu·rodh cha

एउटा अनुरोध छ

Please wake me up at ... o'clock
tomorrow morning.
*ma·lai bho·li bi·hah·na ... ba·je
u·thau·nu·hos*

मलाई भोलि बिहान ... बजे
उठाउनुहोस

Where's the bathroom?
bahth·rum ka·hāh cha?

बाठरूम कहाँ छ ?

Does the hotel have a restaurant?
ho·tel·mah bho·ja·nah·la·ya cha?

होटेलमा भोजनालय छ ?

Where's breakfast served?
*bi·hah·na·ko khah·nah
ka·hāh din·cha?*

बिहानको खाना
कहाँ दिन्छ ?

Can we use the kitchen?
*hah·mi·le bhahm·chah
ca·lau·nu·hun·cha?*

हामिले भान्छा
चलाउनुहुन्छ ?

Is there a laundry nearby?
*e·tah lu·gah·dhu·ne thaū
na·jik cha?*

एता लुगाधुने ठाउँ
नजिक छ ?

Is there somewhere to wash clothes?
lu·gah·dhu·ne thaū pain·cha?

लुगाधुने ठाउँ पाइन्छ ?

Please wash/iron this clothing.
*yo lu·gah (dhu·i di·nu·hos;
is·tri la·gau·nu·hos)*

यो लुगा (धुई दिनुहोस;
ईस्ट्री लगाउनुहोस)

Is my laundry ready?
me·ro lu·gah ta·yahr bha·yo?

मेरो लुगा तयार भयो ?

I need this clothing today/tomorrow.
*me·ro lu·gah ah·jal bho·li
cah·hin·cha*

मेरो लुगा आज/भोलि
चाहिन्छ

Please clean the room.
ko·thah sa·phah gar·nu·hos

कोठा सफा गर्नुहोस

Please change the sheets.
tan·nah pher·nu·hos

तन्ना फेर्नुहोस

Do you have a safe?
*ta·paī·ka·hāh su·ra·chit
thaū cha?*

तपाईकहाँ सुरक्षित
ठाउँ छ ?

Could I leave this to be stored?
    yo ya·hāh choḍ·na sa·kin·cha?   यो यहाँ छोड्न सकिन्छ ?
Could I have a receipt for it?
    yas·ko bil di·nu·hun·cha?   यस्को बिल दिनुहुन्छ ?
Do you change money here?
    ya·hāh pai·sah sāht·nu·hun·cha?   यहाँ पैसा साट्नुहुन्छ ?
Do you arrange tours?
    ya·hāh bhra·maṇ ban·do·bas·ta
    gar·nu·hun·cha?   यहाँ भ्रमण बन्दोबस्त गर्नुहुन्छ ?
Can I leave a message?
    me·ro kha·bar rahkh·nu·hun·cha?   मेरो खबर राख्नुहुन्छ ?
Is there a message board?
    kha·bar·ko ṭhaū cha?   खबरको ठाउँ छ ?
Is there a message for me?
    me·ro lah·gi kha·bar cha?   मेरो लागि खबर छ ?
Could I use the telephone?
    ma phon gar·na sak·chu?   म फोन गर्न सक्छु ?

SELF-CATERING

If you're staying in one area for some time, most guesthouses don't mind if you prepare your own food in your room. Try to find a place near a local market, as fridges are still a luxury item in Nepal except in expensive accommodation. Also, there are no public laundrettes for washing your own clothes, but you'll find plenty of places to have laundry done cheaply, including most hotels.

Do I leave my key at reception?
    sāh·co ri·sep·san·mah choḍ·ne?   साँचो रीसेप्सनमा छोड्ने ?
I've locked myself out.
    sāh·co ko·ṭhah·mah par·yo   साँचो कोठामा पर्यो
We left the key at reception.
    hah·mi·le sāh·co ri·sep·san·mah
    cho·ḍe·ko   हामिले साँचो रीसेप्सनमा छोडेको

ACCOMMODATION

I need (a/another) ...	*ma*·lai ... *cah*·hi·yo	मलाई ...चाहियो
Could we have	*hah*·mi·lai ...	हामीलाई ...
(a/another) ...?	*di*·nu·hun·cha?	दिनुहुन्छ ?
bedding	bi·*chyau*·nah	बिछ्यौना
blanket	*kam*·mal	कम्मल
breakfast	bi·*hah*·na·ko	बिहानको
	khah·nah	खाना
candle	*main*·bat·ti	मैनबत्ती
chair	mec	मेच
curtain	*par*·dah	पर्दा
fan	*pā*·khah	पँखा
the key	*sāh*·co	साँचो

COMPLAINTS   सिकायतहरू

Excuse me, there's a problem
with my room.
 sun·nu·hos, *me*·ro *ko*·ṭhah·mah   सुन्नुहोस, मेरो कोठामा
 sa·*mas*·yah *bha*·yo   समस्या भयो

I don't like this room.
 ma·lai yo *ko*·ṭhah man *par*·dai·na   मलाई यो कोठा मन पर्दैन

Can I change rooms?
 ko·ṭhah *saht*·nu·hun·cha?   कोठा साट्नुहुन्छ ?

The window doesn't open/close.
 jhyahl *khol*·na/*lau*·na sa·ke·na   झ्याल खोल्न ∕ लाउन सकेन

This room smells.
 yo *ko*·ṭhah ga·*naun*·cha   यो कोठा गनाउन्छ

The toilet won't flush.
 bahṭh·rum kahm *gar*·dai·na   बाठरूम काम गर्दैन

There's no (hot) water.
 (*tah*·to) *pah*·ni *chai*·na   (तातो) पानी छैन

The ... doesn't work.
 ... kahm *gar*·dai·na   ... काम गर्दैन

Can you get it fixed?
 yo ba·*nau*·na sa·kin·cha?   यो बनाउन सकिन्छ ?

It's too ...	dhe·rai ... cha	धेरै ... छ
bright	u·jyah·lo	उज्यालो
cold	ci·so	चिसो
dark	ā·dhyah·ro	अँध्यारो
expensive	ma·hā·go	महँगो
hot	tah·to	तातो
light	u·jyah·lo	उज्यालो
noisy	hal·lah	हल्ला
small	sah·no	सानो

This ... is not clean.	yo ... sa·phah chai·na	यो ... सफा छैन
bedding	tan·nah	तन्ना
blanket	kam·mal	कम्मल
pillow	si·rah·ni	सिरानी
pillowcase	si·rah·ni·ko khol	सिरानीको खोल
sheet	tan·nah	तन्ना

ACCOMMODATION

CHECKING OUT
चेक आउट गर्नु

What time do we have to check out?
hah·mi·lai ka·ti ba·je cek
auṭ gar·nu·par·cha?
हामीलाई कति बजे चेक
आउट गर्नुपर्छ ?

I would like to check out ...	ma ... cek auṭ gar·chu	म ... चेक आउट गर्छु
now	a·hi·le	अहिले
at noon	bah·hra ba·je	बाह्र बजे
tomorrow	bho·li	भोलि

We had a great stay, thank you.
hah·mi·le rahm·ro·sā·ga bas·yaū,
dhan·ya·badh
हामिले राम्रोसँग बस्यौ,
धन्यबाद

You've been wonderful.
ta·paī ek·dam rahm·ro bha·yo
तपाई एकदम राम्रो भयो

Thank you for all your help.
ta·paī·le mad·dat di·ye·ko·mah
dhan·ya·bahd
तपाईले मद्दत दियेकोमा
धन्यवाद

ACCOMMODATION

The room was perfect.
ko·thah ek·dam rahm·ro thi·yo

कोठा एकदम राम्रो थियो

We hope we can return some day.
ek din *hah·mi·lai phar·ka·na man lahg·cha*

एक दिन हामिलाई फर्कन मन लाग्छ

I'd like to pay now.
ma *a·hi·le pai·sah tir·chu*

म अहिले पैसा तिर्छु

Can I pay with a travellers cheque?
trah·bhlar cek·le tir·nu·hun·cha?

ट्राभ्लर चेकले तिर्नुहुन्छ ?

There's a mistake in the bill.
bil·mah gal·ti bha·yo

बिलमा गल्ती भयो

Can I leave my backpack here until tonight?
ma *ya·hãh jho·lah be·lu·kah·sam·ma chod·na sa·kin·cha?*

म यहाँ झोला बेलुकासम्म छोड्न सकिन्छ ?

Can you call a taxi for me?
me·ro lah·gi tyahk·si bo·lau·nu·hun·cha?

मेरो लागि ट्चाक्सी बोलाउनुहुन्छ ?

I'm coming back ... ma ... *phar·kin·chu* म ... फर्किन्छु
  in a few days *ke·hi din pa·chi* केहि दिन पछि
  in two weeks *du·i hap·tah pa·chi* दुइ हप्ता पछि

AROUND TOWN

There's plenty to do around town in Nepal. Kathmandu, in particular, is a great place to hang out and is known to some as 'serendipity land'. As well as tourist information centres and a huge tourist industry awaiting you, there are also special tourist police to help out if needed. Most towns have decent banking and telecommunications facilities and a reasonable postal service.

LOOKING FOR ...   ... खोज्नु

I'm looking for a/the ...	ma ... *kho·*je·ko	म ... खोजेको
Where's a/the ...?	... ka·hāh cha?	... कहाँ छ ?
art gallery	ka·*lah·*ko ghar	कलाको घर
bank	baĩk	बैंक
cinema	*si·*ne·mah	सिनेमा
city centre	*sha·*har·ko bic	शहरको बीच
... consulate	... *rahj·*du·tah·vahs	... राजदूतावास
... embassy	... *rahj·*du·tah·vahs	... राजदूतावास
... hotel	... *ho·*ṭel	... होटेल
main square	pra·*mukh* cok	प्रमुख चोक
market	ba·*jahr*	बजार
museum	sã·gra·*hah·*la·ya	संग्रहालय
police	pra·*ha·*ri	प्रहरी
post office	*hu·*lahk *aḍ·*ḍah	हुलाक अड्डा
public toilet	shau·*cah·*la·ya	शौचालय
telephone centre	phon *aḍ·*ḍah	फोन अड्डा
tourist information office	par·*ya·*ṭan kahr·*yah·*la·ya	पर्यटन कार्यालय
town square	*sha·*har·ko cok	शहरको चोक

AT THE BANK   बैंकमा

Changing money and travellers cheques is usually straightforward. International transfers are becoming less complicated and, in major centres, there are even some automatic teller machines (ATMs). With the exception of some expensive hotels and resorts, exchange counters and other places that accept foreign currency don't normally charge much more than the official bank rate.

Remember that it can be difficult to change large bills (100 rupees or more), especially in the countryside, so ask for and carry plenty of small change.

KEEP RECEIPTS

Be sure to keep all your exchange receipts if you want to extend your visa or re-exchange rupees into other currency when you leave the country.

What time does the bank open?
baík ka·ti ba·je khol·cha?   बैंक कति बजे खोल्छ ?
Where can I cash a travellers cheque?
ṭrah·bhlar cek ka·hāh   ट्राभ्लर र चेक कहाँ
sahṭ·nu·hun·cha?   साट्नुहुन्छ ?

I want to change (a) ...   ... *sahṭ·nu·par·yo*   ... साट्नुपर्यो
   cheque   cek   चेक
   some money   *pai·sah a·li·ka·ti*   पैसा अलिकति
   travellers cheque   *ṭrah·bhlar cek*   ट्राभ्लर चेक

Please change this into Nepalese rupees.
yo ne·pah·li ru·pi·yāh·mah   यो नेपाली रुपियाँमा
sah·ṭi di·nu·hos   साटी दिनुहोस
Can I exchange money here?
ya·hāh pai·sah sahṭ·nu·hun·cha?   यहाँ पैसा साट्नुहुन्छ ?
What's the exchange rate today?
ah·ja sahṭ·ne reṭ ka·ti cha?   आज साट्ने रेट कति छ ?

What's your commission?
   ta·*paī*·ko *ah*·yog *ka*·ti cha?   तपाईंको आयोग कति छ ?
How many rupees per US dollar?
   ek *ḍa*·lar·ko *ka*·ti ho?   एक डलरको कति हो ?
Please write it down.
   le·khi·*di*·nu·hos   लेखिदिनुहोस
Where do I sign?
   ka·hāh *sa*·hi *gar*·ne?   कहाँ सही गर्ने ?
Please give me smaller notes.
   khu·drah *pai*·sah *di*·nu·hos   खुद्रा पैसा दिनुहोस
Please give me smaller change for
this note.
   yas·lai *khu*·drah *pai*·sah   यसलाई खुद्रा पैसा
   di·nu·hos   दिनुहोस
Can I have money sent here from
my bank?
   me·ro *baīk*·bah·ṭa *pai*·sah   मेरो बैंकबाट पैसा
   ya·hāh *aun*·cha?   यहाँ आउन्छ ?

How long will it take to arrive?
   pug·na *ka*·ti sa·*ma*·ya *luhg*·cha?   पुग्न कति समय लाग्छ ?
I'm expecting some money from ...
   ...·bah·ṭa *pai*·sah a·*pe*·chah *gar*·chu   ...बाट पैसा अपेक्षा गर्छु
Has my money arrived yet?
   me·ro *pai*·sah *ah*·yo?   मेरो पैसा आयो ?
Can I transfer money from overseas?
   pai·sah bi·*desh*·bah·ṭa *aun*·cha?   पैसा बिदेशबाट आउन्छ ?
Can I use my credit card to
withdraw money?
   kre·ḍiṭ *kahrḍ*·le *pai*·sah   क्रेडिट कार्डले पैसा
   li·nu·hun·cha?   लिनुहुन्छ ?
The ATM swallowed my card.
   pai·*sah*·ko mi·*sin*·le *me*·ro   पैसाको मिसिनले मेरो
   kahrḍ khai *di*·yo   कार्ड खाई दियो

AROUND TOWN

AT THE POST OFFICE

हुलाक अड्डा

Nepal's postal service is slow, but it's cheap and fairly reliable. There aren't many post offices and their hours are short, so be prepared to queue. In Kathmandu, try the small postal counters in Thamel, Chetrapati or Basantapur Square, instead of the GPO (unless you need poste restante). You can also buy stamps and post letters through some bookshops.

SIGNED, SEALED, DELIVERED

Never post anything in letterboxes – even giving it to your hotel can be risky. Make sure you see the clerk postmark the stamps on your mail.

I want to send a/an ...	... pa·*thau*·nu·par·yo	... पठाउनुपर्यो
aerogram	ha·wai·pa·tra	हवाईपत्र
fax	phyahks	फ्याक्स
letter	*ci*·thi	चिठी
parcel	pu·*lin*·dah	पुलिन्दा
telegram	tahr	तार
I want to buy a/an ...	... *kin*·nu·par·yo	... किन्नुपर्यो
postcard	*post*·kahrd	पोस्टकार्ड
stamp	*ti*·kat	टिकट
How much is it	yo ... *ka*·ti *pai*·sah	यो ... कति पैसा
to send this by ...?	*lahg*·cha?	लाग्छ ?
airmail	ha·wai·dahk *gar*·na	हवाईडाक गर्न
ship	ja·*hahj*·bah·ta	जहाजबाट
	pa·*thau*·na	पठाउन

Please give me some stamps.
ma·lai *ti*·kat *di*·nu·hos
मलाई टिकट दिनुहोस

How much is it to send this to ...?
yo ...·mah pa·*thau*·na
ka·ti *lahg*·cha?
यो ...मा पठाउन
कति लाग्छ ?

Please send it by air/surface.

yo ha·wai·ja·*hahj*·bah·*ta*/
gah·ḍi·bah·*ṭa* pa·*ṭhau*·nu·hos

यो हवाईजहाजबाट/
गाडीबाट पठाउनुहोस

Where's the poste restante section?

post res·*ṭāṭ ka*·hāh cha?

पोस्ट रेस्टैंट कहाँ छ ?

Is there any mail for me?

me·ro *ci*·ṭhi·pa·tra cha?

मेरो चिठीपत्र छ ?

airmail	*ha*·wai·ḍahk	हवाईडाक
envelope	khahm	खाम
express mail	*chi*·ṭo post	छिटो पोस्ट
mailbox	pa·tra·*many*·ju·sah	पत्रमञ्जुषा
pen	*ka*·lam	कलम
postcode	*post*·koḍ	पोस्टकोड
registered mail	*dar*·tah·ko post	दर्ताको पोस्ट
surface mail	*gah*·ḍi·bah·ṭa post	गाडीबाट पोस्ट

TELECOMMUNICATIONS टेलेकोमहरू

In Nepalese towns there are now many small communications offices where you can make and receive phone calls and faxes and get on the Internet.

Where's the nearest phone?

na·ji·kai phon *ka*·hāh cha?

नजिकै फोन कहाँ छ ?

Could I please use the telephone?

ma phon *gar*·na *sak*·chu?

म फोन गर्न सक्छु ?

I want to call ...

ma·lai ...·mah phon *gar*·nu·par·yo

मलाई ...मा फोन गर्नुपर्यो

I want to make a reverse-charges/
collect call to ...

ma·lai ya·hāh·bah·*ṭa* ...·mah
phon *gar*·nu·par·yo, *pai*·sah
tya·hāh·bah·*ṭa* *tir*·cha

मलाई यहाँबाट ...मा
फोन गर्नुपर्यो, पैसा
त्यहाँबाट तिर्छ

The number is ...

nam·bar ... ho

नम्बर ... हो

How much is it per minute?

mi·naṭ·ko *ka*·ti ho?

मिनटको कति हो ?

AROUND TOWN

I will speak for (three) minutes.
  (tin) *mi*·naṭ phon *gar*·chu — (तीन) मिनट फोन गर्छु

How many minutes was that?
  ka·ti *mi*·naṭ *bha*·yo? — कति मिनट भयो ?

Please wait a moment.
  ek·chin *par*·kha·nu·hos — एकछिन पर्खनुहोस

What's the area code for ...?
  ...ko koḍ *nam*·bar *ka*·ti ho? — ...को कोड नम्बर कति हो ?

It's engaged.
  phon *bi*·ji cha — फोन बीजी छ

We were cut off.
  lain *kaht*·yo — लाईन काट्यो

I want to send a fax to ...
  ma·lai phyahks ...mah — मलाई फ्याक्स ...मा
  pa·*thau*·nu·par·yo — पठाउनुपर्यो

What's the fax charge per minute to ...?
  ...·mah phyahks pa·*thau*·ne ek — ...मा फ्याक्स पठाउने एक
  mi·naṭ·ko *ka*·ti *pai*·sah *lahg*·cha? — मिनटको कति पैसा लाग्छ ?

fax	phyahks	फ्याक्स
operator	*a*·pre·ṭar	अप्रेटर
phone book	*phon*·ko ki·*tahb*	फोनको किताब
telephone	phon	फोन
urgent	ja·*ru*·ri	जरुरी

Making a Call — फोन गर्नु

Hello, do you speak English?
  na·ma·*ste*, ang·*gre*·ji — नमस्ते, अङ्ग्रेजी
  bol·nu·hun·cha? — बोल्नुहुन्छ ?

Hello? (answering a call)
  ha·*jur*? — हजुर ?

Can I speak to ...?
  ...sā·ga *bol*·na *sak*·chu? — ...सँग बोल्न सक्छु ?

Is ... there?
  ... cha? — ... छ ?

Yes, he's/she's here.
  cha — छ

One moment.
ek·chin
एकछिन

Who's calling?
ya·hāh ko *hu*·nu·hun·cha?
यहाँ को हुनुहुन्छ ?

It's ...
ma ... ho
म ... हो

I'm sorry, (he's/she's) not here.
mahph *gar*·nu·hos,
(wa·hāh) *chai*·na
माफ गर्नुहोस,
(वहाँ) छैन

What time will (he/she) be back?
(wa·hāh) *ka*·ti *ba*·je
phar·kan·cha?
(वहाँ) कति बजे
फर्कन्छ ?

Can I leave a message?
san·desh *chod*·nu·hun·cha?
सन्देश छोड्नुहुन्छ ?

Please tell ... I called.
...lai *mai*·le phon *ga*·re·ko
bhan·ni *di*·nu·hos
...लाई मैले फोन गरेको
भन्नि दिनुहोस

My number is ...
me·ro *nam*·bar ... ho
मेरो नम्बर ... हो

I don't have a contact number.
me·ro *nam*·bar *chai*·na
मेरो नम्बर छैन

I'll call back later.
ma *phe*·ri *pa*·chi phon *gar*·chu
म फेरी पछि फोन गर्छु

What time should I call?
ka·ti *ba*·je *phe*·ri phon *gar*·ne?
कति बजे फेरी फोन गर्ने ?

AROUND TOWN

The Internet
ईंटरनेट

Is there a local Internet cafe?
*ya·*hāh *ī·tar·net kyah·*phe cha?
यहाँ ईंटरनेट क्याफे छ ?

I'd like to get Internet access.
*ma·*lai *ī·tar·net ca·*hi·yo
मलाई ईंटरनेट चहियो

I'd like to check my email.
*i·*mel cek *gar·*nu·par·yo
ईमेल चेक गर्नुपर्यो

I'd like to send an email.
*i·*mel pa·*thau·nu·par·yo
ईमेल पठाउनुपर्यो

HAPPY SNAPS

Always ask people if it's okay to photograph them and be prepared to respect their wishes if they refuse. In particular, people involved in religious ceremonies or washing and bathing may not wish to be photographed. And do send photos if you promise to, as people can be very disappointed otherwise.

SIGHTSEEING
घुमघाम

Nepal is full of fascinating historical and religious sights and local people will be happy to show you around and give background information.

When visiting temples, dress modestly and remove your shoes. At Hindu temples remove any leather items, such as belts, before entering the compound. Normally, only Hindus are permitted right inside a Hindu temple or shrine. You may wish to make a donation or pay a priest to perform a *pu·*jah (पूजा), '*puja* ceremony', for you.

Where's the tourist information office?
*par·*ya·*tan kahr·*yah·la·ya
*ka·*hāh cha?
पर्यटन कार्यालय
कहाँ छ ?

Do you have a local map?
*sthah·*ni·ya *nak·*sah cha?
स्थानीय नक्सा छ ?

I'd like to see ...
ma·lai ... her·na man lahg·yo
मलाई ... हेर्न मन लाग्यो

Do you have a guidebook (in English)?
(ang·gre·ji) gaiḍ ki·tahb cha?
(अङ्ग्रेजी) गाईड किताब छ ?

What are the main attractions?
pra·mukh shu·bha·dar·shan
ke ho?
प्रमुख शुभदर्शन
के हो ?

We only have one/two day(s).
hah·mi·sã·ga ek/du·i din
mah·trai bah·ki cha
हामिसँग एक/दुइ दिन
मात्रै बाकि छ

Is it OK to take photos?
tas·bir khic·nu·hun·cha?
तस्बिर खिच्नुहुन्छ ?

Please take my photo.
me·ro tas·bir khic·nu·hos
मेरो तस्बिर खिच्नुहोस

Can I take your photo?
ta·paī·ko tas·bir
khic·nu·hun·cha?
तपाईंको तस्बिर
खिच्नुहुन्छ ?

I'll send you the photo.
tas·bir ta·paī·lai pa·thaun·chu
तस्बिर तपाईंलाई पठाउन्छु

Please write down your
name and address.
ta·paī·ko nahm ra the·gah·nah
lekh·nu·hos
तपाईंको नाम र ठेगाना
लेख्नुहोस

Getting In
पस्नु

What time does it open/close?
ka·ti ba·je [khol·cha;
ban·da gar·cha]?
कति बजे [खोल्छ;
बन्द गर्छ] ?

How much is the entry fee?
pra·besh shul·ka ka·ti ho?
प्रबेश शुल्क कति हो ?

Is there a	....lai	...लाई
discount for ...?	*gha·tau·nu·hun·cha?*	घटाउनुहुन्छ ?
children	*ke·ṭah·ke·ṭi*	केटाकेटी
students	*bi·dyahr·thi*	बिद्यार्थी
pensioners	*bu·ḍho·bu·ḍhi*	बूढोबूढी

AROUND TOWN

The Sights शुभदर्शन

What's that ...?	tyo ... ke ho?	त्यो ... के हो ?
building	*bha*·wan	भवन
monument	*smah*·rak	स्मारक
temple (Hindu)	*man*·dir	मन्दिर
temple (Buddhist)	*stu*·pah	स्तुपा

How old is it?
ka·ti pu·*rah*·no *bha*·yo? कति पुरानो भयो ?
Who built it?
kas·le ba·*nah*·ya·ko? कसले बनायको ?
What's that?
tyo ke ho? त्यो के हो ?

AROUND TOWN

ancient	*prah*·cin	प्राचीन
cremation	dah·ha·*sā*·skahr	दाहसँस्कार
cremation ghat	ghaṭ	घाट
cultural show	sāh·*skri*·tik	साँस्कृतिक
	pra·*dar*·shan	प्रदर्शन
factory	kahr·*khah*·nah	कारखाना
gardens	ba·*gaī*·cah	बगैंचा
library	pus·ta·*kah*·la·ya	पुस्तकालय
market	ba·*jahr*	बजार
monastery	*gum*·bah	गुम्बा
monument	*smah*·rak	स्मारक
mosque	*mas*·jid	मस्जिद
old city	pu·*rah*·no *sha*·har	पुरानो शहर
pagoda	*ga*·jur	गजुर
palace	*dar*·bahr	दरबार
philosophy	*dhar*·ma	धर्म
religion	*dhar*·ma	धर्म
restaurant	bho·ja·*nah*·la·ya	भोजनालय
statue	*mur*·ti	मूर्ति
temple (Hindu)	*man*·dir	मन्दिर
temple (Buddhist)	*stu*·pah	स्तुपा
university	bi·shwa·bi·*dyah*·la·ya	बिश्वविद्यालय
zoo	*ci*·ḍi·yah·khah·nah	चिडियाखाना

Tours
भ्रमण

Are there regular tours we can join?
hah·mi ba·rah·bar bhra·maṇ
mil·na sak·in·cha?

हामि बराबर भ्रमण
मिल्न सकिन्छ ?

Where can I hire a/an
(English-speaking) guide?
ma·lai (ang·gre·ji bol·ne)
bah·ṭo de·khau·ne mahn·che
ka·hāh pain·cha?

मलाई (अँग्रेजी बोल्ने)
बाटो देखाउने मान्छे
कहाँ पाइन्छ ?

How much is the tour/a guide?
bhra·maṇ·le/ghu·mau·ne
mahn·che·le ka·ti pai·sah lin·cha?

भ्रमणले / घुमाउने
मान्छेले कति पैसा लिन्छ ?

How long is the tour?
bhra·maṇ ka·ti sa·ma·ya lahg·cha?

भ्रमण कति समय लाग्छ ?

Will we have free time?
hah·mi·lai phur·sat hun·cha?

हामिलाई फुर्सत हुन्छ ?

How long are we here for?
hah·mi ya·hāh ka·ti bas·chau?

हामि यहाँ कति बस्छौ ?

What time should we be back?
hah·mi ka·ti ba·je
phar·ka·nu·par·cha?

हामि कति बजे
फर्कनुपर्छ ?

Our guide has paid/will pay.
hahm·ro ghu·mau·ne mahn·che·le
pai·sah ti·re·kol/tir·cha

हाम्रो घुमाउने मान्छेले
पैसा तिरेको / तिर्छ

I'm with them.
ma un·i·ha·ru·sā·ga chu

म उनीहरूसँग छु

I've lost my group.
ma me·ro dal·bah·ṭa ha·rah·yo

म मेरो दलबाट हरायो

Have you seen a group of (Australians)?
ta·paī·le (a·ṣṭre·li·yan) dal
dekh·nu bha·yo?

तपाईले (अष्ट्रेलीयन) दल
देख्नु भयो ?

AT THE EMBASSY
राजदूतावासमा

If you plan to extend your visa, be prepared for long waits at the immigration office. Although visa extensions are often available the following day, it's best to allow more time in case of delays.

Where can I extend my visa?
*bhi·*sah ka·*hãh thap·*ne?
भिसा कहाँ थप्ने ?

I want to extend my visa for ... days.
*ma·*lai ar·*ko ... din·*ko lah·*gi
*bhi·*sah li·*nu par·*yo
मलाई अर्को ... दिनको लागि
भिसा लिनु पर्यो

When can I collect my passport?
*me·*ro rah·ha·*dah·*ni ka·hi·le
li·na au·ne?
मेरो राहदानी कहिले
लिन आउने ?

GOING OUT
बाहिर जानु

There's much more nightlife in Kathmandu (and some other towns) than in the past, as many venues are now permitted to stay open past midnight. There are lots of pubs and bars and a flourishing local scene for live bands. There are also several nightclubs and a number of 24-hour casinos.

Local people tend to stay home after dark, but young Nepalese are beginning to go out more and the streets are still pretty safe at night, especially with the tourist police around.

Where to Go
कहाँ जानु

What's there to do in the evenings?
*be·*lu·kah ke gar·*na sa·kin·cha?
बेलुका के गर्न सकिन्छ ?

Where can I find out what's on?
ke hun·dai·cha ka·sa·ri thah·ha
pau·nu?
के हुन्दैछ कसरी थाह
पाउनु ?

What's on tonight?
*ah·*ja be·*lu·kah ke hun·dai·cha
आज बेलुका के हुन्दैछ ?

I feel like going	ma·lai ····mah jah·na	मलाई ...मा जान
to a/the ...	man lahg·yo	मन लाग्यो
bar	pab	पब
cafe	kyah·phe	क्याफे
cinema	si·ne·mah	सिनेमा
concert	kan·sart	कन्सर्ट
nightclub	klab	क्लब
pub	pab	पब
restaurant	bho·ja·nah·la·ya	भोजनालय
theatre	nahc·ghar	नाचघर

I feel like ...	ma·lai ... man lahg·yo	मलाई ... मन लाग्यो
a stroll	ghum·na	घुम्न
dancing	nahc·na	नाच्न
having a	ka·phi/pi·u·ne	कफी /पिउने
coffee/drink	li·na	लिन

Nightclubs & Bars क्लबहरू

Are there any good nightclubs?
rahm·ro klab·ha·ru chan? राम्रो क्लबहरू छन ?

How do you get to this club?
yo klab·mah ka·sa·ri jah·ne? यो क्लबमा कसरी जाने ?

Do you want to dance?
ta·pai·lai nahc·na man lahg·yo? तपाईलाई नाच्न मन लाग्यो ?

I'm sorry, I'm a terrible dancer.
mahph gar·nu·hos, ma·lai माफ गर्नुहोस, मलाई
nahc·na aun·di·na नाच्न आउन्दिन

Come on!
au·nu·hos nah! आउनुहोस ना !

What type of music do you prefer?
ta·pai·lai kas·to sang·git man तपाईलाई कस्तो सङ्गीत मन
par·cha? पर्छ ?

I really like (reggae).
ma·lai (re·ge) dhe·rai man मलाई (रेगे) धेरै मन
par·cha पर्छ

Do you want to go to a karaoke bar?
ta·pai·lai kah·rah·yo·ke bahr·mah तपाईलाई कारायोके बारमा
jah·na man lahg·yo? जान मन लाग्यो ?

Do you have to pay to enter?
  pra·besh shul·ka di·nu·par·cha?   प्रबेश शुल्क दिनुपर्छ ?
No, it's free.
  di·nu·par·dai·na   दिनुपर्दैन
Yes, it's ...
  di·nu·par·cha, ... ho   दिनुपर्छ, ... हो
This place is great!
  yo *thaū rahm·ro cha!*   यो ठाउँ राम्रो छ !
I'm having a great time!
  ma·lai dhe·rai maj·jah lahg·yo!   मलाई धेरै मज्जा लाग्यो !
I don't like the music here.
  *ma·lai ya·hāh·ko sang·git man
  par·dai·na*   मलाई यहाँको सङ्गीत मन
                पर्दैन
Shall we go somewhere else?
  hah·mi ar·ko thaū·mah jaū?   हामि अर्को ठाउँमा जाउँ ?

Invitations   निम्ताहरू

What are you doing this
evening/weekend?
  *ta·paī be·lu·kah·mah/
  wi·kend·mah ke gar·nu·hun·cha?*   तपाई बेलुकामा/
                विकेन्डमो के गर्नुहुन्छ ?
Would you like to go out somewhere?
  *ta·paī·lai bah·hi·ra jah·na man
  lahg·yo?*   तपाईलाई बाहिर जान मन
              लाग्यो ?
Do you know a good/cheap
restaurant?
  *ta·paī·lai rahm·ro/sas·to
  bho·ja·nah·la·ya thah·ha cha?*   तपाईलाई राम्रो/सस्तो
              भोजनालय थाह छ ?
Would you like to go for a drink/meal?
  *ta·paī·lai pi·u·na/khah·nah
  jah·na man lahg·yo?*   तपाईलाई पिउन/खाना
              जान मन लाग्यो ?
My shout. (I'll buy)
  me·ro pah·li   मेरो पालि

Do you want to come to the ...
concert with me?

ta·*paī*·lai ....ko *kan*·sart·mah   तपाईंलाई ...को कन्सर्टमा
ma·sā·ga *au*·na man *lahg*·cha?   मसँग आउन मन लाग्छ ?

We're having a party.

hahm·ro *pahr*·ṭi cha   हाम्रो पार्टी छ

Come along.

au·nu·hos   आउनुहोस

Responding to Invitations   निम्ताको जवाफ

Sure!

hun·cha!   हुन्छ !

Yes, I'd love to.

hun·cha, ma *aun*·chu   हुन्छ, म आउन्छु

Yes, where shall we go?

hun·cha, *hah*·mi *ka*·hāh *jah*·ne?   हुन्छ, हामि कहाँ जाने ?

No, I'm afraid I can't.

mahph *gar*·nu·hos, ma *sak*·di·na   माफ गर्नुहोस, म सक्दिन

What about tomorrow?

a·ni *bho*·li?   अनि भोलि ?

SIGNS	
बन्द	CLOSED
चिसो	COLD
खतरा	DANGER
प्रवेश	ENTRANCE
निकास	EXIT
तातो	HOT
प्रवेश निषेध	NO ENTRY
धूम्रपान मनाही छ	NO SMOKING
खुला	OPEN
मनाही निषेध	PROHIBITED
बाटो बन्द	ROAD CLOSED
रोक्नुहोस	STOP
शौचालय	TOILETS

AROUND TOWN

Arranging to Meet

भेट् मिलाउनु

What time shall we meet?
  hah·mi ka·ti ba·je bhet·ne?
  हामि कति बजे भेट्ने ?

Where will we meet?
  hah·mi ka·hāh bhet·ne?
  हामि कहाँ भेट्ने ?

Let's meet at (eight o'clock) at the ...
  (*ahth ba·je·ti·ra*) ....*mah bhe·taū*
  (आठ बजेतिर) ...मा भेटौं

OK, I'll see you then.
  *hun·cha, ma ta·paī·lai tyas
  be·lah bhet·chu*
  हुन्छ, म तपाईंलाई त्यस
  बेला भेट्छु

Agreed!/OK!
  hun·cha!
  हुन्छ !

I'll come over at (six).
  ma (cha ba·je·ti·ra) aun·chu
  म (छ बजेतिर) आउन्छु

I'll pick you up at (nine).
  *ma ta·paī·lai (nau ba·je·ti·ra)
  li·na aun·chu*
  म तपाईंलाई (नौ बजेतिर)
  लिन आउन्छु

I'll try to make it.
  ma au·ne ko·sis gar·chu
  म आउने कोसिस गर्छु

If I'm not there by (nine), don't
wait for me.
  *ma (nau) ba·je·sam·ma na·ah·yē
  bhan·ne, ma·lai na·kur·nu·hos*
  म (नौ) बजेसम्म नआयें
  भन्ने, मलाई नकुर्नुहोस

I'll come later.
  ma pa·chi aun·chu
  म पछि आउन्छु

Where will you be?
  ta·paī ka·hāh ho·lah?
  तपाई कहाँ होला ?

See you later/tomorrow.
  pa·chi/bho·li bhe·taū·lah!
  पछि/भोलि भेटौंला !

Sorry I'm late.
  *ma·lai mahph gar·nu·hos,
  dhi·lo bha·yo*
  मलाई माफ गर्नुहोस,
  ढिलो भयो

FAMILY

In Nepal, family life is paramount. In all ethnic groups, the domestic circle is the heart of social and cultural life and a person is identified primarily by their familial associations – and for women, their marital status.

Large families are the norm, and boys are favoured over girls, not only for cultural reasons but because in the absence of any social security system, the elderly need their children (especially sons) to look after them. Another factor is the appallingly high rates of infant (and maternal) mortality: the more likely your children are to die before adulthood, the more children you need to have as a safeguard.

Most Nepalese (especially those who work in tourism) are aware of behavioural norms in different cultures and are generally not offended by the idea that couples may be living together without being married. However, in remote areas of the country it may be easier for everyone if you simply say you're married. For all couples, open displays of affection are not acceptable in Nepalese society: in films, even the romantic leads never kiss!

QUESTIONS   प्रश्नहरू

Are you married?
    ta·*paī*·ko bi·*hah bha*·yo?   तपाईको बिहा भयो ?
Do you have a boyfriend/girlfriend?
    ta·*paī*·ko *pre*·mi/*pre*·mi·kah cha?   तपाईको प्रेमि／प्रेमिका छ ?
Do you have any children?
    ta·*paī*·ko cho·rah·*cho*·ri chan?   तपाईको छोराछोरी छन् ?
How many children do you have?
    ta·*paī*·ko cho·rah·*cho*·ri ka·ti   तपाईको छोराछोरी कति
    ja·nah chan?   जना छन् ?
Who looks after the children?
    cho·rah·*cho*·ri·lai *kas*·le   छोराछोरीलाई कसले
    rekh·dekh *gar*·nu·hun·cha?   रेखदेख गर्नुहुन्छ ?
Do you have grandchildren?
    ta·*paī*·ko nah·ti·*nah*·ti·ni chan?   तपाईको नातिनातिनी छन् ?

FAMILY

How many brothers/sisters do
you have?
  ta·*paī*·ko dah·ju·*bhai*/
  di·di·*ba*·hi·ni *ka*·ti *ja*·nah chan?

तपाईंको दाजुभाइ/
दिदीबहिनी कति जना छन् ?

How old are they?
  u·ni·ha·ru *ka*·ti *bar*·sa *bha*·yo?

उनीहरू कति बर्ष भयो ?

How many in your family?
  ta·*paī*·ko pa·ri·bahr·mah *ka*·ti
  ja·nah chan?

तपाईंको परिबारमा कति
जना छन् ?

Do you live with your family?
  ta·*paī* pa·ri·bahr·mah
  bas·nu·hun·cha?

तपाईं परिबारमा
बस्नुहुन्छ ?

Is your husband/wife here?
  ta·*paī*·ko *sri*·mahn/*sri*·*ma*·ti
  ya·hāh *hu*·nu·hun·cha?

तपाईंको श्रीमान/श्रीमती
यहाँ हुनुहुन्छ ?

Are your parents alive?
  ta·*paī*·ko *ah*·mah, *bu*·wah
  a·hi·le·sam·ma ji·*un*·dai
  hu·nu·hun·cha?

तपाईंको आमा, बुबा
अहिलेसम्म जिउँदै
हुनुहुन्छ ?

REPLIES   जवाफहरू

I'm married/not married.
  me·ro bi·*hah bha*·yo/*bha*·ya·ko
  chai·na

मेरो बिहा भयो/भयको
छैन

I'm ...	ma ... hū	म ... हुँ
divorced	*cho*·de·ko	छोडेको
single	*ek*·lai	एक्ले
separated	*chuṭ*·ṭai	छुट्टै
widowed	bi·dha·wah	बिधवा

I have a partner.
  me·ro *ji*·ban *sah*·thi cha

मेरो जीबन साथी छ

We live together but we're not married.
  hah·mi *sā*·gai bas·chaū *ta*·ra
  hahm·ro bi·*hah bha*·ya·ko *chai*·na

हामि सँगै बस्छौं तर
हाम्रो बिहा भयको छैन

I don't have any children.
  me·ro cho·rah·*cho*·ri *chai*·na

मेरो छोराछोरी छैन

I have (two) children.
*me·ro (du·i) ja·nah
cho·rah·cho·ri chan*   मेरो (दुइ) जना
छोराछोरी छन

I have a daughter/son.
*me·ro ek ja·nah cho·ri/
cho·rah cha*   मेरो एक जना छोरी/
छोरा छ

I live with my family.
me·ro pa·ri·bahr·mah bas·chu   मेरो परिबारमा बस्छु

IT'S A GAY LIFE

Be aware that Nepalese culture is very homophobic, more so toward gay men than lesbians, as male homosexuality is often confused with paedophilia. But, of course, a gay underground exists. Openly gay behaviour is not tolerated and homosexual activity is, in fact, illegal. Harassment can occur, even from officials, so it's best to be discreet.

FAMILY   परिबार

baby	*bac·cah*	बच्चा
boy	*ke·ṭah*	केटा
brothers	*dah·ju·bhai*	दाजुभाइ
children (general)	*ke·ṭah·ke·ṭi*	केटाकेटी
children (own)	*cho·rah·cho·ri*	छोराछोरी
dad	*bah*	बा
daughter	*cho·ri*	छोरी
elder brother's wife	*bhau·jyu*	भाउज्यू
extended family	*san·tahn*	सन्तान
family	*pa·ri·bahr*	परिबार
family name	*thar*	थर
father	*bu·wah*	बुबा
father-in-law	*sa·su·rah*	ससुरा
girl	*ke·ṭi*	केटी
given name	*shu·bha·nahm*	शुभनाम
grandfather	*bah·je*	बाजे
grandmother	*ba·jyai*	बज्यै
grandparents	*bah·je ba·jyai*	बाजे बज्यै

FAMILY

husband (general)	*sri·*mahn	श्रीमान
husband (own)	*log·*ne	लोग्ने
mother	*ah·*mah	आमा
mother-in-law	*sah·*su	सासू
mum	*ah·*mai	आमै
nickname	*u·*pa·nahm	उपनाम
parents	*ah·*mah *bu·*wah	आमा बुवा
sisters	di·di·*ba·*hi·ni	दिदीबहिनी
son	*cho·*rah	छोरा
wife (general)	sri·*ma·*ti	श्रीमती
wife (own)	*swahs·*ni	स्वास्नी
wife's in-laws	ja·*hahn*	जहान

TALKING WITH PARENTS   बा आमासँग गफ गर्नु

When is your baby due?
  ta·*paī·*ko bac·cah ka·hi·le
  *aun·*cha?
तपाईंको बच्चा कहिले
आउन्छ ?

What are you going to call your baby?
  ta·*paī·*ko bac·cah·lai ke
  nahm *di·*nu·hun·cha?
तपाईंको बच्चालाई के
नाम दिनुहुन्छ ?

Is this your first child?
  yo ta·*paī·*ko pa·hi·lo
  *bac·*cah ho?
यो तपाईंको पहिलो
बच्चा हो ?

How old are your children?
  ta·*paī·*ko cho·rah·cho·ri ka·ti
  *bar·*sa *bha·*yo?
तपाईंको छोराछोरी कति
बर्ष भयो ?

Does he/she attend school?
  *u·*ni bi·*dyah·*la·ya·mah *jahn·*cha?
ऊनी बिद्यालयमा जान्छ ?

Is it a private or government school?
  bi·*dyah·*la·ya ah·*pas·*ko ho
  ki sar·*kahr·*ko ho?
बिद्यालय आपसको हो
कि सरकारको हो ?

What's the baby's name?
  *bac·*cah·ko nahm ke ho?
बच्चाको नाम के हो ?

Is it a boy or a girl?
  *cho·*rah ho, ki *cho·*ri?
छोरा हो, कि छोरी ?

Does he/she let you sleep at night?
  *u·*ni·le ta·*paī·*lai *sut·*na
  *din·*cha?
ऊनीले तपाईंलाई सुत्न
दिन्छ ?

He's/She's very big for his/her age!
u·ni·ko *u*·mer·mah *thu*·lo cha!

उनीको उमेरमा ठूलो छ !

What a beautiful child!
kas·to *rahm*·ro *bac*·cah!

कस्तो राम्रो बच्चा !

He/She looks like you.
u·ni ta·*paī jas*·tai cha

उनी तपाई जस्तै छ

Who does he/she look like, Mum
or Dad?
u·ni *ah*·mah *jas*·tai cha,
ki *bu*·wah?

उनी आमा जस्तै छ,
कि बुवा ?

LITTLE ADULTS

Nepal is an extremely poor country and many families
can't afford to send all or any of their children to school,
even where schooling is free, because they can't
manage without the children's input into the family
household or business. Many children, especially girls,
work instead of going to school (or leave school very early),
although only a minority work in commercial employment.
In fact, some children work to pay for the education of
their younger siblings.

TALKING WITH CHILDREN

केटाकेटीसँग गफ गर्नु

What's your name?
tim·ro nahm ke ho?

तिम्रो नाम के हो ?

How old are you?
ti·mi *ka*·ti *bar*·sa *bha*·yo?

तिमी कति बर्ष भयो ?

When's your birthday?
tim·ro *jan*·ma·din *ka*·hi·le ho?

तिम्रो जन्मदिन कहिले हो ?

Do you have brothers and sisters?
tim·ro dah·ju·*bhai* di·di·*ba*·hi·ni
chan?

तिम्रो दाजुभाइ दिदीबहिनी
छन ?

Do you have a pet at home?
tim·ro *ghar*·mah *pahl*·tu
ja·*nah*·war cha?

तिम्रो घरमा पाल्तु
जनावर छ ?

FAMILY

Do you go to school or kindergarten?
*ti·*mi is·*kul jahn·*cha ki
nar·sa·ri?

तिमी इस्कुल जान्छ कि
नर्सरी ?

Is your teacher nice?
*tim·*ro *shi·*chak rahm·*ro cha?

तिम्रो शिक्षक राम्रो छ ?

Do you like school?
*ti·*mi·lai is·*kul man par·*cha?

तिमीलाई इस्कुल मन पर्छ ?

Do you play sport?
*ti·*mi khel·*kud khel·*cha?

तिमी खेलकुद खेल्छ ?

What sport do you play?
*ti·*mi kun khel·*kud khel·*cha?

तिमी कुन खेलकुद खेल्छ ?

What do you do after school?
is·*kul·*pa·chi *ti·*mi ke gar·*cha?

इस्कुलपछि तिमी के गर्छ ?

Do you learn English?
*ti·*mi ang·*gre·ji bhah·*sah
paḍh·*cha?

तिमी अङ्ग्रेजी भाषा
पढ्छ ?

We speak a different language in
my country, so I don't understand
you very well.
*me·*ro desh·*mah *hah·*mi ar·*ko
bhah·*sah bol·*chaũ, *tya·sai·le
*mai·*le *ti·*mi·lai rahm·*ro
bu·*jhi·na

मेरो देशमा हामि अर्को
भाषा बोल्छौ, त्यसैले
मैले तिमीलाई राम्रो
बुझीन

I come from very far away.
ma *dhe·*rai ṭah·ḍhah·bah·ṭa
ah·ya·ko

म धेरै टाढाबाट
आयको

Do you want to play?
*ti·*mi·lai khel·*na man *lahg·yo?

तिमीलाई खेल्न मन लाग्यो ?

What will we play?
*hah·*mi ke khel·*ne?

हामि के खेल्ने ?

Many travellers visit Nepal for trekking, but there are plenty of other activities to suit all tastes. These include rafting, kayaking and mountain biking and there's a fascinating array of cultural activities to observe and participate in for anthropology, history and architecture buffs. Religion and spirituality may also be of interest, especially Buddhism or yoga and meditation.

TALKING ABOUT TRAVELLING यात्राको गफ

Have you travelled much?
ta·*paī*·le *dhe*·rai *yah*·trah
gar·nu *bha*·yo?
तपाईंले धेरै यात्रा
गर्नु भयो ?

How long have you been travelling?
ta·*paī*·ko *yah*·trah *ka*·ti *bha*·yo?
तपाईको यात्रा कति भयो ?

I've been travelling for (two) months.
me·ro *yah*·trah (*du*·i) *ma*·hi·nah
bha·yo
मेरो यात्रा (दुइ) महीना
भयो

When did you come to Nepal?
ta·*paī* ne·*pahl*·mah *ka*·hi·le
au·nu *bha*·ya·ko?
तपाई नेपालमा कहिले
आउनु भयको ?

(Two weeks) ago.
(*du*·i *hap*·tah) *bhu*·yo
(दुइ हप्ता) भयो

How long will you stay?
ka·ti *bas*·nu·hun·cha?
कति बस्नुहुन्छ ?

I'll stay in Nepal for (one year).
ma ne·*pahl*·mah (ek *bar*·sa) *bas*·chu
म नेपालमा (एक बर्ष) बस्छु

Where have you been?
ta·*paī* *ka*·hāh *jah*·nu *bha*·yo?
तपाई कहाँ जानु भयो ?

I've been to ...
ma ...·mah *ga*·yē
म ...मा गयें

Did you go alone?
ta·*paī* *ek*·lai *jah*·nu *bha*·yo?
तपाई एक्लै जानु भयो ?

What did you think of (Pokhara)?
ta·*paī*·lai (*po*·kha·rah) *kas*·to
lahg·yo?
तपाईलाई (पोखरा) कस्तो
लाग्यो ?

INTERESTS

I thought it was ...	*ma·lai ... lahg·*yo	मलाई ... लाग्यो
boring	*wahk·*ka	वाक्क
great	*ek·*dam *rahm·*ro	एकदम राम्रो
horrible	*na·rahm·*ro	नराम्रो
OK	*ṭhi·*kai	ठीकै
too expensive	*dhe·*rai ma·*hā·*go	धेरै महँगो

There are too many tourists there.
   *tya·*hāh par·*ya·*ṭak *dhe·*rai chan
   त्यहाँ पर्यटक धेरै छन

Not many people speak (English).
   *tho·*rai *ja·*na·tah (ang·*gre·*ji)
   *bol·*chan
   थोरै जनता (अङ्ग्रेजी)
   बोल्छन

I was ripped off in ...
   ...*mah ma·lai *ṭhag·*yo
   ...मा मलाई ठग्यो

People are really friendly there.
   *tya·*hāh *ja·*na·tah *dhe·*rai
   ra·*mai·*lo chan
   त्यहाँ जनता धेरै
   रमाइलो छन

What's there to do in (Chitwan)?
   (*chit·*wan)·mah ke *gar·*na
   *paun·*cha?
   (चित्वन)मा के गर्न
   पाउन्छ ?

The best time to go is in (Dasain).
   *tya·*hāh *jah·*na *sab·*bhan·dah
   *rahm·*ro *be·*lah (*da·*saī) ho
   त्यहाँ जान सबभन्दा
   राम्रो बेला (दसैं) हो

I'm going to Pokhara for
(three weeks).
   ma (tin *hap·*tah)·ko *lah·*gi
   *po·*kha·rah·mah *jan·*chu
   म (तीन हप्ता)को लागि
   पोखरामा जान्छु

Is it expensive?
   ma·*hā·*go cha?
   महँगो छ ?

Is it safe for women travellers on
their own?
   *ek·*lai *nah·*ri *yah·*tri·ko *lah·*gi
   su·*ra·chit cha?
   एक्लै नारी यात्रीको लागि
   सुरक्षित छ ?

Is it safe to hitch?
   lipht *li·nu su·*ra·chit cha?
   लिफ्ट लिनु सुरक्षित छ ?

COMMON INTERESTS

संयुक्त चाखहरू

What do you do in your spare time?

ta·*paī*·ko *phur*·sat·mah ke *gar*·nu·hun·cha?	तपाईंको फुर्सतमा के गर्नुहुन्छ ?

Do you have any hobbies?

ta·*paī*·ko *ke*·hi sokh cha?	तपाईंको केही सोख छ ?

Do you like ...?

ta·*paī*·lai ... man *par*·cha?	तपाईंलाई ... मन पर्छ ?

I like/don't like ...

ma·lai ... man *par*·cha/*par*·dai·na	मलाई ... मन पर्छ/पर्दैन

basketball	*bahs*·ket·bal	बास्केट्बल
football	*laht*·te *bha*·kun·do	लात्ते भकुन्डो
trekking	*pai*·dal *hīḍ*·na	पैदल हिड्न
music	*sang*·git	सङ्गीत
photography	*tas*·bir *khic*·na	तस्विर खिच्न
playing cards	tahs *khel*·na	तास खेल्न
playing games	khel *khel*·na	खेल खेल्न
playing sport	*khel*·kud *khel*·na	खेलकुद खेल्न
reading	*paḍh*·na	पढ्न
seeing films	cal·*ci*·tra *her*·na	चलचित्र हेर्न
shopping	*kin*·mel *gar*·na	किनमेल गर्न
skiing	is·*ki khel*·na	इस्की खेल्न
swimming	*pau*·ḍi *khel*·na	पौडी खेल्न
talking	*ku*·rah *gar*·na	कुरा गर्न
travelling	*yah*·trah *gar*·na	यात्रा गर्न
watching sport	*khel*·kud *her*·na	खेलकुद हेर्न

I make ...

	ma ... ba·*naun*·chu	म ... बनाउन्छु
pottery	*mah*·ṭah·kah *bhāh*·ḍah	माटाका भाँडा
jewellery	*ga*·ha·nah	गहना

I collect ...

	ma ... ja·*maun*·chu	म ... जमाउन्छु
books	ki·*tahb*	किताब
coins	*mu*·drah	मुद्रा
dolls	*pu*·ta·li	पुतली
stamps	*ṭi*·kaṭ	टिकट

It's fun.

	maj·jah *lahg*·cha	मज्जा लाग्छ

INTERESTS

MUSIC   सङ्गीत

Do you like ...?	ta·*paī*·lai ... man *par*·cha?	तपाईंलाई ... मन पर्छ ?
to dance	*nahc*·na	नाच्न
listening to music	*sang*·git *sun*·na	सङ्गीत सुन्न

Do you ...?	ta·*paī*·lai ... *aun*·cha?	तपाईंलाई ... आउन्छ?
play an instrument	*bah*·jah ba·*jau*·na	बाजा बजाउन
sing	git *gau*·na	गीत गाउन

What sort of music do you like?
ta·*paī*·lai ke *sang*·git
man *par*·cha?
तपाईंलाई के सङ्गीत
मन पर्छ ?

Which bands do you like?
ta·*paī*·lai ke bahṇḍ
man *par*·cha?
तपाईंलाई के बाण्ड
मन पर्छ ?

I like (the) ...
ma·lai ... man *par*·cha
मलाई ... मन पर्छ

Have you heard the latest release by ...?
ta·*paī*·le ...ko ah·*dhu*·nik git
sun·nu *bha*·yo?
तपाईंले ...को आधुनिक
गीत सुन्नु भयो ?

TRADITIONAL MUSIC

Music and song are fundamental to all the cultures of Nepal. Traditional Nepalese music is generally either classical/religious or folk music. Classical ragas originated in India but have acquired a Nepalese character. Hinduism and Buddhism each have distinctive styles of religious song, including the blast of Tibetan horns.

Folk music themes include love, nature and heroic sagas, performed by traditional singers called *gaine* who play the *sarangi*, a small stringed instrument. *Damai* or members of the musical caste traditionally play instruments such as the *sahnai* (a stringed instrument), *narsingha* (large trumpets) and various kinds of drums, but these days their profession mainly involves playing Hindi film music on brass instruments for wedding processions.

INTERESTS

Which radio station plays good music?
kun *re·ḍi·yo* is·*ṭe*·san·mah   कुन रेडियो इस्टेसनमा
rahm·ro sang·git su·*naun*·cha?   राम्रो सङ्गीत सुनाउन्छ ?

What frequency is it on?
kun *re·ḍi·yo beṇḍ*·mah cha?   कुन रेडियो बेण्डमा छ ?

This radio station, is it FM or AM?
yo *re·ḍi·yo* is·*ṭe*·san *eph*·em   यो रेडियो इस्टेसन एफएम
ho ki *ai*·em?   हो कि ऐएम ?

Where can you hear traditional
music around here?
ya·*hāh* sāh·*skri*·tik *sang*·git   यहाँ साँस्कृतिक सङ्गीत
ka·*hāh sun*·ne?   कहाँ सुन्ने ?

THEY MAY SAY ...

mahph *gar*·nu·hos, *ṭi*·kaṭ *sa*·bai *be*·ci·yo
Sorry, we're sold out.

CINEMA & THEATRE   सिनेमा र अभिनय

Most of the cinemas are hugely crowded and show only Hindi
(Indian) and occasionally Nepali films – without subtitles – but
you can find some European films and live theatre, and there
are plenty of Nepalese cultural performances. Some restaurants
also show English-language videos, although they're often poor
quality pirated versions.

I feel like going	ma·lai ... her·na	मलाई ... हेर्न
to a ...	man *lahg*·yo	मन लाग्यो
film	philm	फिल्म
play	*li*·lah	लीला

What's on at the cinema tonight?
be·lu·kah *si*·ne·mah *hal*·mah ke cha?   बेलुका सिनेमा हलमा के छ ?

Where can I find a cinema guide?
si·ne·mah *a*·kha·bahr ka·*hāh*   सिनेमा अखबार कहाँ
paun·cha?   पाउन्छ ?

Are there any tickets for ...?
...ko *ṭi*·kaṭ *paun*·cha?   ...को टिकट पाउन्छ ?

INTERESTS

Is the performance in English?
nah·tak ang·*gre*·ji·mah cha?

नाटक अङ्ग्रेजीमा छ ?

Does it have English subtitles?
ang·*gre*·ji *le*·khe·ko cha?

अङ्ग्रेजी लेखेको छ ?

Shall we sit or stand?
bas·āu ki u·*ṭhi*·bas·ne?

बसौं कि उठिबस्ने ?

Where shall we sit?
ka·hāh *bas*·ne?

कहाँ बस्ने ?

Are those seats taken?
ti *ṭhāu*·ha·ru·mah *ko*·hi
ba·se·cha?

ती ठाउँहरूमा कोही बसेछ ?

NEPALESE DANCE

Traditional Nepalese dance is either classical/religious/
festival dance or folk dance, and there are many varieties of
each. Classical dances include the Hindu *Bhairav-Kali* and
the Buddhist *Bajra-Yogini*, while mask dances, such as
the *Newar Lakhe* dance, are performed during religious
festivals. Popular folk dances include the *Tharu* Stick dance,
the women's *Sakhi* dance, the *Maruni* dance (sung and
danced by a group of men and a group of women), and
the *Panche* dance (performed during wedding processions).

OPINIONS   भनाइहरू

Do you agree?
ta·*paī mahn*·nu·hun·cha?   तपाई मान्नुहुन्छ ?

I agree/disagree.
ma *mahn*·chu/*mahn*·di·na   म मान्छु/मान्दिन

What do you think?
ta·*paī*·ko bi·*cahr* ke ho?   तपाईको बिचार के हो ?

I think that ...
me·ro bi·*cahr*·mah ...   मेरो बिचारमा ...

That's my opinion.
tya·hi *me*·ro bi·*cahr* ho   त्यही मेरो बिचार हो

Do you like it?
ta·*paī*·lai yo man *par*·cha?   तपाईलाई यो मन पर्छ ?

I like/don't like it.
ma·lai yo man *par*·cha/*par*·dai·na   मलाई यो मन पर्छ/पर्दैन

That's true/not true.
tyo *sa*·tya ho/*hoi*·na   त्यो सत्य हो/होइन

This is good/bad.
yo *rahm*·ro/kha·*rahb* cha   यो राम्रो/खराब छ

POLITICS   राजनीति

Democracy only came to Nepal after the 1990 people's uprising and as yet it's failed to meet the people's high expectations. The Maoist People's War (since 1996) and rampant corruption have also contributed to an atmosphere of insecurity and repression. However, the Nepalese do love to debate politics, so it's not a taboo subject – just be sensitive to the current, somewhat difficult, political climate.

What do you think of the current
government?
a·hi·le·ko *sar*·kahr ke bi·*cahr*   अहिलेको सरकार के बिचार
gar·nu·hun·cha?   गर्नुहुन्छ ?

INTERESTS

I agree/don't agree with their policy on ...	...ko sar·*kah*·ri *ni*·ti ma *mahn*·chu/ *mahn*·di·na	...को सरकारी नीति म मान्छु/ मान्दिन
drugs	*o*·kha·ti	ओखती
the economy	*ar*·tha	अर्थ
education	*shi*·chah	शिक्षा
the environment	bah·tah·*ba*·raṇ	बाताबरण
social welfare	sah·*mah*·jik *bha*·lai	सामाजिक भलाइ

I'm against ...
ma ...ko bi·*rodh* hū   म ...को बिरोध हुँ

I'm in favour of ...
ma ...ko *pa*·cha *lin*·chu   म ...को पक्ष लिन्छु

Who do you vote for?
ta·*paī* kas·lai mat
kha·*sahl*·nu·hun·cha?   तपाईं कस्लाई मत
खसाल्नुहुन्छ ?

I support the ... party.	ma ... *dal*·lai sa·*mar*·than *gar*·chu	म ... दललाई समर्थन गर्छु
I'm a member of the ... party.	ma ...ko *dal*·ko sa·*das*·ya hū	म ...को दलको सदस्य हुँ
communist	*sahm*·ya·bah·di	साम्यबादी
conservative	pu·*rah*·tan·*bah*·di	पुरातनबादी
green	*ha*·ri·yo	हरियो
social democratic	sah·*mah*·jik pra·*jah*·tan·tra	सामाजिक प्रजातन्त्र
socialist	sa·*mahj*·bah·di	समाजबादी

I don't vote.
ma mat kha·*sahl*·di·na   म मत खसाल्दिन

In my country we have a (socialist) government.
me·ro *desh*·mah (sa·*mahj*·bah·di)
sar·kahr cha   मेरो देशमा (समाजबादी)
सरकार छ

Politicians are all the same.
rahj·*ni*·ti·gyā *sa*·bai *e*·kai ho   राजनीतिज्ञ सबै एकै हो

INTERESTS

candidate's speech	u·*me*·da·bahr·ko *bhah*·saṇ	उमेदबारको भाषण
corrupt	*bhras*·ṭa	भ्रष्ट
counting of votes	mat *gan*·nu	मत गन्नु
democracy	pra·*jah*·tan·tra	प्रजातन्त्र
demonstration	ju·*lus*	जुलूस
... election	... cu·*nahb*	... चुनाब
local council	na·gar·*pah*·li·kah	नगरपालिका
regional	prah·*de*·shik	प्रादेशिक
national	*rah*·stri·ya	राष्ट्रिय
electorate	*mat*·dah·tah sa·*mu*·ha	मतदाता समूह
exploitation	*sho*·saṇ	शोषण
to legalise	*kah*·nu·ni *ah*·dhahr *di*·nu	कानुनी आधार दिनु
to legislate	*ni*·yam *nir*·mahṇ *gar*·nu	नियम निर्माण गर्नु

misogyny	ai·mai·*pra*·ti·ko *ghri*·ṇah	आइमाईप्रतिको घृणा
parliament	*sā*·sad	संसद
policy	*ni*·ti	नीति
political speech	*rahj*·nai·tik *bhah*·saṇ	राजनैतिक भाषण
polling	*mat*·dahn	मतदान
president	*rah*·stra·pa·ti	राष्ट्रपति
prime minister	pra·*dhahm man*·tri	प्रधान मन्त्री
racism	*jah*·ti·bahd	जातिबाद
rally	ja·*maht*	जमात
sexism	ai·mai·*pra*·ti·ko *ghri*·ṇah	आइमाईप्रतिको घृणा
strike	*haḍ*·tahl	हडताल
trade union	*kahm*·ko sa·*mi*·ti	कामको समिति
unemployment	be·*kah*·ri	बेकारी
vote	mat	मत
to vote	mat kha·*sahl*·nu	मत खसाल्नु

ENVIRONMENT   बातावरण

Does Nepal have a pollution problem?
 ne·*pahl*·ko *du*·sit sa·*ma*·syah cha?   नेपालको दुषित समस्या छ ?

Does Kathmandu have a recycling
programme?
 kahth·mah·*ḍāu*·ko ri·*sai*·kal   काठ्माडौंको रीसाइकल
 yo·ja·nah cha?   योजना छ ?

Is this recyclable?
 yo ri·*sai*·kal gar·na sa·ki·ne   यो रीसाइकल गर्न सकिने
 bas·tu ho?   बस्तु हो ?

Are there any protected ... in Nepal?
 ne·*pahl*·mah ke·hi   नेपालमा केही
 ba·*cah*·ya·ko ... cha?   बचायको ... छ ?

Is this a	yo ba·*cah*·ya·ko	यो बचायको
protected ...?	... ho?	... हो ?
forest	ban	बन
park	u·*dyahn*	उद्यान
species	bar·ga	बर्ग

Where do you stand on ...?
 ...bah·re ta·*paī*·ko   ...बारे तपाईंको
 bi·*cahr* ke ho?   बिचार के हो ?

conservation	*sā*·ra·chaṇ	सँरक्षण
deforestation	ban·bi·*nahs*	बनबिनास
to dispose of	*phyāhk*·nu	फ्याँक्नु
drought	*suk*·khah	सुक्खा
endangered species	*kha*·ta·rah·mah	खतरामा
	par·ne bar·ga	पर्ने बर्ग
hunting	*shi*·kahr	शिकार
industrial pollution	au·*dyo*·gik	औद्योगिक
	du·sit	दुषित
irrigation	*sī*·cai	सिंचाइ
pollution	*du*·sit	दुषित
recycling	ri·*sai*·kal	रीसाइकल
reservoir	*pah*·ni *po*·kha·ri	पानी पोखरी

STAYING IN TOUCH — नबिर्सनु

(Tomorrow) is my last day here.
*(bho·*li) *ya·*hāh *me·*ro *an·*tim
din ho

(भोलि) यहाँ मेरो अन्तिम
दिन हो

Let's swap addresses.
*hahm·*ro *the·gah·*nah *sah·*ṭaū

हाम्रो ठेगाना साटौं

Do you have a pen and paper?
ta·*paī·*sā·ga *ka·*lam ra
*kah·*gaj cha?

तपाईंसँग कलम र
कागज छ ?

Do you have an email address?
ta·*paī·*ko *i·*mel *the·gah·*nah cha?

तपाईंको ईमेल ठेगाना छ ?

What's your (email) address?
ta·*paī·*ko (*i·*mel) *the·gah·*nah
ke ho?

तपाईंको (ईमेल) ठेगाना
के हो ?

Here's my (email) address.
yo *me·*ro (*i·*mel) *the·gah·*nah ho

यो मेरो (ईमेल) ठेगाना हो

Do you have access to a fax machine?
ta·*paī* phyahks *gar·*na
*sa·*kin·cha?

तपाईं फ्याक्स गर्न
सकिन्छ ?

INTERESTS

If you ever visit (Scotland), please
come and visit us.
ta·*paī* (is·*kaṭ·*laīḍ)·mah *ah·*yo
*bha·*ne, *hah·*mi·lai *bheṭ·*na
*au·*nu·hos

तपाईं (इस्कट्लैंड)मा आयो
भने, हामीलाई भेट्न
आउनुहोस

If you come to (Birmingham),
you have a place to stay.
ta·*paī* (*bahr·*ming·ham)·mah *ah·*yo
*bha·*ne, ta·*paī·*lai bahs *hun·*cha

तपाईं (बार्मिङ्हम)मा आयो
भने, तपाईंलाई बास हुन्छ

I'll send you copies of the photos.
ma ta·*paī·*lai *tas·*bir
pa·*thaun·*chu

म तपाईंलाई तस्विर
पठाउन्छु

INTERESTS

Don't forget to write!
   ma·lai ci·thi pa·ṭhau·na
   na·bir·sa·nu·hos!

मलाई चिठी पठाउन
नबिर्सनुहोस !

It's been great meeting you.
   ma·lai ta·paī·sã·ga
   bhe·ṭe·ko·mah rahm·ro lahg·yo

मलाई तपाईंसँग
भेटेकोमा राम्रो लाग्यो

Keep in touch!
   ma·lai na·bir·sa·nu·hos!

मलाई नबिर्सनुहोस !

SHOPPING

In Kathmandu and other towns most shopkeepers speak some English, but outside the more populated areas this is not always the case. To address a shopkeeper, follow the suggestions in the Meeting People chapter (see page 35). He or she may respond with 'speak', *bhan·nu·hos* (भन्नुहोस्). Remember that 'please' and 'thank you' are not necessary in Nepali. Just state what you want and add 'please give', *di·nu·hos* (दिनुहोस्).

LOOKING FOR ...   ... खोज्नु

Where's the nearest ...?	*na·ji·kai ... ka·hāh cha?*	नजिकै ... कहाँ छ ?
bank	*baĩk*	बैंक
barber	*ha·jahm*	हजाम
book shop	*ki·tahb pa·sal*	किताब पसल
camera shop	*kyah·me·rah pa·sal*	क्यामेरा पसल
chemist	*au·sa·dhi pa·sal*	औषधी पसल
clothing store	*lu·gah pa·sal*	लुगा पसल
cobbler	*sahr·ki*	सार्की
fruit shop	*phal·phul pa·sal*	फलफूल पसल
handicraft shop	*has·ta·ka·lah pa·sal*	हस्तकला पसल
laundry	*lu·gah·dhu·ne ṭhaũ*	लुगाधुने ठाउँ
market	*ba·jahr*	बजार
music shop	*sang·git pa·sal*	सङ्गीत पसल
newsagency	*a·kha·bahr pa·sal*	अखबार पसल
optician	*cash·mah pa·sal*	चश्मा पसल
pharmacy	*au·sa·dhi pa·sal*	औषधी पसल
shoe shop	*jut·tah pa·sal*	जुता पसल
souvenir shop	*ci·no pa·sal*	चिनो पसल
stationer	*ci·ṭhi·pa·tra pa·sal*	चिठीपत्र पसल
supermarket	*su·par·mahr·keṭ*	सुपरमार्केट
teashop	*ci·yah pa·sal*	चिया पसल
travel agency	*yah·trah li·ne pa·sal*	यात्रा लिने पसल
vegetable shop	*tar·kah·ri pa·sal*	तरकारी पसल

MAKING A PURCHASE   सामान किन्नु

I'm just looking.	*her*·dai·chu	हेर्दैछु

Where can I buy ...?	... *ka*·hāh *kin*·na *pain*·cha?	... कहाँ किन्न पाइन्छ ?
paper	*kah*·gaj	कागज
soap	*sah*·bun	साबुन
string	*ḍo*·ri	डोरी

Do you have a ...?	ta·*paī*·ka·*hāh* ... cha?	तपाईंकहाँ ... छ ?
hat	*ṭo*·pi	टोपी
newspaper	*a*·kha·bahr	अखबार
pencil	*si*·sah·ka·lam	सिसाकलम

SHOPPING

MAKING RUPEE

The Nepalese currency is the rupee, ru·*pi*·yāh (रुपियाँ), which is divided into 100 *pai*·sah (पैसा), which is also the word for 'money'.

How much is this (pen)?
  yo (*ka*·lam)·ko *ka*·ti *pai*·sah ho?   यो (कलम)को कति पैसा हो ?

How much do (eggs) cost?
  (*phul*)·ko *ka*·ti ho?   (फुल)को कति हो ?

Four rupees each.
  eu·*ṭah*·ko cahr ru·*pi*·yāh   एउटाको चार रुपियाँ

Please write down the price.
  mol lekh·*di*·nu·hos   मोल लेखदिनुहोस

I'd like to buy ...
  ... *kin*·na man *lahg*·yo   ... किन्न मन लाग्यो

Do you have any others?
  ar·ko *ku*·nai cha?   अर्को कुनै छ ?

There is/are none.
  chai·na   छैन

Which one? This one?
  kun *cah*·hĩ? yo *cah*·hĩ?   कुन चाहिं ? यो चाहिं ?

Show it to me.
  ma·lai de·*khau*·nu·hos
मलाई देखाउनुहोस

Please show me the price.
  mol de·*khau*·nu·hos
मोल देखाउनुहोस

May I/we see it?
  he·raũ?
हेरौं ?

I like/don't like this.
  ma·lai yo man *par*·cha/*par*·dai·na
मलाई यो मन पर्छ/पर्दैन

What's it made of?
  ke·le *ba*·ne·ko?
केले बनेको ?

Where was it made?
  ka·*hãh ba*·ne·ko?
कहाँ बनेको ?

I'll take it.
  lin·chu
लिन्छु

What else do you need?
  a·ru *ke*·hi *cah*·hin·cha?
अरु केही चाहिन्छ ?

That's all. How much is it?
  te·ti *mah*·trai, ka·ti *bha*·yo?
तेति मात्रै, कति भयो ?

Do you accept credit cards?
  kre·ḍiṭ kahrḍ *hun*·cha?
क्रेडिट कार्ड हुन्छ ?

Could I have a receipt please?
  bil *di*·nu·hun·cha?
बिल दिनुहुन्छ ?

Does it have a guarantee?
  tyas·ko *bah*·cah·cha?
त्यसको बाचा छ ?

Can I have it sent abroad?
  bi·*desh*·mah pa·*thau*·nu·hun·cha?
बिदेशमा पठाउनुहुन्छ ?

Please wrap it.
  ber·nu·hos
बेर्नुहोस

I'd like to return this.
  yo phar·*kau*·nu·par·cha
यो फर्काउनुपर्छ

It's faulty.
  yo kahm *gar*·dai·na
यो काम गर्दैन

It's broken.
  yo *bi*·gre·ko cha
यो बिग्रेको छ

I'd like my money back.
  me·ro *pai*·sah *phar*·kai *di*·nu·hos
मेरो पैसा फर्काइ दिनुहोस

SHOPPING

BARGAINING
मोलतोल गर्नु

It's customary to bargain, *mol·tol gar·*nu (मोलतोल गर्नु), especially for tourist and luxury goods and transport. As in most Asian countries, friendly bargaining is a way of life and foreigners are presumed wealthier than locals. With a little patience and goodwill, you'll be able to reduce the price of most items to the satisfaction of both yourself and the shopkeeper. But there will generally be a going price for basic household goods and foodstuffs.

Really?
*sāh·*cai?
साँचै ?

That's expensive!
ma·*hā·*go cha!
महँगो छ !

It's cheap!
*sas·*to cha!
सस्तो छ !

The price is too high.
mol *dhe·*rai ma·*hā·*go cha
मोल धेरै महँगो छ

It's too much for us.
*hahm·*ro *lah·*gi *dhe·*rai *bha·*yo
हाम्रो लागि धेरै भयो

I don't have that much money.
ma·*sā·*ga *te·*ti *pai·*sah *chai·*na
मसँग तेति पैसा छैन

Could you lower the price a little?
*a·*li·ka·ti gha·*tau·*nu·hun·cha?
अलिकति घटाउनुहुन्छ ?

I'll give (200) rupees.
(*du·*i·say) ru·*pi·*yāh *din·*chu
(दुइसय) रुपियाँ दिन्छु

That's not possible, give me (250).
*hun·*dai·na, (*du·*i·say pa·*cahs*)
*di·*nu·hos
हुन्दैन, (दुइसय पचास) दिनुहोस

OK.
*hun·*cha
हुन्छ

I don't want it.
*cah·*hin·dai·na
चाहिन्दैन

Do you have something cheaper?
*a·*ru *ku·*nai *sas·*to cha?
अरु कुनै सस्तो छ ?

No more than ...
...*bhan·*dah kam
...भन्दा कम

SOUVENIRS

चिनोहरू

anklet	*pau*·ju	पाउजु
bangle	*cu*·rah	चुरा
brassware	*pi*·tal·ko *sah*·mahn	पितलको सामान
carpet	ga·*laī*·cah	गलैंचा
chain	*si*·kri	सिक्री
doll	*pu*·ta·li	पुतली
(a pair of) earrings	(ek jor) ṭap	(एक जोर) टप
embroidery	*buṭ*·ṭah	बुट्टा
gem/jewel	ju·*hah*·raht	जुहारात
gold	sun	सुन
handicraft	*has*·ta·ka·lah	हस्तकला
incense burner	dhup *dah*·ni	धूप दानि
jewellery	ga·ha·nah	गहना
mask	ma·*kuṇ*·ḍo	मकुण्डो

necklace	*mah*·lah	माला
Nepalese knife	*khu*·ku·ri	खुकुरी
Nepalese painting	*thahṅg*·kah	थाङ्का
ornament	*a*·laṅg·kahr	अलङ्कार
painting	*ci*·tra	चित्र
pottery	*mah*·ṭah·kah *bhāh*·ḍah	माटाका भाँडा
puppet	*kaṭh*·pu·ta·li	कठपुतली
ring	*aū*·ṭhi	औठी
rug	*sah*·no ga·*laī*·cah	सानो गलैंचा
silver	*cāh*·di	चाँदी
statue	*mur*·ti	मूर्ति
tapestry	*ci*·tra·paṭ	चित्रपट
wooden article	*kahṭh*·bah·ṭa	काठबाट बनेको
	ba·ne·ko *bas*·tu	बस्तु

ESSENTIAL ITEMS
आवश्यक सामानहरू

Where can I find (a) ...?	... *ka*·hāh *kin*·na *pain*·cha?	... कहाँ किन्न पाइन्छ ?
I'd like (a) ...	*ma*·lai ... *cah*·hi·yo	मलाई ... चाहियो
batteries	*ma*·sa·lah	मसला
candles	*main*·bat·ti	मैनबत्ती
gas cyclinder	gyāhs *si*·liṇ·ḍar	ग्याँस सिलीण्डर
matches	*sa*·lai	सलाइ
shampoo	*dhu*·lai	धुलाइ
soap	*sah*·bun	साबुन
toilet paper	*ṭwai*·leṭ *pe*·par	ट्वाईलेट पेपर
toothpaste	*many*·jan	मञ्जन
washing powder	*lu*·gah·dhu·ne *sah*·bun	लुगाधुने साबुन

CLOTHING
लुगा

Nepalese national dress comprises a sari, *sah*·ḍi (साडी), and blouse, *co*·lo (चोलो), for women, and a cap, *ṭo*·pi (टोपी), tunic, *dau*·rah (दाउरा), and drawstring trousers, *su*·ru·wahl (सुरुवाल), for men.

belt	*pe*·ṭi	पेटी
boots	buṭ	बुट
button	ṭāhk	टाँक
cap	*ṭo*·pi	टोपी
clothing	*lu*·gah	लुगा
coat	koṭ	कोट
dress	*jah*·mah	जामा
gloves	*pan*·jah	पन्जा
hat	*ṭo*·pi	टोपी
jacket	*jyah*·keṭ	ज्याकेट
jeans	*jin*·painṭ	जीनपाइन्ट
jumper	*swi*·ṭar	स्विटर
muffler	gal·*ban*·di	गलबन्दी

pants (trousers)	*paint*	पाइन्ट
Nepalese trousers	*su*·ru·wahl	सुरुवाल
sandals	*cap*·pal	चप्पल
scarf	*do*·*pat*·tah	दोपट्टा
shirt	ka·*mij*	कमिज
shoes	*jut*·tah	जुत्ता
shorts	*kat*·tu	कट्टु
singlet	*gan*·ji	गन्जी
socks	*mo*·jah	मोजा
sweater	*swi*·tar	स्विटर
trousers	*paint*	पाइन्ट
T-shirt	*gan*·ji	गन्जी
underpants	*kat*·tu	कट्टु
vest/waistcoat	*is*·ta·kot	ईस्टकोट्

Can I try it on?
la·gai *her*·nu·hun·cha? — लगाई हेर्नुहुन्छ ?

My size is ...
me·ro saij ... ho — मेरो साइज ... हो

It fits well/doesn't fit.
thik cha/*chai*·na — ठीक छ/छैन

Can you make this in my size?
ma·lai yo *lu*·gah *ba*·nai·di·na *sa*·kin·cha? — मलाई यो लुगा बनाईदिन सकिन्छ ?

It's too ...	*dhe*·rai ... cha	धेरै ... छ
big	*thu*·lo	ठूलो
small	*sah*·no	सानो
short	*cho*·to	छोटो
long	*lah*·mo	लामो
tight	*ka*·sin	कसि
loose	*khu*·ku·lo	खुकुलो

SHOPPING

MATERIALS

भौतिकहरू

brass	*pi*·tal	पितल
cotton	*su*·ti	सुती
glass	kāhc	काँच
gold	sun	सुन
handmade	*haht*·le *ba*·ne·ko	हातले बनेको
leather	*chah*·lah	छाला
metal	*dhah*·tu	धातु
plastic	*plah*·stik	प्लास्टिक
pottery	*mah*·tah·kah *bhāh*·dah	माटाका भाँडा
silk	*re*·sham	रेशम
silver	*cāh*·di	चाँदी
wood	kahth	काठ
wool	un	ऊन
sheep wool	*bhe*·dah·ko un	भेडाको ऊन
yak wool	*caū*·ri·ko un	चौरीको ऊन

COLOURS

रङहरू

dark ...	*gah*·dhah ...	गाढा ...
light ...	*phi*·kah ...	फिका ...
bright ...	*ca*·ha·ki·lo ...	चहकिलो ...
pale ...	*phi*·kah ...	फिका ...
black	*kah*·lo	कालो
blue	*ni*·lo	निलो
brown	*khai*·ro	खैरो
green	*ha*·ri·yo	हरियो
grey	*kai*·lo	कैलो
multicoloured	*rang*·gin	रँङीन
orange	*sun*·ta·lah rang	सुन्तला रङ
pink	gu·*lah*·phi	गुलाफी
purple	*pyah*·ji	प्याजी
red	*rah*·to	रातो
white	*se*·to	सेतो
yellow	pa·*hē*·lo	पहेंलो

TOILETRIES
बाठरुमको सामान

comb	*kaī*·yo	काईयो
condoms	ḍhahl	ढाल
hairbrush	*ka*·pahl *kor*·ne *bu*·rus	कपाल कोर्ने बुरुस
laxative	ju·*lahph*	जुलाफ
sanitary	ma·hi·nah·bah·ri·ko	महीनाबारीको
products	*sah*·mahn	सामान
moisturiser	*mukh*·mah	मुखमा लगाउने
(face cream)	la·*gau*·ne krim	क्रीम

razor	*chu*·rah	छुरा
razor blades	*pat*·ti	पत्ती
shampoo	*dhu*·lai	धुलाइ
shaving cream	*khau*·ra·ne krim	खौरने क्रीम
soap	*sah*·bun	साबुन
tissues	*kah*·gaj·ko ru·*mahl*	कागजको रुमाल
toilet paper	*ṭwai*·leṭ *pe*·par	ट्वाईलेट पेपर
toothbrush	dāht *mahjh*·ne *bu*·rus	दाँत माझ्ने बुरुस
toothpaste	*many*·jan	मञ्जन

SHOPPING

SHOPPING NIRVANA

Nepalese clothing, handicraft and souvenir shops are full of wonderful things to buy. Look out for shawls, waistcoats and embroidered T-shirts, all kinds of bags, handmade paper items, woodcarvings, brassware and jewellery. Other popular items include handwoven carpets, *thahng*·kah (थाङ्का) paintings, traditional masks, pottery and Nepalese dolls and puppets. When you buy from handicraft cooperatives, you can be sure of paying a fair price and supporting local employment and training initiatives into the bargain!

STATIONERY & PUBLICATIONS

चिठीपत्र र प्रकाशनहरू

Is there an English-language bookshop nearby?
ya·hāh na·ji·kai ang·gre·ji ki·tahb pa·sal cha?
यहाँ नजिकै अङ्ग्रेजी किताब पसल छ ?

Do you have any books in English by ...?
ta·paī·ka·hāh ...·le lekh·yo ang·gre·ji ki·tahb cha?
तपाईंकहाँ ...ले लेख्यो अङ्ग्रेजी किताब छ ?

Do you sell ...?	*ya·hāh ... bec·cha?*	यहाँ ... बेच्छ ?
magazines	*pa·tri·kah*	पत्रिका
newspapers	*a·kha·bahr*	अखबार
postcards	*post·kahrḍ*	पोस्टकार्ड

aerogram	*ha·wai·pa·tra*	हवाईपत्र
book	*ki·tahb*	किताब
dictionary	*shab·da·kosh*	शब्दकोश
envelope	*khahm*	खाम
exercise book	*kah·pi*	कापी
ink	*ma·si*	मसी
letterpad	*ci·thi·lekh·ne kah·pi*	चिठीलेख्ने कापी
map	*nak·sah*	नक्सा
... map	*...·ko nak·sah*	...को नक्सा
city	*sha·har*	शहर
regional	*che·tra*	क्षेत्र
road	*bah·ṭo*	बाटो
notebook	*kah·pi*	कापी
novel	*u·pan·yahs*	उपन्यास
paper	*kah·gaj*	कागज
pen	*ka·lam*	कलम
pencil	*si·sah·ka·lam*	सिसाकलम
safety pin	huk	हुक
scissors	*kaī·ci*	कैंची
stamp	*ṭi·kaṭ*	टिकट
writing pad/paper	*lekh·ne kah·pi*	लेख्ने कापी

MUSIC सङ्गीत

I'm looking for a ... CD.
ma ...·ko si·ḍi khoj·dai·chu
म ...को सीडी खोज्दैछु

Do you have any ...?
ta·pai·ka·hāh ... cha?
तपाईंकहाँ ... छ ?

What's his/her best recording?
us·ko sab·bhan·dah rahm·ro
git kun ho?
उसको सबभन्दा राम्रो
गीत कुन हो ?

I heard a band/singer called ...
mai·le ... bhan·ne bahnḍ/
gah·yak sun·nē
मैले ... भन्ने बाण्ड/
गायक सुन्नें

Can I listen to this CD here?
yo si·ḍi ya·hāh sun·nu·hun·cha?
यो सीडी यहाँ सुन्नुहुन्छ ?

I need a blank tape.
ma·lai khah·li ṭep cah·hi·yo
मलाई खाली टेप चाहियो

SHOPPING

PHOTOGRAPHY तस्बिर खिच्ने कला

How much is it to process this film?
eu·ṭah ril priṇṭ gar·na, ka·ti
pai·sah lahg·cha?
एउटा रील प्रिन्ट गर्न, कति
पैसा लाग्छ ?

When will it be ready?
ka·hi·le ta·yahr hun·cha?
कहिले तयार हुन्छ ?

Please give me a film for this camera.
yo kyah·me·rah·lai eu·ṭah ril
di·nu·hos
यो क्यामेरालाई एउटा रील
दिनुहोस

Do you fix cameras?
kyah·me·rah ba·nau·nu·hun·cha?
क्यामेरा बनाउनुहुन्छ ?

battery	ma·sa·lah	मसला
B&W film	kah·lo se·to ril	कालो सेतो रील
colour film	rang·gin ril	रँगीन रील
film	ril	रील
videotape	bhi·ḍi·yo	भिडीयो

SHOPPING

SMOKING   धूम्रपान

Smoking is still very common in Nepal, particularly among men.
Locally produced, often unfiltered, cigarettes (from government-
owned factories) are the cheapest, while better quality, imported
cigarettes and tobacco are quite expensive in local terms.

A packet of cigarettes, please.
  ek *baṭ*·ṭah *cu*·roṭ *di*·nu·hos   एक बट्टा चुरोट दिनुहोस

Are these cigarettes strong or mild?
  yo *cu*·roṭ *ka*·ḍah ho ki   यो चुरोट कडा हो कि
  ma·*dhu*·ro?   मधुरो ?

Do you have a light?
  sa·lai cha?   सलाइ छ ?

Do you mind if I smoke?
  mai·le *dhum*·ra·pahn   मैले धूम्रपान
  gar·na *hun*·cha?   गर्न हुन्छ ?

Please don't smoke.
  dhum·ra·pahn na·*gar*·nu·hos   धूम्रपान नगर्नुहोस

I'm trying to give up.
  choḍ·na *ko*·sis *gar*·dai·chu   छोड्न कोसिस गर्दैछु

THROUGH THE HAZE ...

Tobacco smoking is still very common in Nepal – it's
permitted in all public places, including restaurants, halls
and cinemas. Dubious advertising is everywhere. The
government makes a good profit from the manufacture
and sale of cigarettes, so public health messages about the
risks of smoking are taking a while to be sent out.

cigarettes	*cu*·roṭ	चुरोट
cigarette papers	*cu*·roṭ *kah*·gaj	चुरोट कागज
hookah	*huk*·kah	हुक्का
lighter	*lai*·ṭar	लाईटर
matches	*sa*·lai	सलाइ
pipe	*cu*·roṭ paip	चुरोट पाईप्
tobacco	*sur*·ti	सुर्ती

SIZES & COMPARISONS

कत्रो र तुलनाहरू

a little	*a*·li *a*·li	अलि अलि
a little bit	a·li·*ka*·ti	अलिकति
also	*pa*·ni	पनि
any	ke·hi/*ku*·nai	केही / कुनै
big	*ṭhu*·lo	ठूलो
enough	pra·*shas*·ta	प्रशस्त
few	*tho*·rai	थोरै
heavy	*ga*·hraũ	गहौँ
less	kam	कम
light	ha·*lu*·kah	हलुका
long	*lah*·mo	लामो
(too) many/much	*dhe*·rai	धेरै
more	*a*·jha *dhe*·rai	अझ धेरै
most	*dhe*·rai·ja·so	धेरैजसो
short	*cho*·ṭo	छोटो
small	*sah*·no	सानो
some	ke·hi/*ku*·nai	केही / कुनै
tall	*a*·glo	अग्लो
too	*sah*·hrai	साह्रै

WEIGHTS & MEASURES   भार र नापहरू

The metric system is in common use, but there are some measures particular to Nepal, approximating the following:

50 grams	*mu*·thi	मुथी
100 grams	*cau*·thai	चौथाइ
200 grams	pau	पाउ
400 grams/0.5 litre	*mah*·nah	माना
800 grams	ser	सेर
2 kg (2.5 ser)	*dhahr*·ni	धार्नी
3.2 kg (4 ser)	*pah*·thi	पाथी
64 kg (20 *pah*·thi)	*mu*·ri	मुरी
180 grains	*to*·lah	तोला
span (0.25 m)	*bit*·to	बित्तो
metre	gaj	गज

SHOPPING

FOOD

In larger towns, especially Kathmandu, restaurants serve all kinds of dishes, including a wide range of Western-style food. In the countryside and on trekking routes, however, only a few different food items will be available at any time of year.

The most typical Nepali meal is dahl bhaht tar·kahri (दाल भात तरकारी) – lentils, boiled rice and vegetable curry. Curries are usually mild, but often served with a fresh pickle or relish, a·cahr (अचार), which may be spicy, pi·ro (पिरो). If you don't want spicy food, request pi·ro na·hahl·nu·hos (पिरो नहाल्नुहोस). Potatoes, corn, millet and other carbohydrates are also staple foods up in the hills.

ONE ESSENTIAL WORD

The verb khah·nu (खानु), 'to eat', is also commonly used for drinking and smoking:

I eat rice/food.	
ma bhaht khahn·chu	म भात खान्छु
I drink tea.	
ma ci·yah khahn·chu	म चिया खान्छु
I don't smoke cigarettes.	
ma cu·roṭ khahn·di·na	मा चुरोट खान्दिन

THROUGH THE DAY   दिनभरि

In Nepal, eating two meals a day is the norm: one late in the morning around 10 or 11 am and the second at 7 or 8 pm, with just a glass of tea (and perhaps a sweet snack) first thing. In less touristy areas, you may find it difficult to get a Western-style breakfast or much food before 10 am, or lunch after midday or so.

breakfast	bi·hah·na·ko khah·nah	बिहानको खाना
lunch	ca·me·nah	चमेना
dinner/food/meal	bhaht	भात
snack	khah·jah	खाजा

VEGETARIAN &
SPECIAL MEALS

साकाहारी र
बिशेष खाना

Vegetarian meals are widely available, due to the fact that high-caste Hindus are traditionally vegetarian and meat is relatively scarce – although Newar cuisine is renowned for its many meat dishes. Dairy products are also uncommon, except for yogurt (which is a luxury food), so vegans will have few difficulties. Soy products apart from tofu are not often available.

I'm vegetarian.
   ma sah·kah·*hah*·ri hū

म साकाहारी हुँ

Do you have any vegetarian dishes?
   ta·*paī*·ka·hāh sah·kah·*hah*·ri
   khah·nah cha?

तपाईंकहाँ साकाहारी
खाना छ ?

Does this dish have (meat)?
   yo *khah*·nah·mah (*mah*·su) cha?

यो खानामा (मासु) छ ?

Can I get this without (meat)?
   yo (*mah*·su) na·*hah*·le·ko
   paun·cha?

यो (मासु) नहालेको
पाउन्छ ?

Does it contain (eggs)?
   yo *khah*·nah·mah (phul) cha?

यो खानामा (फुल) छ ?

I'm allergic to (peanuts).
   ma (*ba*·dahm) *khah*·nu *hun*·dai·na

म (बदाम) खानु हुन्दैन

TABLE MANNERS

In Hindu Nepal, there are strict rules about keeping food and drink ritually pure and unpolluted. Food becomes 'contaminated', *jhu·*to (जुठो), if touched by someone else's hand or mouth, or by a serving plate or utensil. So take care when handling food (only use your right hand), and remember sharing food from your plate (or someone else's) is a big no-no. You should also be careful not to contaminate a buffet table of food by placing your used plate on it. Nepalese people share a common drinking vessel (jug or cup) by tipping the water straight into their upturned mouths without touching. This is quite a skill!

I don't eat ...	ma ... *khahn*·di·na	मा ... खान्दिन
chicken	*ku*·khu·rah·ko *mah*·su	कुखुराको मासु
dairy products	*dudh*·ko *khah*·nah	दूधको खाना
fish	*mah*·chah	माछा
meat	*mah*·su	मासु
pork	*sū*·gur·ko *mah*·su	सुँगुरको मासु
spicy food	*pi*·ro	पिरो

SNACKS

खाजाहरू

Various snacks can be bought on Nepalese streets, mainly from mobile stalls. Most of these are cold snack-type food, except for the occasional evening stall selling fresh hot *mo*·mo (मो:मो), which are like dim sims, wontons or dumplings. Fruit is mostly available at stalls and you can bargain. Street ice cream is not hygienically prepared and best avoided (although ice cream shops are OK). One favourite snack is a mix of dried peas, chickpeas and puffed rice, made up for you with onion, lemon and chilli to your taste, *bhu*·jah (भुजा). Another great street snack is corn on the cob, cooked over hot coals.

corn	*ma*·kai	मकै
ice cream	*khu*·wah *ba*·raph	खुवा बरफ
mixed dried peas	*bhu*·jah	भुजा
momo	*mo*·mo	मो:मो
pappadam	*pah*·paḍ	पापड
peanuts	*ba*·dahm	बदाम
popcorn	*bhu*·ṭe·ko *ma*·kai	भुटेको मकै

FOOD

A MATTER OF TASTE

bitter	*ti*·to	तीतो
hot (spicy)	*pi*·ro	पिरो
salty	nu·*ni*·lo	नुनीलो
sour	a·*mi*·lo	अमीलो
spicy	*pi*·ro	पिरो
stale	*bah*·si	बासी
sweet	*gu*·li·yo	गुलियो

FOOD

EATING OUT
बाहिर खानु

Restaurants in tourist areas have wildly ambitious menus offering all kinds of cuisine from Tibetan, Chinese and Thai to American, Italian, German and Mexican! However, the dish that actually arrives may not bear an exact resemblance to what you were expecting. These restaurants have little on offer when it comes to Nepalese food, although some do a set meal of curry, rice, dahl and pickle. In Kathmandu there are several high-priced restaurants that specialise in Nepalese and Newar food in traditional surroundings, some with entertainment as well. If it's within your budget, this experience is well worth it.

TAXES & TIPS

As with accommodation, middle-priced and expensive restaurants charge government tax on top of the bill, while cheaper places usually don't bother. Tipping is not mandatory but will be greatly appreciated as wages are very low. Leave around 5% in budget restaurants and a bit more in others.

Waiter!
   dah·jyu! (man)/bhai! (boy)
   di·di! (woman)/*ba*·hi·ni! (girl)

दाज्यू !/भाइ !
दिदी !/बहिनी !

A table for (five), please.
   (pāhc) *ja*·nah·ko *lah*·gi *ṭe*·bul
   di·nu·hos

(पाँच) जनाको लागि टेबुल दिनुहोस

Please give me/us the menu.
   men·yu *di*·nu·hos

मेन्यु दिनुहोस

Could you recommend something?
   su·jhahb *di*·nu·hun·cha?

सुझाब दिनुहुन्छ ?

I'll have what they're having.
   u·ni·ha·ru·le ke *lin*·chan *ma*·lai
   pa·ni *ṭe*·hi *di*·nu·hos

उनीहरूले के लिन्छन मलाई पनि तेही दिनुहोस

What's in that dish?
   tyo *pa*·ri·kahr·mah ke cha?

त्यो परिकारमा के छ ?

Please give me (a little) ...	(*a*·li·ka·ti) ... *di*·nu·hos	(अलिकति) ... दिनुहोस
drinking water	*khah*·ne *pah*·ni	खाने पानी
rice	bhaht	भात
soup	*su*·ru·wah	सुरुवा

Please give me (a) ...	*ma*·lai ... *di*·nu·hos	मलाई ... दिनुहोस
cold beer	*ci*·so *bi*·yar	चिसो बियर
meal/food	*khah*·nah	खाना

Please bring me a/an/the ...	*ma*·lai ... *lyau*·nu·hos	मलाई ... ल्याउनुहोस
ashtray	*ahsh*·tre	आश्ट्रे
bill	bil	बिल
fork	*kāh*·tah	काँटा
glass of water	ek gi·*lahs pah*·ni	एक गिलास पानी
with ice	*ba*·raph·sā·ga	बरफसँग
without ice	*ba*·raph na·*hah*·le·ko	बरफ नहालेको
knife	*cak*·ku	चक्कु
plate	thahl	थाल

Do I get it myself or do they bring it to me?
ah·phai *li*·ne ki *be*·rah·le
lyaun·cha?
आफै लिने कि बेराले
ल्याउन्छ ?

What's this/that?
yo/tyo ke ho?
यो/त्यो के हो ?

I'm hungry/thirsty.
ma·lai bhok/*tir*·khah *lahg*·yo
मलाई भोक/तिर्खा लाग्यो

No ice in my drink, please.
me·ro *pahn*·mah *ba*·raph
na·*hahl*·nu·hos
मेरो पानमा बरफ
नहाल्नुहोस

How do you like the food?
khah·nah *kas*·to *lahg*·yo?
खाना कस्तो लाग्यो ?

The meal was delicious.
khah·nah *mi*·tho *lahg*·yo
खाना मीठो लाग्यो

The food isn't hot. (temperature)
khah·nah *tah*·to chai·na
खाना तातो छैन

FOOD

I love this dish.
   ma·lai yo *pa*·ri·kahr *ek*·dam
   man *par*·cha

मलाई यो परिकार एकदम मन पर्छ

We love the local cuisine.
   hah·mi·lai swa·*de*·shi *khah*·nah
   ek·dam man *par*·cha

हामिलाई स्वदेशी खाना एकदम मन पर्छ

Our compliments to the chef.
   bhahn·se·lai *hahm*·ro *tah*·riph
   di·nu·hos

भान्सेलाई हाम्रो तारीफ दिनुहोस

Is service included in the bill?
   se·bah *bil*·sa·met ho?

सेबा बिलसमेत हो ?

HOME TRUTHS

When invited into a private home always remove your shoes, leaving them outside the door or where everyone else leaves theirs.

Hindus, particularly those of high caste, don't usually eat in company and it's a great honour to be asked to share a meal. However, the Newars of Kathmandu and most hill people are mainly Buddhists and don't place so much emphasis on privacy. All Nepalese are generally very sociable and love a good feast. But don't be too surprised if you're the only person eating or if the women don't participate in the meal except to serve it.

Remember that there are strict rules about food in Nepal (more on page 122). It's important to wash or rinse your right hand and your mouth before sitting down – and again after eating – for both etiquette and hygiene. Don't touch your mouth to a common drinking vessel and wait to be served food rather than serving yourself. You'll often be treated as an honoured guest and your plate refilled (several times) without your asking!

When sharing a meal, you usually sit on a mat on the floor with your legs crossed. You eat from a dish placed on the floor, using your right hand only. You can use your left hand to hold a glass.

FOOD

TYPICAL DISHES पक्का परिकारहरू

a·cahr अचार
freshly made pickle or relish, served with curry and made from vegetables such as tomato, potato or radish; often spicy

ah·lu kau·li आलु काउलि
potato and cauliflower curry

ah·lu tah·mah आलु तामा
popular soup-like dish made from potatoes, bamboo shoots and beans

bhu·tu·wah भुटुवा
fried meat curry, usually goat or water buffalo (all meat in Nepal comes from castrated male animals)

cau·cau चाउचाउ
fried noodles with meat and/or vegetables

cyu·rah च्यूरा
flat, crunchy dried rice often eaten with snacks or at feasts instead of boiled rice

dahl bhaht tar·kahri दाल भात तरकारी
Nepal's national dish – lentils, rice and vegetable curry

gun·druk गुन्द्रुक
dried bitter mustard, radish or cauliflower leaves, served as a side dish or soup

mo·mo मो:मो
very popular snack of meat or vegetable dumplings, steamed or fried, often served with tomato pickle; usually round but sometimes crescent-shaped and then called *ko·the* (कोथे) (Tibetan)

rah·yo·ko sahg रायोको साग
mustard greens

shel ro·ti शेल रोटी
fried rice-flour bread shaped like thin doughnuts

su·ku·ti सुकुति
fried air-dried meat (usually water buffalo)

FOOD

Newar Food   नेवारी खाना

bhu·tan   भुतन
fried chopped intestines

ca·tāh·ma·ri   चताँमरि
rice-flour pancakes served with meat/egg filling or
with a curry

chwe·lah   छ्वेला
dish of boiled (sometimes grilled) spicy water buffalo

gwah·rah·ma·ri   ग्वारामरि
deep-fried sweet dough balls (like doughnuts)

ka·ci·lah   कचिला
raw, spiced minced water buffalo (like steak tartare)

kwah·ti   क्वाति
soup of mixed beans (usually nine kinds)

mus·yah   मुस्या
soybeans; served fresh as a side dish or roasted as a
snack

se·ku·wah   सेकुवा
roasted or grilled water buffalo

swā̃·pu·kah   स्वँ:पुका
stuffed fried goat lung

ta·khah   त:खा
jellied meat (usually water buffalo)

wo/bah·ḍah   वा/बाडा
savoury patties made from mung or other beans ground
into a wet paste, pan-fried (*wo*) or deep-fried (*bah·ḍah*)

FOOD

Sweets मिठाई

bar·phi बर्फि
soft, fudge-like sweet made from milk

je·ri/ju·le·bi जेरी/जुलेबि
large (*je·ri*) or small (*ju·le·bi*) orange flower-shaped sweets, deep-fried then soaked in sugar syrup

khir खिर
rice pudding

lad·du लड्डु
sweet yellow chickpea-flour balls, often used as an offering to the gods, especially Ganesh

lahl mo·han लाल मोहन
sweet, milky dough balls, deep-fried and then soaked in sugar syrup

si·kar·ni सिकर्नि
sweet yogurt pudding

Tibetan Food तिबेतको खाना

thuk·pah थुक्पा
noodle soup with meat and/or vegetables

ti·be·tan ci·yah तिबेतन चिया
Tibetan tea made in a churn with butter and salt

tsam·pah त्सम्पा
barley or other flour, eaten mixed with milk, water or tea

tum·bah तूम्बा
mildly alcoholic drink of fermented millet topped with hot water and served in a large wooden receptacle

FOOD

AT THE MARKET

बजारमा

Where's the weekly market?
haht ba·*jahr* ka·*hāh* cha?

हात बजार कहाँ छ ?

When's the weekly market?
haht ba·*jahr* ka·hi·le *hun*·cha?

हात बजार कहिले हुन्छ ?

How much per kilo?
ek *ki*·lo·ko *ka*·ti ho?

एक किलोको कति हो ?

Do you have anything cheaper?
tyo·bhan·dah *sas*·to ke cha?

त्योभन्दा सस्तो के छ ?

What's the local speciality?
swa·de·*shi* bi·*shes*·tah ke ho?

स्वदेशी बिशेषता के हो ?

Give me (half a/one) kilo please.
ma·lai *(ah*·dhah/ek) *ki*·lo
di·nu·hos

मलाई (आधा/एक) किलो
दिनुहोस

I'd like (sixes slices of cheese).
ma·lai (cha *ţuk*·rah cij)
cah·hi·yo

मलाई (छ टुका चीज)
चाहियो

May I taste it?
ma·lai *cahkh*·na *paun*·cha?

मलाई चाख्न पाउन्छ ?

That's all. How much is it?
te·ti *mah*·trai, *ka*·ti *bha*·yo?

तेति मात्रै, कति भयो ?

Where can I find ...?
I'd like some ...

... ka·*hāh paun*·cha?
ma·lai ... *cah*·hi·yo

... कहाँ पाउन्छ ?
मलाई ... चाहियो

bread (loaf)	*pau*·ro·ţi	पाउरोटी
butter	ma·khan	मखन
cauliflower	*kau*·li	काउली
cheese	cij	चीज
chilli	khur·*sah*·ni	खुर्सानी
chocolate/candy	*cak*·leţ	चक्लेट
eggs	phul	फुल
flour	*pi*·ţho	पीठो
garlic	*la*·sun	लसुन
ginger	a·du·wah	अदुवा
ghee	ghi·u	घिउ
honey	ma·ha	मह
leafy greens	*sahg*·paht	सागपात

FOOD

milk	dudh	दूध
oil	tel	तेल
pepper	*ma*·ric	मरिच
potato	*ah*·lu	आलु
rice (uncooked)	*cah*·mal	चामल
salt	nun	नुन
sugar	*ci*·ni	चिनी
tea leaves	*ci*·yah *pat*·ti	चिया पत्ती
yogurt	*da*·hi	दही

Meat मासु

Meat is scarce and expensive, and tends to be served mainly on festival days and other special occasions. Remember that in Hindu Nepal, cows are sacred and beef is not eaten (it's illegal). Popular meat includes buff (water buffalo), goat, chicken and yak.

beef	*gai*·ko *mah*·su	गाईको मासु
brain	*gi*·di	गिदी
buff (water buffalo)	*rāh*·gah·ko *mah*·su	राँगाको मासु
chicken	*ku*·khu·rah·ko *mah*·su	कुखुराको मासु
dried meat	*su*·ku·ti	सुकुति
duck meat	*hāhs*·ko *mah*·su	हाँसको मासु
eel	bahm	बाम
(dried) fish	(*su*·ke·ko) *mah*·chah	(रुकेको) माछा
goat meat	*kha*·si·ko *mah*·su	खसीको मासु
head	*ṭau*·ko	टाउको
intestines	ahn·drah·*bhū*·ḍi	आन्द्राभुँडी
lamb	*bhē*·ḍah·ko *mah*·su	भेँडाको मासु
liver	*ka*·le·jo·ko *mah*·su	कलेजोको मासु
lung	*phok*·so	फोक्सो
mutton	*bhē*·ḍah·ko *mah*·su	भेँडाको मासु
pork	*sū*·gur·ko *mah*·su	सुँगुरको मासु
prawn	*jhing*·ge *mah*·chah	झिङ्गे माछा
skin	*chah*·lah	छाला
tongue	*ji*·bro	जिब्रो
venison	*mri*·ga·ko *mah*·su	मृगको मासु
yak meat	*caū*·ri·gai·ko *mah*·su	चौँरीगाईको मासु

FOOD

Vegetables

तरकारी

asparagus	*ku*·ri·lo	कुरिलो
bamboo shoot	*tah*·mah	तामा
beans	*si*·mi	सिमी
beetroot	cu·*kan*·dar	चुकन्दर
broad beans	*ba*·ku·lah	बकुला
cabbage	ban·dah·*ko*·bi	बन्दाकोबि
carrot	*gah*·jar	गाजर
cauliflower	*kau*·li	काउली
chilli	khur·*sah*·ni	खुर्सानी
choko squash	is·*kus*	इस्कुस
corn	*ma*·kai	मकै
cucumber	*kāh*·kro	काँक्रो
dried vegetable	*gun*·druk	गुन्द्रुक
eggplant (long)	*bhahn*·ṭah	भाण्टा
eggplant (ovoid)	*brin*·jal	ब्रीन्जल
garlic	*la*·sun	लसुन
green beans	*ha*·ri·yo *si*·mi	हरियो सिमी
green garlic	*ha*·ri·yo *la*·sun	हरियो लसुन
green/spring onion	*ha*·ri·yo pyahj	हरियो प्याज
green pepper	*bhē*·dah khur·*sah*·ni	भेंडा खुर्सानी
leafy greens	*sahg*·paht	सागपात
lettuce	*ji*·ri·ko sahg	जिरीको साग
mushroom	cyau	च्याउ
mustard greens	*rah*·yo·ko sahg	रायोको साग
nettles	*sis*·nu	सिस्नु
okra	rahm·*to*·ri·yah	राम्तोरिया
onion	pyahj	प्याज
peas	*ke*·rau	केराउ
potato	*ah*·lu	आलु
pumpkin	*phar*·si	फर्सि
radish	*mu*·lah	मुला
spinach	pah·*lung*·go	पालुङ्गो
squash (bitter gourd)	ka·*re*·lo	करेलो
squash (long green)	*lau*·kah	लौका
squash (zucchini)	ghi·*raū*·lo	घिरौंलो

FOOD

sweet potato	*sa*·khar *khaṇ*·ḍa	सखर खण्ड
tomato	gol·*bhē*·ḍah	गोलभेंडा
turnip	*sal*·gam	सल्गाम
yam	*ta*·rul	तरुल
zucchini	ghi·*raū*·lo	घिरौंलो

TABLE ARTICLES

cup	kap	कप
dish/utensil	*bhāh*·ḍah	भाँडा
dishes/utensils	bhāh·ḍah·*kū*·ḍah	भाँडाकुँडा
glass	gi·*lahs*	गिलास
jug	su·*rah*·hi	सुराही
napkin/towel	ru·*mahl*	रुमाल
spoon	*cam*·cah	चम्चा
toothpick	*sin*·ko	सिन्को

Cereal & Legumes

दाल खालको अन्नहरू

barley	jau	जौ
buckwheat	*phah*·par	फापर
chickpea	*ca*·nah	चना
lentils (black)	*kah*·lo dahl	कालो दाल
lentils (brown)	*khai*·ro dahl	खैरो दाल
lentils (red)	*mu*·sur dahl	मुसुर दाल
lima beans	*ba*·ku·lah	बकुला
millet	*ko*·do	कोदो
oats	jai	जइ
red kidney beans	*rah*·to *su*·ke·ko *si*·mi	रातो सुकेको सिमी
rice (beaten)	*cyu*·rah	च्यूरा
rice (cooked)	bhaht	भात
rice (uncooked)	*cah*·mal	चामल
rice (unhusked)	dhahn	धान
semolina	*su*·ji	सुजि
soybeans	*bhaṭ*·mahs	भटमास
wheat	*ga*·hū	गहूँ
white dried beans	*se*·to *su*·ke·ko *bo*·di	सेतो सुकेको बोदि

FOOD

FOOD

Fruit & Nuts   फलफूल र बदामहरू

almond	*ma*·di·se *ba*·dahm	मदिसे बदाम
apple	syau	स्याउ
apricot	khur·*pah*·ni	खुरपानी
banana	*ke*·rah	केरा
berry	*ba*·yar	बयर
betel nut	su·*pah*·ri	सुपारी
blackberry	*phā*·ḍer	फँडेर
blueberry	*cu*·tro	चुत्रो
cashew	*kah*·ju	काजु
cherry	pai·*yū*·khahl·ko phal	पैयूँखालको फल
coconut	*na*·ri·wal	नरिवल
custard apple	*sa*·riph	सरिफ
date (hard)	*kha*·jur	खजुर
date (soft)	cho·*ha*·rah	छोहरा
fig	*an*·jir	अन्जीर
grape	*ā*·gur	अँगुर
grapefruit	*bho*·ga·ṭe	भोगटे
guava	*am*·bah	अम्बा
jackfruit	*rukh*·ka·ṭa·har	रूखकटहर
lapsi	*a*·mi·li	अमीली
lemon	*kah*·ga·ti	कागती
lime	*jya*·mir	ज्यमीर
lychee	*li*·ci	लीची
mandarin	*sun*·ta·lah	सुन्तला
mango	āhp	आँप
melon	*tar*·bu·jah	तरबुजा
mulberry	*kim*·bu	किम्बु
orange	*sun*·ta·lah	सुन्तला
papaya	*me*·wah	मेवा
peach	*ah*·ru	आरु
peanut	*ba*·dahm	बदाम
pear	*nahs*·pah·ti	नास्पाती
persimmon	*ha*·lu·wah·bed	हलुवाबेद
pineapple	*bhuī*·ka·ṭa·har	भुइँकटहर

pistachio	*pis*·tah	पिस्ता
plum	ah·ru·*ba*·kha·ḍah	आरुबखडा
pomegranate	a·*nahr*	अनार
pomelo	*bho*·ga·ṭe	भोगटे
raisin	dahkh	दाख
raspberry	*ai*·sa·lu	ऐसलु
strawberry	kau·wah·*kah*·phal	कौवाकाफल
sweet lime	*mu*·sam	मूसम
walnut	*o*·khar	ओखर
watermelon	*khar*·bu·jah	खरबुजा

Bread रोटी

bread	*ro*·ṭi	रोटी
flat bread	ca·*pah*·ti	चपाती
deep fried bread	*pu*·ri	पुरी
loaf of bread	*pau*·ro·ṭi	पाउरोटी
flour	*pi*·ṭho	पीठो
chickpea flour	*be*·san	बेसन
fine wheat flour	*mai*·dah	मैदा
wholemeal flour	*aht*·tah	आत्ता

Spices & Condiments मसलाहरू

aniseed	soph	सोफ
asafoetida	hing	हिंङ्ग
basil	*tul*·si	तुलसी
bay leaf	*tej*·paht	तेजपात
cardamom (black)	a·*laī*·ci	अलैंची
cardamom (green)	*su*·ku·mel	सुकुमेल
chilli	khur·*sah*·ni	खुर्सानी
chives	*chyah*·pi	छचापी
cinnamon	*dahl*·ci·ni	दाल्चिनी
cloves	lwahng	ल्वाङ्ग
coriander (dried)	*dha*·ni·yāh	धनियाँ
coriander (fresh)	ha·ri·yo *dha*·ni·yāh	हरियो धनियाँ
cumin	*ji*·rah	जीरा
fennel	soph	सोफ

fenugreek	*me·*thi	मेठी
ginger (dried)	*su·*tho	सूठो
ginger (fresh)	*a·du·*wah	अदुवा
honey	*ma·*ha	मह
horseradish	*sar·*syu	सर्स्यु
jam	jahm	जाम
lapsi	*a·*mi·li	अमिलि
mango powder	*am·*cur	अम्चुर
mint	*bah·*ba·ri	बाबरी
mixed spice	*ga·*ram *ma·*sa·lah	गरम मसला
molasses	*cah·*ku/*khu·*do	चाक/खुदो
mustard oil	*to·*ri·ko tel	तोरीको तेल
mustard seed	*to·*ri·ko bi·*u*	तोरीको बिउ
nutmeg	*jai·*phal	जाईफल
oil	tel	तेल
parsley	*jwah·*nu	ज्वानु

peanut butter	*ba·*dahm·ko	बदामको
	*ma·*khan	मखन
pepper(corn)	*ma·*ric	मरिच
pickle	a·*cahr*	अचार
... powder	...ko *dhu·*lo	...को धूलो
relish	a·*cahr*	अचार
saffron	*ke·*sahr	केशर
salt	nun	नुन
sesame seeds	*til·*ko bi·*u*	तिलको बिउ
sugar (brown)	*sak·*kar	सक्कर
sugar (white)	*ci·*ni	चिनी
sugar cane	*u·*khu	उखु
tamarind	*a·*mi·li	अमिलि
turmeric	*be·*sahr	बेसार
vinegar	*sir·*khah	सिर्खा
yeast	*kham·*bir	खम्बिर

FOOD

Dairy Products   दूधको खाना

butter	*ma*·khan	मखन
cheese	cij	चीज
cream	tar	तर
egg	phul/*aṇ*·ḍah	फुल/अण्डा
ghee	ghi·*u*	घिउ
ice cream	*khu*·wah *ba*·raph	खुवा बरफ
milk	dudh	दूध
yogurt (curd)	*da*·hi	दही

DRINKS   पानहरू

There's a great variety of drinks available. Most water, however, is undrinkable unless boiled or treated with iodine (filtering alone is not sufficient). Local licensed bottlers produce the usual softdrinks, but the Nepalese speciality, lemon juice with (club) soda (and sugar or even salt), is much more refreshing!

Hot Drinks   तातो पानहरू

As far as hot drinks go, Nepalese tea is always safe and available everywhere, while coffee is usually instant although coffee beans are grown locally and some places do serve real coffee. Hot chocolate is available and another local favourite is lemon juice with hot water, 'hot lemon', *tah*·to *pah*·ni·mah *kah*·ga·ti (तातो पानीमा कागती).

FOOD

ci·yah	चिया

Nepalese tea – hot, sweet and milky (cai in India)

ti·*be*·tan *ci*·yah	तिबेतन चिया

Tibetan tea – made in a churn with butter and salt

black tea	*kah*·lo *ci*·yah	कालो चिया
lemon tea	*kah*·ga·ti *ci*·yah	कागती चिया
black coffee	*kah*·lo *ka*·phi	कालो कफी
milk coffee	dudh *ka*·phi	दूध कफी
hot chocolate	*tah*·to *cak*·leṭ	तातो चक्लेट

Cold Drinks   चिसो पानहरू

boiled water	*u·mah·le·ko pah·ni*	उमालेको पानी
fresh lemon juice	*kah·ga·ti·ko ras*	कागतीको रस
lemon soda	*so·dah·mah kah·ga·ti*	सोडामा कागती
water	*pah·ni*	पानी
yogurt drink (sweet or salty)	*la·si*	लसि

Alcoholic Drinks   रक्सीको पानहरू

All kinds of alcohol are widely available, both locally-made and imported versions (which can be more expensive than at home). Except for some high castes, the Nepalese like a drink and their traditional drinks, including *rak·si* (रक्सी), the local firewater, are extremely cheap. Western-style bars serve beer and all kinds of cocktails.

chyahng   छचाङ्ग
  mildly alcoholic rice beer made at home (sometimes also from corn, barley or millet); also called jāhḍ (जाँड) in Nepali and thō (थों) in Newari
rak·si   रक्सी
  local distilled liquor; can be very rough
bi·yar   बियर
  Western-style beer (many brands brewed locally)
tum·bah   तूम्बा
  mildly alcoholic Tibetan drink of fermented millet topped with hot water, served in a large wooden receptacle

FOOD

TREKKING &
MOUNTAINEERING

Nepal is well known for having some of the best trekking in the world. Naturally, most trekking areas are remote, and the Nepalese who live in the mountains and high valleys are still more traditional than those in Kathmandu and other towns. Most people you meet while trekking will speak Nepali, even if it's not their first language.

The hillpeople are generally devout and observant of local customs, which are deeply rooted in their religion, a harmonious mixture of Hinduism, Buddhism and ancient Tantrism. As you walk along you'll come across holy buildings, stupas (white domes with prayer flags) and walls of prayer stones. Always walk around these clockwise, keeping them on your right as you pass.

DID YOU KNOW ...

Eight of the world's 14 highest mountains are found in Nepal and its northern frontier is the mighty Himalaya (which is pronounced with the stress on the second, not third, syllable: hi·*mah*·la·ya).

REQUESTING INFORMATION   जानकारी सोध्नु

Where can I find out about trekking trails in the region?

yo *che*·tra·mah, *tre*·king
bah·ṭo·ko *jahn*·kah·ri
ka·hāh *pain*·cha?

यो क्षेत्रमा, ट्रेकिङ
बाटोको जानकारी
कहाँ पाइन्छ ?

I'd like to talk to someone who knows this area.

ma·lai yo *che*·tra·ko·bah·re
thah·ha *hu*·ne *mahn*·che·sā·ga
ku·rah gar·na man *lahg*·yo

मलाई यो क्षेत्रकोबारे
थाह हुने मान्छेसँग
कुरा गर्न मन लाग्यो

Where can I hire mountain gear?
pa·*hahd cadh*·ne *sah*·mahn
ka·hāh *bhah*·ḍah·mah *li*·ne? पहाड चढ्ने सामान
कहाँ भाडामा लिने ?

Where can we buy supplies?
cah·hi·ne *sah*·mahn ka·hāh *kin*·ne? चाहिने सामान कहाँ किन्ने ?

Is it safe to climb this mountain?
yo pa·*hahd cadh*·na su·*ra*·chit cha? यो पहाड चढ्न सुरक्षित छ ?

Do I need a guide?
bah·ṭo de·*khau*·nu·par·cha? बाटो देखाउनुपर्छ ?

Are you going by yourself?
ta·*paĩ ek*·lai *jah*·ne? तपाई एक्लै जाने ?

How long is the trail?
bah·ṭo *ka*·ti *lah*·mo cha? बाटो कति लामो छ ?

Is the track (well-)marked?
bah·ṭo·mah (*rahm*·ro·sā·ga)
ci·no la·*gah*·ya·ko cha? बाटोमा (राम्रोसँग)
चिनो लगायको छ ?

BED & BREAKFAST

If you order an evening meal on less popular trekking routes, the price quoted to you traditionally includes accommodation for the night.

How high is the climb?
ka·ti *u*·co *cadh*·nu·par·cha? कति उचो चढ्नुपर्छ ?

Is there a lodge up there?
u *mah*·thi laj cha? उ माथि लज छ ?

Can I get there on foot?
tya·hāh hĩ·ḍe·ra *jah*·na sa·kin·cha? त्यहाँ हिंडेर जान सकिन्छ ?

Which is the shortest/easiest route?
sab·bhan·dah *cho*·ṭo/*sa*·ji·lo
bah·ṭo kun ho? सदभन्दा छोटो/सजिलो
बाटो कुन हो ?

Is the path open?
bah·ṭo *kho*·le·ko cha? बाटो खोलेको छ ?

When does it get dark?
ka·ti *be*·lah ā·*dhyah*·ro *hun*·cha? कति बेला अँध्यारो हुन्छ ?

Is it very scenic?
dri·shya *rahm*·ro cha? दृश्य राम्रो छ ?

HIRING PORTERS   भरिया लिनु

It's well worth the relatively small expense of hiring a guide or
porter, *bha·ri·yah* (भरिया), as you learn much more about the area
and you could practise your new-found language skills with your
companions. You'll also get cheaper rates.

GUIDES V. PORTERS

Trekking guides and porters carry out different roles.
A guide will know the trails, speak English, arrange
accommodation and supervise porters, but will not carry
a load or cook. In addition to carrying a load, versatile
porters sometimes act as guides and cook too.

Excuse me, will you go with me to ...?
 e, ta·*paī ma*·sā·ga ....sam·ma   ए, तपाई मसँग ...सम्म
 jah·nu·hun·cha?   जानुहुन्छ ?
How long will it take,
to get there and back?
 jah·na, *au*·na, *ka*·ti sa·*ma*·ya   जान, आउन, कति समय
 lahg·cha?   लाग्छ ?
How much are you asking?
 ta·*paī ka*·ti *li*·nu·hun·cha?   तपाई कति लिनुहुन्छ ?
With/Without food?
 khah·nah sa·*met*/ *bah*·hek?   खाना समेत / बाहेक ?
With/Without a load?
 bhah·ri sa·*met*/ *bah*·hek?   भारी समेत / बाहेक ?
I'll give you ... rupees per day.
 ma ta·*paī*·lai *din*·ko ...   म तपाईलाई दिनको ...
 ru·*pi*·yāh *din*·chu   रुपियाँ दिन्छु
We'll leave on (Monday at 10 am).
 hah·mi (*som*·bahr, das *ba*·je)   हामि (सोमबार, दस बजे)
 jahn·chaũ   जान्छौं
We'll meet at (Tatopani).
 (tah·to·*pah*·ni)·mah *bhet*·ne   (तातोपानी)मा भेट्ने

ASKING DIRECTIONS   बाटो सोध्नु

To get your bearings along the way, you'll probably need to ask
directions, the names of villages and distances. It's better to ask
'Which is the way to ...?' rather than 'Is this the way to ...?' as
people would hate you to feel lost and so will usually answer 'yes'
to the second question, whether it's true or not!

Distances are often measured in kos (कोस): one *kos* is about
three kilometres. If the answer is *du*·i kos (दुइ कोस), two *kos*, this
is not literally true but a common expression meaning 'not far'.

Which is the way to (Lukla)?
   (luk·lah) *jah*·ne *bah*·to kun ho?   (लुक्ला) जाने बाटो कुन हो ?
Does this path go to ...?
   yo *bah*·to ....*mah jahn*·cha?   यो बाटो ...मा जान्छ ?
What's the next village?
   au·ne gaū·ko nahm ke ho?   आउने गाउँको नाम के हो ?
How far is it to ...?
   ... *ka*·ti *ṭah*·ḍhah cha?   ... कति टाढा छ ?
Which direction?
   kun *di*·shah?   कुन दिशा ?
I'm lost.
   ma ha·*rah*·yē   म हरायें
Are there any tourist attractions near here?
   ya·hāh *ka*·tai par·*ya*·ṭak   यहाँ कतै पर्यटक
   shu·bha·*dar*·shan cha?   शुभदर्शन छ ?
May I cross your property?
   ma ta·*paī*·ko *jag*·gah·bah·ṭa   म तपाईको जग्गाबाट
   jah·na *hun*·cha?   जान हुन्छ ?
Can we go through here?
   hah·mi ya·*hāh*·bah·ṭa   हामि यहाँबाट
   jah·na *hun*·cha?   जान हुन्छ ?
Can I swim here?
   ya·hāh *pau*·ḍi *khel*·na *sa*·kin·cha?   यहाँ पौडी खेल्न सकिन्छ ?
Where have you come from?
   ka·*hāh*·bah·ṭa *au*·nu *bha*·ya·ko?   कहाँबाट आउनु भयको ?

From (Pokhara).
   (po·kha·rah)·bah·ṭa   (पोखरा)बाट

How long did it take you?
   ta·paī·lai ka·ti sa·ma·ya   तपाईंलाई कति समय
   lahg·yo?   लाग्यो ?

How many hours/days?
   ka·ti ghaṇ·ṭah/din?   कति घण्टा / दिन ?

It takes us (three) hours.
   hah·mi·lai (tin) ghaṇ·ṭah   हामीलाई (तिन) घण्टा
   lahg·cha   लाग्छ

For you, it'll take (four to five) hours.
   ta·paī·lai (cahr·pāhc)   तपाईंलाई (चारपाँच)
   ghaṇ·ṭah lahg·cha   घण्टा लाग्छ

PARKS & PLAINS

Nepal has a good number of national parks, plus wildlife reserves, conservation areas and hunting reserves. The best-known for tourism are the Sagarmatha National Park and Annapurna Conservation Area Project (ACAP) in the mountains, and the Royal Chitwan National Park in the Terai plains bordering India. All parks and reserves maintain a careful balance between the conservation of animals and environment and people's needs.

downward	*ta·la·ti·ra*	तलतिर
downhill	*o·rah·lo*	ओरालो
steep downhill	*bhi·rah·lo*	भिरालो
level	*ter·so*	तेर्सो
straight ahead	*si·dhah*	सिधा
this side	*wah·ri*	वारी
that side	*pah·ri*	पारी
upward	*mahs·ti·ra*	मास्तिर
uphill	*u·kah·lo*	उकालो
steep uphill	*ṭhah·ḍo*	ठाडा

ON THE PATH

बाटोमा

Where can I spend the night?
  bahs *bas·*na *ka·*hāh *pain·*cha   बास बस्न कहाँ पाइन्छ ?

Can I leave some things here for a while?
  *me·*ro *sah·*mahn *ya·*hāh   मेरो सामान यहाँ
  *chod·*na *sak·*chu?   छोड्न सक्छु ?

There are (three) of us.
  *hah·*mi (tin) *ja·*nah chaū   हामि (तिन) जना छौं

Do you provide meals?
  *khah·*nah *paun·*cha?   खाना पाउन्छ ?

What kind of food?
  ke *khah·*nah *paun·*cha?   के खाना पाउन्छ ?

Is this water OK to drink?
  yo *pah·*ni *khah·*nu·hun·cha?   यो पानी खानुहुन्छ ?

I have to rest.
  *ma·*lai *ah·*rahm *li·*nu·par·cha   मलाई आराम लिनुपर्छ

Let's sit in the shade.
  *shi·*tal *ṭhaū·*mah *ba·*saū   शीतल ठाउँमा बसौं

I need to go to the toilet.(urinate/defecate)
  *ma·*lai *pi·*sahb/*di·*sah *lahg·*yo   मलाई पिसाब/दिसा लाग्यो

Please ask about ...	...*bah·*re *sodh·*nu·hos	...बारे सोध्नुहोस
boiled water	u·*mah·*le·ko *pah·*ni	उमालेको पानी
bread	*ro·*ṭi	रोटी
food	*khah·*nah	खाना
tea	*ci·*yah	चिया
Please give me ...	*ma·*lai ... *di·*nu·hos	मलाई ... दिनुहोस
cooked rice	bhaht	भात
lentils	dahl	दाल
liquor	*rak·*si	रक्सी
rice beer	chyahng	छ्याङ
shelter	bahs	बास
tobacco	*sur·*ti	सुर्ती
vegetables	tar·*kah·*ri	तरकारी

Where's the ...?	... ka·hāh cha?	... कहाँ छ ?
bridge	pul	पुल
inn	bhaṭ·ṭi	भट्टी
resting place tree	cau·tah·rah	चौतारा
statue	mur·ti	मूर्ति
teashop	ci·yah pa·sal	चिया पसल
village	gaũ	गाउँ

Do you have (a) ...?	ta·paĩ·sã·ga ... cha?	तपाईंसँग ... छ ?
bag	jho·lah	झोला
carry basket	ḍo·ko	डोको
firewood	dau·rah	दाउरा
knife	cak·ku	चक्कु
Nepalese knife	khu·ku·ri	खुकुरी
stove	sṭobh	स्टोभ

What time are you ...?	ka·ti ba·je ...?	कति बजे ... ?
getting up	uṭh·ne	उठ्ने
going to sleep	sut·na jah·ne	सुत्न जाने

altitude	uc·cai	उच्चाइ
binoculars	dur·bin	दूरबीन
camping	shi·bir	शिबिर
candles	main·bat·ti	मैनबत्ती
compass	di·shah·su·cak yan·tra	दिशासूचक यन्त्र
flashlight	ṭarc	टर्च
gloves	pan·jah	पन्जा
guide	bah·ṭo de·khau·ne	बाटो देखाउने
	mahn·che	मान्छे
hunting	shi·kahr	शिकार
ledge	cheu	छेउ
lookout	dau	दाउ
map	nak·sah	नक्सा
mountain climbing	pa·hahḍ caḍh·ne	पहाड चढ्ने
pickaxe	gaĩ·ti	गैंती
provisions	khah·dya sah·ma·gri	खाद्य सामग्री
rope	ḍo·ri	डोरी
signpost	sang·ket·cin·ha	सङ्केतचिन्ह
trekking	pai·dal yah·trah	पैदल यात्रा

CAMPING

शिबिर गर्नु

Independent camping is uncommon and there are few public camping grounds. However, people may allow you to set up a tent on their property. Many trekking companies have their own sites, which aren't generally available to independent travellers.

Is there a camp site nearby?
  ya·hāh ke·hi shi·bir na·jik cha?   यहाँ केही शिबिर नजिक छ ?
Am I allowed to camp here?
  ya·hāh shi·bir gar·nu·hun·cha?   यहाँ शिबिर गर्नुहुन्छ ?
Who owns this land?
  yo *jag·gah kas·ko ho?*   यो जग्गा कस्को हो ?
Can I talk to him/her?
  ma·lai wa·hāh·sā·ga ku·rah gar·na sak·chu?   मलाई वहाँसँग कुरा गर्न सक्छु ?
Are there shower facilities?
  snahn *kak·sha cha?*   स्नान कक्श छ ?
Where can I hire a tent?
  pahl *ka·hāh bhah·ḍah·mah pain·cha?*   पाल कहाँ भाडामा पाइन्छ ?

I want to hire a ...	*ma·lai ... bhah·ḍah·mah cah·hi·yo*	मलाई ... भाडामा चाहियो
backpack	*jho·lah*	झोला
sleeping bag	*sut·ne jho·lah*	सुल्ने झोला
stove	*stobh*	स्टोभ
tent	pahl	पाल

TOILET TRAINING

All villages have a communal pit toilet, a *car·pi* (चर्पी), which trekkers are welcome to use. If you do need to go outside, keep well away from water sources and out of sight. Dig a hole, and burn your toilet paper, as nothing looks worse than piles of paper littering the landscape! The Nepalese don't use toilet paper, they use a waterjug, **lo·tah** (लोता), and their left hand, which is not used for anything else (giving or receiving, shaking hands or eating!)

WEATHER मौसम

What's the weather like?
   mau·sam *kas*·to cha?   मौसम कस्तो छ ?
The weather is ... today.
   ah·ja *mau*·sam ... cha   आज मौसम ... छ

Will it be ... (tomorrow)?	(*bho*·li) *mau*·sam ... *ho*·lah?	(भोली) मौसम ... होला ?
bad	kha·*rahb*	खराब
cloudy	*bad*·li	बदली
cold	*jah*·do	जाडो
foggy	ku·*i*·ro	कुइरो
frosty	tu·*sah*·ro	तुसारो
good	*rahm*·ro	राम्रो
hot	*gar*·mi	गर्मी
humid	*bahs*·pi·ya	बाष्पीय
rainy	*pah*·ni *par*·cha	पानी पर्छ
sunny	gha·*mai*·lo	घमाईलो
windy	*hah*·wah *lahg*·ne	हावा लाग्ने

It's raining heavily.	*pah*·ni *ek*·dam *par*·dai·cha	पानी एकदम पर्दैछ
It's raining lightly.	*pah*·ni *a*·li *a*·li *par*·dai·cha	पानी अलि अलि पर्दैछ
It's flooding.	*bah*·dhi *aun*·cha	बाढी आउन्छ

blizzard	*hiū*·ko *āh*·dhi	हिउँको आँधी
climate	hah·wah·*pah*·ni	हावापानी
cloud	*bah*·dal	बादल
ice	*ba*·raph	बरफ
lightning	bi·ju·li *cam*·kai	बिजुली चम्काई
mud	*hi*·lo	हिलो
rainbow	in·*dre*·ni	इन्द्रेनी
sky	*ah*·kahsh	आकाश
snow	hiū	हिउँ
storm	*hu*·ri	हुरी
sun	*sur*·ya	सूर्य
thunder	*gar*·jan	गर्जन

SEASONS

ऋतुहरू

summer	*gar*·mi *mau*·sam	गर्मी मौसम
autumn	*sha*·rad *ri*·tu	शरद ऋतु
winter	*jah*·do ma·hi·nah	जाडो महीना
spring	*ba*·san·ta *ri*·tu	बसन्त ऋतु
monsoon	*bar*·khah	बर्खा
rainy season	*bar*·saht	बर्सात

GEOGRAPHICAL TERMS

भूगोलीक शब्द

beach	ba·*lau*·ṭe ki·*nahr*	बलौटे किनार
bridge	pul	पुल
cave	*gu*·phah	गुफा
cliff	bhir	भीर
creek	*kho*·lah	खोला
earthquake	bhuĩ·*cah*·lo	भुइँचालो
farm	*khet*·bah·ri	खेतबारी
footpath	*go*·re·ṭo	गोरेटो
forest	ban	बन
gap	*khah*·li ṭhaũ	खालि ठाउँ
hanging bridge	*jho*·lung·ge pul	झोलुङ्गे पुल
hill	*ḍāh*·ḍah	डाँडा
hot spring	*tah*·to *pah*·ni mul	तातो पानी मूल

BANYAN REUNION

Along trails and in villages, you'll come across a kind of community resting or meeting place, made by building rocks and stones into a comfortable seating area at the base of a large, shady banyan or peepal tree. This is called a **cau**·*tah*·**rah** (चौतारा) and the locals will be more than happy for you to join them there. The resting areas are easy to recognise and are commonly referred to when giving directions. One of the most well-known **cau**·*tah*·**rahs** is in New Road, Kathmandu (where newspaper sellers, shoe-shiners and camera shops are found).

island	*ṭah*·pu/dwip	टापु/द्वीप
jungle	ban	बन
lake	tahl	ताल
landslide	*pa*·hi·ro	पहिरो
mountain	pa·*hahḍ*	पहाड
mountain path	pa·*hah*·ḍi *bah*·ṭo	पहाडी बाटो
high mountain path	hi·*mahl*·ko *bah*·ṭo	हिमालको बाटो
pass	*bhan*·jyahng	भन्ज्याङ
narrow pass	*sāh*·ghu·ro *bhan*·jyahng	साँघुरो भन्ज्याङ
peak	cu·*cu*·ro	चुचुरो
plains	ma·desh/ta·*rai*	मदेश/तराई
pond	*po*·kha·ri	पोखरी
river	na·di	नदी
scenery	*dri*·shya	दृश्य
sea	sa·*mu*·dra	समुद्र
snow peak	hi·*mahl*	हिमाल
trail	*sah*·no *bah*·ṭo	सानो बाटो
valley	u·*pa*·tya·kah	उपत्यका
waterfall	*jhar*·nah	झर्ना

FAUNA
जनावरहरू

Nepal's national animal is the cow, which is sacred in Hinduism.

What's that animal called?
tyo ja·*nah*·war·lai ke *bhan*·cha?   त्यो जनावरलाई के भन्छ ?

bat	*ca*·me·ro	चमेरो
bear	*bhah*·lu	भालु
buffalo	*rāh*·gah/	राँगा/
	bhaī·si (m/f)	भैंसी
camel	ūṭ	ऊँट
cat	bi·*rah*·lo	बिरालो
cobra	*go*·man	गोमन
cow	gai	गाई
crocodile	*go*·hi	गोही
deer	*mri*·ga/*ha*·riṇ	मृग/हरिण
black buck	*nil*·gai	नीलगाई
musk	*kas*·tu·ri *mri*·ga	कस्तूरी मृग
sambar	*sahm*·bahr	सामबार
spotted	*ci*·tal	चितल
dog	*ku*·kur	कुकुर
donkey	*ga*·dhah	गधा
eel	bahm	बाम
elephant	*haht*·ti	हात्ती
fish	*mah*·chah	माछा
fox	*phyau*·ro	फ्याउरो
frog	*bhyah*·gu·to	भ्यागुतो
goat	*bahkh*·ro	बाख्रो
castrated goat	*kha*·si	खसी
horse	*gho*·dah	घोडा
jackal	syahl	स्याल
leopard	*ci*·tu·wah	चितुवा
snow leopard	*se*·to *ci*·tu·wah	सेतो चितुवा
lion	*sī*·ha	सिंह
lizard	che·*pah*·ro	छेपारो
mole	chu·*cun*·dro	छुचुन्द्रो
mongoose	*nyau*·ri *mu*·sah	न्याउरी मूसा
monkey	*bāh*·dar	बाँदर

mouse	*mu·sah*	मूसा
mouse hare	*pi·kah*	पीका
otter	ôt	ओत
ox	*go·ru*	गोरु
pig	*sū·gur*	सुँगुर
porcupine	*dum·si*	दुम्सी
rabbit	kha·*rah·yo*	खरायो
rat	*mu·sah*	मूसा
red panda	*rah·to pahṇ·ḍah*	रातो पाण्डा
rhinoceros	*gaī·ḍah*	गैंडा
sheep	*bhē·ḍah*	भेंडा
snake	*sar·pa*	सर्प
squirrel	*lo·khar·ke*	लोखर्के
tiger	bahgh	बाघ
tortoise/turtle	*ka·chu·wah*	कछुवा
wolf	*bwāh·so*	ब्वाँसो
yak	*caū·ri·gai*	चौंरीगाई
yeti	*ye·ti*	येति

Insects

कीराहरू

ant	ka·*mi·lah*	कमिला
bee	*mau·ri*	मौरी
butterfly	*pu·ta·li*	पुतली
cockroach	*sāhng·glo*	साँङ्लो
flea	u·*pi·yāh*	उपियाँ
fly	*jhī·gah*	झिंगा
leech	*ju·kah*	जुका
louse	*jum·rah*	जुम्रा
mosquito	*lahm·khuṭ·ṭe*	लामखुट्टे
scorpion	*bic·chi*	बिच्छी
snail	*shā·kha·ki·rah*	शंखकीरा
spider	*mah·ku·rah*	माकुरा
tick	*kir·no*	किनो
worm	*ki·rah*	कीरा

Birds

चराहरू

chicken	*ku·*khu·rah	कुखुरा
crane	*sah·*ras	सारस
crow	kahg	काग
cuckoo	*koi·*li	कोइली
dove	*dhu·*kur	धुकुर
duck	hāhs	हाँस
eagle	cil	चील
falcon	bahj	बाज
hen	*ku·*khu·ri	कुखुरी
heron	ba·*kul·*lah	बकुल्ला
kite	cil	चील
mynah	*mai·*nah	मैना
owl	*ul·*lu	उल्लु
parrot	*su·*gah	सुगा
peacock	ma·*yur*	मयुर
pheasant	*kah·*lij	कालिज
pigeon	*pa·*re·wah	परेवा
stork	*dha·*nesh/*nil·*ca·rah	धनेश / नीलचरा
vulture	*gid·*dha	गिद्ध

DID YOU KNOW ...
Nepal is home to over 800 bird species, which is close to 10% of the global total. The Royal Chitwan National Park is one of the top ten places for bird-watching in the world. Nepal's national bird is the *dāh·*phe (डाँफे), 'Impeyan pheasant', a rare bird found in the high Himalaya.

FLORA & AGRICULTURE   फूल र खेतीपाती

What tree/flower is that?
    tyo rukh/phul ke ho?   त्यो रूख/फूल के हो ?
What's it used for?
    tyo *ke*·ko *lah*·gi u·pa·*yuk*·ta cha?   त्यो केको लागि उपयुक्त छ ?
Can you eat the fruit?
    tyas·ko phul *khah*·nu·hun·cha?   त्यस्को फूल खानुहुन्छ ?

banyan	*bar*·ko rukh	बरको रूख
cedar	*de*·wa·dahr	देवदार
chestnut	*ka*·ṭus rukh	कटुस रूख
deodar	*de*·wa·dahr	देवदार
elephant grass	*haht*·ti ghās	हात्ती घाँस
grassland	*phahn*·tah	फान्ता
juniper	dhu·pi·*sal*·lah	धुपीसल्ला
peepal	*pi*·pal	पीपल
pine	*sal*·lah·ko rukh	सल्लाको रूख
rosewood	*gu*·lahph·ko rukh	गुलाफको रूख
sal	sahl	साल

Herbs, Flowers & Crops   जडीबुटी, फूल र बाली

Nepal's national flower is the red rhododendron lah·li·*gu*·rāhs (लालीगुराँस), which grows in the Himalaya.

agriculture	*khe*·ti·pah·ti	खेतीपाती
bamboo	bāhs	बाँस
barley	jau	जौ
branch	*hāh*·gah	हाँगा
bush (bushland)	*jhah*·di	झाडी
bush (shrub)	boṭ	बोट
corn	*ma*·kai	मकै
crops	*bah*·li	बाली
fern	*un*·yu	उन्यू
flower	phul	फूल
harvest (n)	*bah*·li·nah·li	बालीनाली
irrigation	*sī*·cai	सिंचाइ

jasmine	*ca·*me·li	चमेली
leaf	paht	पात
marigold	*sa·*ya·pa·tri phul	सयपत्री फूल
millet	*ko·*do	कोदो
orchard	*vah·*ṭi·kah	वाटिका
orchid	*ar·*kiḍ	अर्किड
poinsettia	lah·li·*pah·*te	लालीपाते
rhododendron	*gu·*rāhs	गुराँस
red rhododendron	lah·li·*gu·*rāhs	लालीगुराँस
rice field/paddy	*dhahn·*bah·ri	धानबारी
stick	*laṭh·*ṭhi	लट्ठी
sugar cane	*u·*khu	उखु
terraced land	*ga·*rah	गरा
tobacco	*sur·*ti	सुर्ती
tree	rukh	रूख
wheat	*ga·*hū	गहुँ
wood	kahṭh	काठ

Western-style clinics are more expensive than local ones, however, communication will be easier and service may be quicker. Kathmandu has good medical facilities, as do some other towns. But if you have an accident or fall ill while trekking, you may need some help from the locals to reach a doctor.

AT THE DOCTOR
डाक्टरमा

I'm sick.
ma bi·*rah*·mi chu म बिरामी छ

My friend is sick.
me·ro *sah*·thi bi·*rah*·mi cha मेरो साथी बिरामी छ

I need a doctor (who speaks English).
ma·lai (ang·*gre*·ji *bol*·ne) मलाई (अङ्ग्रेजी बोल्ने)
ḍahk·ṭar *cah*·hi·yo डाक्टर चाहियो

Where can I find a good doctor?
rahm·ro ḍahk·ṭar ka·hāh *paun*·chu? राम्रो डाक्टर कहाँ पाउन्छु ?

Please call a doctor.
ḍahk·ṭar·lai bo·*lau*·nu·hos डाक्टरलाई बोलाउनुहोस

Where's the/a ...? ... ka·hāh cha? ... कहाँ छ ?
chemist/pharmacy *au*·sa·dhi *pa*·sal औषधी पसल
dentist *dāht*·ko ḍahk·ṭar दाँतको डाक्टर
doctor ḍahk·ṭar डाक्टर
health post/clinic ci·kit·*sah*·la·ya चिकित्सालय
hospital *as*·pa·tahl अस्पताल

Where's the nearest hospital?
na·ji·kai as·pa·tahl ka·hāh cha? नजिकै अस्पताल कहाँ छ ?

I need a porter.
ma·lai bha·ri·yah *cah*·hi·yo मलाई भरिया चाहियो

Please carry me to ...
...·sam·ma ma·lai *bok*·nu·hos ...सम्म मलाई बोक्नुहोस

Please send a message.
kha·bar pa·*thau*·nu·hos खबर पठाउनुहोस

HEALTH

THE DOCTOR MAY ASK ...

ke *bha*·yo? के भयो ?
  What's the matter?

khah·nah *khah*·nu *bha*·yo? खाना खानु भयो ?
  Have you eaten?

au·sa·dhi *khah*·nu *bha*·yo? औषधी खानु भयो ?
  Have you taken any medicine?

ka·tai du·khe·ko cha? कतै दुखेको छ ?
  Do you feel any pain?

ka·*hāh* dukh·cha? कहाँ दुख्छ ?
  Where does it hurt?

ta·*paī*·ko ma·hi·nah·bah·ri तपाईंको महीनाबारी
bha·ya·ko cha? भयको छ ?
  Are you menstruating?

ta·*paī*·ko ja·ro cha? तपाईंको जरो छ ?
  Do you have a temperature?

ka·hi·le de·khi *bha*·yo? कहिले देखी भयो ?
  How long have you been like this?

ta·*paī*·lai yas·to pa·hi·lah तपाईंलाई यस्तो पहिला
ka·hi·le *bha*·ya·ko cha? कहिले भयको छ ?
  Have you had this before?

ta·*paī* dhum·ra·pahn तपाई धूम्रपान
gar·nu·hun·cha? गर्नुहुन्छ ?
  Do you smoke?

ta·*paī* jāhḍ·*rak*·si तपाई जाँड-रक्सी
pi·*u*·nu·hun·cha? पिउनुहुन्छ ?
  Do you drink?

ta·*paī* o·kha·ti ki na·*sah*·lu तपाई ओखती कि नसालु
au·sa·dhi *li*·nu·hun·cha? औषधी लिनुहुन्छ ?
  Do you take medication
  or illegal drugs?

ta·*paī*·ko ke·hi a·*lahr*·ji cha? तपाईंको केही अलार्जि छ ?
  Are you allergic to anything?

ta·*paī* gar·bha·va·ti hu·nu·hun·cha? तपाई गर्भवती हुनुहुन्छ ?
  Are you pregnant?

AILMENTS

दुःखहरू

I don't feel well.
  ma·lai san·co chai·na   मलाई सन्चो छैन

I feel nauseous.
  ma·lai wahk·wahk lahg·yo   मलाई वाकवाक लाग्यो

I've been vomiting.
  mai·le bahn·tah ga·rē   मैले बान्ता गरें

I can't sleep.
  ma sut·na sa·ki·na   म सुत्न सकिन

I feel dizzy/weak.
  ma·lai ring·ga·ṭah/   मलाई रिङ्गटा/
  kam·jor lahg·yo   कमजोर लाग्यो

I've been bitten.
  ma·lai ṭok·yo   मलाई टोक्यो

I'm having trouble breathing.
  ma·lai sahs pher·na gah·hro   मलाई सास फेर्न गाह्रो
  lahg·yo   लाग्यो

HEALTH

I have (a/an) ...	*ma·lai ... lahg·yo*	मलाई ... लाग्यो
I've had (a/an) ...	*ma·lai ... lah·ge·ko thi·yo*	मलाई ... लागेको थियो

addiction	lat	लत
anaemia	*rak·ta·chin·tah*	रक्तक्षीणता
arthritis	bahth	बाथ
bite	*ṭo·kai*	टोकाइ
blister	*pho·kah*	फोका
bronchitis	swahs *na·li·ko* rog	स्वास नलीको रोग
cancer	*kyahn·sar*	क्यानसर
chicken pox	*ṭheu·lah*	ठेउला
cholera	*hai·jah*	हैजा
cold	*ru·ghah*	रुघा
constipation	*di·sah ka·se·ko*	दिसा कसेको
cough	*kho·ki*	खोकी
cramp	*baū·ḍyai*	बौंडचाइ
cut/wound	ghau	घाउ

HEALTH

diarrhoea	*jhah*·ḍah/*pa*·khah·lah	झाडा/पखाला
disease	rog	रोग
dysentery	ra·gat·*mah*·si	रगतमासी
fever	*ja*·ro	जरो
food poisoning	*khah*·nah kha·*rahb*	खाना खराब
frostbite	tu·*sah*·ro·le *khah*·ya·ko	तुसारोले खायको
gastroenteritis	*gyah*·strik	ग्यास्ट्रिक
glandular fever	*gāh*·ṭho·ko ja·ro	गाँठोको जरो
headache	ṭau·ko dukh·yo	टाउको दुख्यो
heart condition	*mu*·ṭu·ko bi·*rah*·mi	मुटुको बिरामी
hepatitis	*ka*·le·jo·ko rog	कलेजोको रोग
illness	rog	रोग
indigestion	*a*·pac	अपच
inflammation	*sun*·ni·ya·ko *a*·bas·thah	सुन्नीयको अबस्था
influenza	ru·ghah·*kho*·ki·ko ja·ro	रुघाखोकीको जरो
itch	ci·*lau*·na	चिलाउन

jaundice	*ka*·mal·pit·ta	कमलपित्त
kidney disease	mir·*gau*·lah·ko rog	मिर्गौलाको रोग
leprosy	*kus*·ṭa·rog	कुष्टरोग
lice	*jum*·rah	जुम्रा
lump	ḍal·lo	डल्लो
malaria	*au*·lo	औलो
measles	dah·*du*·rah	दादुरा
meningitis	me·nī·*jai*·ṭis	मेनिंजाइटीस
nausea	*wahk*·wah·ki	वाकवाकि
pain	du·*khai*	दुःखाई
paralysis	*pa*·cha·baht	पक्षबात
poliomyelitis	*po*·li·yo	पोलियो
rash	sujh	सुझ
rheumatism	bahth	बाथ
sore throat	*ghāh*·ṭi *du*·khe·ko	घाँटी दुखेको
sprain	*mar*·kai	मर्काइ

HEALTH

stomachache	*peṭ du·*khe·ko	पेट दुखेको
sunburn	ḍa·*dhau·*na	डढाउन
sunstroke	lu	लु
swelling	*su·*jan	सुजन
tetanus	*dha·*nu·rog	धनुरोग
toothache	dāht *du·*khe·ko	दाँत दुखेको
travel sickness	*gah·*di·mah *lahg·*ne	गाडीमा लाग्ने
	*wahk·*wahk	वाकवाक
tuberculosis	*cha·*ya·rog	क्षयरोग
typhoid	*ṭai·*phaiḍ	टाइफाइड
urinary infection	*pi·*sahb·ko rog	पिसाबको रोग
venereal disease	*bhi·*rī·gi	भिरिंगि
worms	*ju·*kah	जुका

It hurts here.
  *ya·*hāh *dukh·*yo — यहाँ दुख्यो

I feel better/worse.
  *ma·*lai ṭhik/jhan *na·*rahm·ro — मलाई ठीक / झान नराम्रो
  *lahg·*yo — लाग्यो

This is my usual medicine.
  ma yo *au·*sa·dhi *li·*ne *gar·*thē — म यो औषधी लिने गर्थें

I've been vaccinated.
  *mai·*le khop *li·*sa·kē — मैले खोप लिसकें

Can I have a receipt for my insurance?
  *me·*ro *bi·*mah·ko *lahg·*gi bil — मेरो बिमाको लागि बिल
  *di·*nu·hun·cha? — दिनुहुन्छ ?

I'm feeling fine now.
  *a·*hi·le ṭhik *bha·*yo — अहिले ठीक भयो

blood pressure	*rak·*ta·cahp	रक्तचाप
blood test	*ra·*gat·ko jāhc	रगतको जाँच
examination	jāhc	जाँच
injection	*su·*i	सूई
health	*swahs·*thya	स्वास्थ्य
patient (n)	*ro·*gi	रोगी
test	jāhc	जाँच

HEALTH

ALTITUDE SICKNESS

Acute mountain sickness (AMS) or altitude sickness is the most dangerous environmental hazard trekkers may face. Know the symptoms (breathlessness, dizziness, fatigue, insomnia, mental confusion, a pounding heart) and be alert for their appearance. Other potential health hazards for all travellers include heatstroke, prickly heat rash, sunburn and hypothermia.

WOMEN'S HEALTH   महिलाको स्वास्थ्य

Could I see a female doctor?
    ma *ai*·mai *ḍahk*·ṭar *her*·na   म आइमाई डाक्टर हेर्न
    sak·chu?   सक्छु ?
I haven't menstruated for ...
    me·ro *ma*·hi·nah·bah·ri   मेरो महीनाबारी
    na·*bha*·ya·ko ... *bha*·yo   नभयको ... भयो
I think I'm pregnant.
    ma *gar*·bha·va·ti chu   म गर्भवती छु
    ma bi·*cahr gar*·chu   म बिचार गर्छु
I'd like to have a pregnancy test.
    ma·lai *gar*·bha·va·ti·ko jāhc   मलाई गर्भवतीको जाँच
    cah·hi·yo   चाहियो
I'm (... weeks) pregnant.
    ma *gar*·bha·va·ti chu   म गर्भवती छु
    (... *hap*·tah *bha*·yo)   (... हप्ता भयो)

I'm taking the contraceptive pill.
ma pa·ri·bahr ni·yo·jan·ko
au·sa·dhi lin·dai·chu

म परिवार नियोजनको
औषधी लिन्दैछु

I'd like to use contraception.
ma·lai pa·ri·bahr ni·yo·jan·ko
au·sa·dhi li·na man lahg·yo

मलाई परिवार नियोजनको
औषधी लिन मन लाग्यो

I'd like to get the morning-after pill.
ma·lai mar·ning·ahph·ṭar·pil
cah·hi·yo

मलाई मर्निङ्गआफ्टरपिल
चाहियो

HEALTH

HIT THE BOTTLE

Never drink tap or river water unless it has been boiled and preferably also filtered. You may need to insist on properly sterilised water. Water that's only been filtered (in a basic Nepalese sandstone filter) is still unsafe to drink, but not all Nepalese people are aware of this. Water purification tablets are useless against Nepal's waterborne amoebae, and only iodine (or chlorine) is effective. Bottled water is widely available and quite cheap, but does lead to litter. Remember also to avoid ice and street icecream.

abortion	*gar·bha·paht*	गर्भपात
contraceptive device	*pa·ri·bahr ni·yo·jan·ko sah·dhan*	परिवार नियोजनको साधन
cystitis	*pi·sahb·ko rog*	पिसाबको रोग
family planning	*pa·ri·bahr ni·yo·jan*	परिवार नियोजन
menstruation	*ma·hi·nah·bah·ri*	महीनाबारी
miscarriage	*rak·ta·paht*	रक्तपात
period pain	*ma·hi·nah·bah·ri·ko du·khai*	महीनाबारीको दुःखाई
the Pill	*pa·ri·bahr ni·yo·jan·ko au·sa·dhi*	परिवार नियोजनको औषधी
pregnancy test kit	*gar·bha·va·ti jāhc·ne sah·mahn*	गर्भवती जाँच्ने सामान

HEALTH

SPECIAL HEALTH NEEDS

बिशेष स्वास्थ्य आबश्यकता

I have ...	*ma*·lai ... *lahg*·yo	मलाई ... लाग्यो
asthma	*dam*·ko *bya*·thah	दमको ब्यथा
diabetes	ma·dhu·*me*·ha	मधुमेह
epilepsy	*chah*·re rog	छारे रोग

I'm allergic to ...	*ma*·lai ... *li*·nu hun·dai·na	मलाई ... लिनु हुन्दैन
antibiotics	ahn·ṭi·bi·*yo*·ṭik	आण्टीबीयोटीक
aspirin	*ais*·pi·rin	आईसपिरिन्
bees	*mau*·ri	मौरी
dairy products	*dudh*·ko *khah*·nah	दूधको खाना
penicillin	pe·ni·*si*·lin	पेनिसिलिन
pollen	pa·*rahg*	पराग
that medicine	tyo *au*·sa·dhi	त्यो औषधी

I have a skin problem.
me·ro *chah*·lah·ko sa·*mas*·yah cha

मेरो छालाको समस्या छ

I have high/low blood pressure.
me·ro *rak*·ta·cahp *bha*·de·ko/ *gha*·ṭe·ko cha

मेरो रक्तचाप भदेको/ घटेको छ

I have a weak heart.
me·ro *mu*·ṭu *kam*·jor cha

मेरो मुटु कमजोर छ

I've had my vaccinations.
me·ro khop *li*·sak·yo

मेरो खोप लिसक्यो

I have my own syringe.
ma·sā·ga *ahph*·no *si*·rinj cha

मसँग आफ्नो सिरिन्ज छ

Is that a new syringe you're using?
tyo *su*·i ra *si*·rinj *na*·yāh ho?

त्यो सूई र सिरिन्ज नयाँ हो ?

HEALTH

I don't want a blood transfusion.
*ma·lai ra·*gat *li·*na man *par·*dai·na   मलाई रगत लिन मन पर्दैन
I'm on medication for ...
ma ...ko *au·*sa·dhi *lin·*dai·chu   म ...को औषधी लिन्दैछु
I'm on a special diet.
ma *khah·*nah *bāh·*dhe·ko chu   म खाना बाँधेको छु
I need a new pair of glasses.
*ma·*lai *na·*yāh *cash·*mah *cah·*hi·yo   मलाई नयाँ चश्मा चाहियो

ALTERNATIVE TREATMENTS   अर्को उपचारहरू

Traditional Ayurvedic medicines from plants are prepared in Nepal, while Tibetan medicines are another alternative. Massage therapists are everywhere and chiropractors can also be found.

Ayurvedic medicine	ah·yur·*be·*dah	आयुर्बेदा
Ayurvedic tonic	ra·*sah·*di	रसादि
faith healer	*dhah·*mi/*jhāh·*kri	धामी / झाँक्री
herbal treatment	ja·ḍi·*bu·*ṭi	जडीबूटी
massage	*mah·*lis	मालिस
meditation	dhyahn	ध्यान
midwife	dhai	धाई
shaman/witchdoctor	*jahn·*ne	जान्ने
Tibetan medicine	ti·*be·*tan ḍahk·ṭa·ri	तिबेतन डाक्टरी
traditional doctor	*bai·*dha	बैध
witch (m/f)	*bok·*si	बोक्सी
yoga	*yo·*gah	योगा

HEALTH

PARTS OF THE BODY   अङ्गप्रत्यङ्ग

My ... hurts.
  me·ro ... dukh·yo   मेरो ... दुख्यो
I have a pain in my ...
  me·ro ...mah du·khai cha   मेरो ...मा दुखाई छ
I've burned my ...
  me·ro ....mah pol·yo   मेरो ...मा पोल्यो
I can't move my ...
  me·ro ... ca·lau·na sak·di·na   मेरो ... चलाउन सक्दिन
He/She broke his/her ...
  wa·hāh·ko ... bhāhc·yo   वहाँको ... भाँच्यो

ankle	go·li·*gāh*·tho	गोलीगाँठो
anus	*mal*·dwahr	मलद्वार
appendix	*a*·pen·diks	अपेण्डीक्स
arm	*pah*·khu·rah	पाखुरा
back	*pi*·thū	पिठ्युँ
backbone	ḍhaḍ	ढाड
bladder	*mu*·trah·sha·ya	मूत्राशय
blood	*ra*·gat	रगत
body	ji·*u*	जीउ
bone	hahḍ	हाड
brain	*gi*·di	गिदी
breast	stan	स्तन
buttock	cahk	चाक
calf	pī·*ḍu*·lah	पिंडुला
cheek	*gah*·lah	गाला
chest	*chah*·ti	छाती
ear	kahn	कान
elbow	ku·*hi*·no	कुहिनो
eye	*āh*·khah	आँखा
face	*a*·nu·hahr	अनुहार

HEALTH

finger	*aū*·lah	औंला
foot	*khut*·ṭah	खुट्टा
hair	ka·*pahl*	कपाल
hand	haht	हात
head	*ṭau*·ko	टाउको
heart	*mu*·ṭu	मुटु
hip	cahk	चाक
jaw	bang·*gah*·rah	बङ्गारा
joint	*jor*·ni	जोर्नी
kidney	mir·*gau*·lah	मिर्गौला
knee	*ghū*·ḍah	घुँडा
leg	*go*·ḍah	गोडा
lips	oṭh	ओठ
liver	*ka*·le·jo	कलेजो
lung	*phok*·so	फोक्सो
mouth	mukh	मुख
muscle	*māh*·sha·pe·shi	मांशपेशी
nails	nang	नङ
neck	*ghāh*·ṭi	घाँटी

nose	nahk	नाक
penis	*ling*·ga	लिङ्ग
rib	*ka*·rang	करङ
shoulder	kāhdh	काँध
skin	*chah*·lah	छाला
stomach	peṭ	पेट
teeth/tooth	dāhṭ	दाँत
testicles	*aṇ*·ḍa	अण्ड
throat (inside)	*ga*·lah	गला
throat (outside)	*ghāh*·ṭi	घाँटी
tongue	*ji*·bro	जिब्रो
vagina	*yo*·ni	योनि
vein	*na*·sah	नसा
womb/uterus	*pah*·the·ghar	पाठेघर
wrist	*nah*·ḍi	नाडी

HEALTH

AT THE CHEMIST

औषधी पसलमा

Nepalese pharmacies stock a wide range of Western medicines, available without prescription. They can be good places to go for medical advice.

I need something for ...
...ko *lah*·gi, *au*·sa·dhi
di·nu·hos

...को लागि, औषधी
दिनुहोस

Please give me ...	ma·lai ... di·nu·hos	मलाई ... दिनुहोस
aspirin	*ais*·pi·rin	आईसपिरिन्
bandages	*paṭ*·ṭi	पट्टी
iodine	*ai*·ḍin	आईडीन्
medicine	*au*·sa·dhi	औषधी

Do I need a prescription for ...?
...ko *lah*·gi *au*·sa·dhi·vi·dhi
li·nu·par·cha?

...को लागि औषधिविधि
लिनुपर्छ ?

I have a prescription.
me·ro *au*·sa·dhi·vi·dhi cha

मेरो औषधिविधि छ

How many times a day?
din·ko *ka*·ti pa·ṭak?

दिनको कति पटक ?

(Twice) a day.
din·ko (*du*·i·pa·ṭak)

दिनको (दुइपटक)

With food.
khah·nah·sā·ga

खानासँग

Can I drive on this medication?
yo *au*·sa·dhi *li*·e·ra, *gah*·ḍi
ca·*lau*·nu·hun·cha?

यो औषधी लिएर, गाडी
चलाउनुहुन्छ ?

SPECIFIC NEEDS

TRAVELLING WITH THE FAMILY

परिबारमा यात्रा
गर्नु

The Nepalese love children and they're welcome everywhere. Having them around is a great way to interact with the locals. You won't find many facilities specific to children, such as high chairs or kids' menus, and there are few playgrounds or swimming pools (except in five-star hotels). The staff in hotels, restaurants and other places, however, will often go to considerable lengths to ensure your children are well looked after.

Are there facilities for babies?
bac·cah·ko su·bi·dhah cha?
बच्चाको सुबिधा छ ?

Do you have a child-minding service?
bac·cah her·ne se·bah cha?
बच्चा हेर्ने सेबा छ ?

Could someone look after my child?
me·ro bac·cah·lai her·na sa·kin·cha?
मेरो बच्चालाई हेर्न सकिन्छ ?

Where can I find a/an (English-speaking) babysitter?
(ang·gre·ji bol·ne) bac·cah her·ne mahn·che ka·hāh pain·cha?
(अङ्ग्रेजी बोल्ने) बच्चा हेर्ने मान्छे कहाँ पाइन्छ ?

Can you put an (extra) bed/cot in the room?
(thap) khahṭ/kha·ṭi·yah ko·ṭhah·mah rahkh·nu·hun·cha?
(थप) खाट / खटिया कोठामा राख्नुहुन्छ ?

Is it suitable for children?
bac·cah·ko lah·gi su·hau·ne cha?
बच्चाको लागि सुहाउने छ ?

Is there a family discount?
pa·ri·bahr·ko chuṭ cha?
परिबारको छुट छ ?

Is there a discount for children?
bac·cah·ko lah·gi kam hun·cha?
बच्चाको लागि कम हुन्छ ?

Are children allowed?
bac·cah·lai lyau·nu·hun·cha?
बच्चालाई ल्याउनुहुन्छ ?

Do you have a children's menu?
bac·cah·ko men·yu cha?
बच्चाको मेन्यु छ ?

Are there any activities for children?
bac·cah·ha·ru·ko *lah*·gi *ke*·hi
kah·rya·kram cha?

बच्चाहरूको लागि केही
कार्यक्रम छ ?

Is there a playground nearby?
khel·ne ṭhaũ *na*·ji·kai cha?

खेल्ने ठाउँ नजिकै छ ?

SPECIFIC NEEDS

DISABLED TRAVELLERS   अपाङ्ग यात्रीहरू

I'm disabled.
ma a·*pahng*·ga hū

म अपाङ्ग हुँ

I need assistance.
ma·lai *mad*·dat *cah*·hi·yo

मलाई मद्दत चाहियो

What services do you have for
disabled people?
a·*pahng*·ga·ha·ru·lai ke
se·bah·ha·ru chan?

अपाङ्गहरूलाई के सेबाहरू
छन् ?

Is there wheelchair access?
pahng·grah *bha*·ya·ko *mec*·ko
pa·hũc cha?

पाङ्ग्रा भयको मेचको
पहुँच छ ?

I'm deaf.
ma *ba*·hi·ro hū

म बहिरो हुँ

Speak more loudly, please.
ṭhu·lo *swar*·le
bhan·nu·hos

ठूलो स्वरले
भन्नुहोस

Are guide dogs permitted?
gaiḍ *ku*·kur·ko *a*·nu·ma·ti cha?

गाइड कुकुरको अनुमति छ ?

braille	*an*·dhah·ha·ru·ko *padh*·ne *yan*·tra	अन्धाहरूको पढ्ने यन्त्र
disabled person	a·*pahng*·ga *mahn*·che	अपाङ्ग मान्छे
guide dog	gaiḍ *ku*·kur	गाइड कुकुर
wheelchair	*pahng*·grah *bha*·ya·ko mec	पाङ्ग्रा भयको मेच

PILGRIMAGE & RELIGION   तीर्थयात्रा र धर्म

Most Nepalese are Hindu or Buddhist or a mix of both; some are Muslims. Travellers from Western countries are generally assumed to be Christian. As there are few Christians in Nepal, the Nepalese do not differentiate between different types of Christians, such as Catholics and Protestants.

What's your religion?
ta·*paī* kun *dhar*·ma
mahn·nu·hun·cha?

तपाई कुन धर्म
मान्नुहुन्छ ?

I'm ...   ma ... *mahn*·chu   म ... मान्छु
  Buddhist   *bud*·dha *dhar*·ma   बुद्ध धर्म
  Christian   *i*·sai *dhar*·ma   इसाई धर्म
  Hindu   *hin*·du *dhar*·ma   हिन्दु धर्म

I'm ...   ma ... hū   म ... हुँ
  Jewish   ya·*hu*·di   यहुदि
  Muslim   *mu*·sal·mahn   मुसलमान

I'm not religious.
ma *ku*·nai *dhar*·ma *mahn*·di·na

म कुनै धर्म मान्दिन

I'm (Christian), but not practising.
ma (*i*·sai *dhar*·ma) *mahn*·chu,
ta·ra ma *prahr*·tha·nah gar·di·na

म (इसाई धर्म) मान्छु,
तर म प्रार्थना गर्दिन

I think I believe in God.
me·ro bi·*cahr*·mah,
bha·ga·bahn·lai bi·*shwahs* gar·chu

मेरो बिचारमा,
भगबानलाई बिश्वास गर्छु

I believe in destiny/fate.
ma *bhahg*·ya bi·*shwahs* gar·chu

म भाग्य बिश्वास गर्छु

I'm interested in astrology/philosophy.
ma·lai *jyo*·tis·bi·*dyah*·mah/
dar·*shan*·*shah*·stra·mah cahkh
lahg·cha

मलाई ज्योतिषबिद्यामा/
दर्शनशास्त्रमा चाख
लाग्छ

I'm an atheist.
ma *nah*·stik hū

म नास्तिक हुँ

I'm agnostic.
ma jaḍ·*bah*·di hū

म जडबादी हुँ

Can I attend this ceremony/ritual?
    ma yo *ut*·sab·mah/*pu*·jah·mah   म यो उत्सबमा/पूजामा
    u·*pas*·thit *hu*·na *sak*·chu?   उपस्थित हुन सक्छु ?
Can I pray here?
    ma *ya*·hāh *prahr*·tha·nah   म यहाँ प्रार्थना
    gar·nu·hun·cha?   गर्नुहुन्छ ?
Where can I pray/worship?
    ma *ka*·hāh *prahr*·tha·nah/*pu*·jah   म कहाँ प्रार्थना/पूजा
    gar·na *sak*·chu?   गर्न सक्छु ?

SPECIFIC NEEDS

Brahmin	*bah*·hun	बाहुन
Buddhist monk	*bhi*·chu	भिक्षु
Buddhist priest	*lah*·mah	लामा
church	*gir*·jah·ghar	गिर्जाघर
funeral	ma·*lahm*	मलाम
funeral rites	*shrahd*·dha	श्राद्ध
god/goddess	*de*·va·tah	देवता
Hindu priest	bah·hun·*bah*·je	बाहुनबाजे
pilgrimage	tir·tha·*yah*·trah	तीर्थयात्रा
prayer	*prahr*·tha·nah	प्रार्थना
priest	pu·*jah*·ri	पूजारी
relic	*pun*·ya·sma·raṇ *bas*·tu	पुण्यस्मरण बस्तु
religious festival procession	*jah*·trah	जात्रा
ritual	*pu*·jah	पूजा
saint (Hindu)	ma·*haht*·mah	महात्मा
saint (Muslim)	pir	पीर
shrine	*de*·wal	देवल
temple (Buddhist)	*stu*·pah	स्तूपा
temple (Hindu)	*man*·dir	मन्दिर
worship	*pu*·jah	पूजा

TIMES, DATES & FESTIVALS

TELLING THE TIME
समय हेर्नु

Telling the time in Nepali is similar to English, using phrases equivalent to quarter past, half past and quarter to the hour (rather than 9.15, 9.30, 9.45 and so on). The 24-hour clock is not often employed, so bi·*hah*·na (बिहान), 'morning', and be·lu·kah (बेलुका), 'evening', indicate am and pm.

What time is it?
  ka·ti *ba*·jyo?   कति बज्यो ?
  (lit: how-much clock-of?)
It's two o'clock.
  du·i *ba*·jyo   दुइ बज्यो
  (lit: two clock-of)
At what time?
  ka·ti *ba*·je·ti·ra?   कति बजेतिर ?
  (lit: how-much clock-at?)
At two o'clock.
  du·i *ba*·je·ti·ra   दुइ बजेतिर
  (lit: two clock-at)
At ten o'clock in the morning.
  bi·*hah*·na das *ba*·je·ti·ra   बिहान दस बजेतिर
  (lit: morning ten clock-at)

quarter past	*sa*·wah	सवा
	(lit: plus-a-quarter)	
half past	*sah*·dhe	साढे
	(lit: plus-a-half)	
quarter to	*pau*·ne	पौने
	(lit: minus-a-quarter)	

| It's early. | *sa*·be·rai ho | सबेरै हो |
| It's late. | *ḍhi*·lo cha | ढिलो छ |

Quarter to two.
  pau·ne du·i ba·jyo   पौने दुइ बज्यो
  (lit: quarter-to two clock-of)
Quarter past two.
  sa·wah du·i ba·jyo   सवा दुइ बज्यो
  (lit: quarter-past two clock-of)
Half past two.
  sah·ḍhe du·i ba·jyo   साढे दुइ बज्यो
  (lit: half-past two clock-of)
Twenty to one.
  ek *baj·na·lai* bis *mi·naṭ*   एक बज्नलाई बीस मिनट
  bāh·ki cha   बाँकी छ
  (lit: one clock-to twenty
  minute remain is)

DAYS OF THE WEEK   बारहरू

What day is it today?
  ah·ja ke *bahr?*   आज के बार ?

Monday	*som·bahr*	सोमबार
Tuesday	*mang·gal·bahr*	मङ्गलबार
Wednesday	*bu·dha·bahr*	बुधबार
Thursday	*bi·hi·bahr*	बिहिबार
Friday	*su·kra·bahr*	शुक्रबार
Saturday	*sa·ni·bahr*	शनिबार
Sunday	*ai·ta·bahr*	आइतबार

TIME, DATES & FESTIVALS

THE NEPALESE CALENDAR   बिक्रम सम्बत्

The Hindu calendar *Bikram Sambat* is used in Nepal. It's a lunar-solar system, 57 years ahead of the Gregorian calendar, *Isvi Sambat*, so that 2002 AD is 2059 BS. Both have 365 days and 12 months, but the number of days in a Nepalese month varies from 29 to 32.

There are three other calendars which are less widely used: the *Shakya Sambat* for astrology, the Newars' *Nepal Sambat*, of the Kathmandu Valley and the Tibetan 60-year cyclical calendar. The first Nepalese month begins in mid-April.

THE NEPALESE CALENDAR

bai·sahkh mid-April to mid-May	बैसाख
jeth mid-May to mid-June	जेठ
a·sahr mid-June to mid-July	असार
saun mid-July to mid-August	साउन
bha·dau mid-August to mid-September	भदौ
a·soj mid-September to mid-October	असोज
kaht·tik mid-October to mid-November	कात्तिक
mang·sir mid-November to mid-December	मङ्सिर
pus mid-December to mid-January	पुस
mahgh mid-January to mid-Februray	माघ
phah·gun mid-February to mid-March	फागुन
cait mid-March to mid-April	चैत

TIME, DATES &
FESTIVALS

Each lunar month is divided into two fortnights, and each of the fourteen days has a name; e·*kah*·da·si (एकादसी) is the eleventh day, an inauspicious day when meat is to be avoided.

ma·*sahn*·ta   मसान्त
  last day of a Nepalese month

sang·*krahn*·ti   सङ्क्रान्ति
  first day of a Nepalese month

DATES   मितिहरू

The Hindu calendar uses the word *ga*·te (गते) to indicate the date:

What Nepali date is it today?
  ah·ja *ka*·ti *ga*·te?   आज कति गते ?
The first of the Nepali month.
  ek *ga*·te   एक गते
It's 1 *Magh*.
  mahgh ek *ga*·te ho   माघ एक गते हो

The Gregorian calendar uses the word *tah*·rikh (तारिख) to indicate the date. Like *ga*·te, *tah*·rikh follows the number:

What date is it today?
  ah·ja *ka*·ti *tah*·rikh?   आज कति तारिख ?
The third of the month.
  tin *tah*·rikh   तीन तारिख
It's 18 October.
  ok·*to*·bar a·*thah*·ra *tah*·rikh ho   ओक्टोबर अठार तारिख हो

day	din	दिन
fortnight	*pan*·dhra din	पन्ध्र दिन
hour	*ghan*·ṭah	घण्टा
minute	*mi*·naṭ	मिनट
month	*ma*·hi·nah	महीना
public holiday	sar·*kah*·ri *bi*·dah	सरकारी बिदा
week	*hap*·tah	हप्ता
year	*bar*·sa/sahl	बर्ष/साल

PRESENT बर्तमान

now	*a*·hi·le	अहिले
nowadays	hi·jo·*ah*·ja	हिजोआज
this morning	*ah*·ja bi·*hah*·na	आज बिहान
this evening	*ah*·ja *be*·lu·kah	आज बेलुका
this month	yo *ma*·hi·nah	यो महीना
this week	yo *hap*·tah	यो हप्ता
this year	yo *bar*·sa	यो बर्ष
today	*ah*·ja	आज
tonight	*ah*·ja *rah*·ti	आज राति

PAST भूतकाल

a while ago	*ek*·chin *bha*·yo	एकछिन भयो
after	pa·chi	पछि
(five) years ago	(pāhc) *bar*·sa *bha*·yo	(पाँच) बर्ष भयो
(three) days ago	(tin) din *bha*·yo	(तीन) दिन भयो
(half an hour) ago	(*ah*·dhah *ghan*·ṭah) *bha*·yo	(आधा घण्टा) भयो
last Friday	ga·ya·ko *su*·kra·bahr	गयको शुक्रबार
last night	hi·jo *rah*·ti	हिजो राति
last week	ga·ya·ko *hap*·tah	गयको हप्ता
last month	ga·ya·ko *ma*·hi·nah	गयको महीना
last year	ga·ya·ko *bar*·sa	गयको बर्ष
long ago	*dhe*·rai sa·*ma*·ya *bha*·yo	धेरै समय भयो
recently	*hahl*·sah·lai	हालसालै
since (May)	(mai)·de·khi	(माइ)देखि
the day before yesterday	as·ti	अस्ति
yesterday	hi·jo	हिजो
yesterday evening	hi·jo *be*·lu·kah	हिजो बेलुका
yesterday morning	hi·jo bi·*hah*·na	हिजो बिहान

FUTURE   भविष्य

coming year	*au*·ne *bar*·sa	आउने बर्ष
in (five) minutes	(pāhc) *mi*·naṭ *pa*·chi	(पाँच) मिनट पछि
in (six) days	(cha) din *pa*·chi	(छ) दिन पछि
next week	*ar*·ko *hap*·tah	अर्को हप्ता
next month	*ar*·ko ma·*hi*·nah	अर्को महीना
next year	*ar*·ko *bar*·sa	अर्को बर्ष
soon	*cāh*·ḍai	चाँडै
the day after tomorrow	*par*·si	पर्सि
tomorrow	*bho*·li	भोलि
tomorrow morning	*bho*·li bi·*hah*·na	भोलि बिहान
tomorrow afternoon	*bho*·li *diū*·so	भोलि दिउँसो
tomorrow night	*bho*·li *rah*·ti	भोलि राति
until (June)	(*jun*)·sam·ma	(जुन)सम्म
within an hour/ month	ek *ghaṇ*·ṭah·bhi·tra/ ma·hi·nah·bhi·tra	एक घण्टाभित्र/ महिनाभित्र

DURING THE DAY   दिनमा

afternoon	*diū*·so	दिउँसो
all day	*din*·bha·ri	दिनभरि
dawn	bi·*hahn*	बिहान्
dusk	*san*·dhyah·kahl	सन्ध्याकाल
early	*sa*·be·rai	सबेरै
evening	*be*·lu·kah	बेलुका
late	*ḍhi*·lo	ढिलो
lunchtime	*ca*·me·nah·ko *be*·lah	चमेनाको बेला
midday	ma·*dhyahn*·ha	मध्यानह
midnight	ma·*dhya*·raht	मध्यरात
morning	bi·*hah*·na	बिहान
night	raht	रात
noon	ma·*dhyahn*·ha	मध्यानह
sunrise	*sur*·yo·da·ya	सूर्योदय
sunset	sur·*yahs*·ta	सूर्यास्त

GODS & PROMINENT BEINGS   देवताहरू

Religion is a significant part of Nepalese culture and you'll find it easier to gain some cultural understanding if you're familiar with religious terminology. Most temples are dedicated to one or other of a multitude of gods, each known by various names or forms. There are said to be 300 million Hindu deities!

Brahma   *brah·ma*   ब्राम्ह
Supreme Being of the Hindu Trinity, Great Creator of all worldly things. His consort is Saraswati and his animal is a swan or goose.

Buddha   *bud·*dhah   बुद्ध
The Enlightened One of Buddhism; for Hindus, the ninth incarnation of Vishnu.

Ganesh   *ga·*nesh   गणेश
Elephant-headed god of wisdom, prosperity and success, and the remover of obstacles. Elder son of Shiva and Pahrvati, and easily the most popular god in Nepal. His animal is the shrew, a symbol of wisdom. Ganesh is also called Vinayak.

Laxmi   *lach·*mi   लक्ष्मी
goddess of wealth and prosperity, consort of Vishnu

Manjushri   *mahn·*jush·ri   मन्जुश्री
god of divine wisdom, founder of Nepalese civilisation and creator of the Kathmandu Valley

Pahrvati   *pahr·va·*ti   पार्वती
peaceful consort of Shiva representing his female and, through Kahli and Durga, his fearsome side. Pahrvati's symbol is the *yoni*, which complements Shiva's *lingam*.

TIME, DATES &
FESTIVALS

Kumari   ku·*mah*·ri   कुमारी
young virgin Newar girl who's worshipped by the
Nepalese as a living goddess

Pashupati   pa·shu·*pa*·ti   पशुपती
a benevolent form of Shiva. Lord of Beasts and keeper
of all living things. Supreme god of Nepal.

Shiva   *shi*·va   शिव
second member of the Hindu Trinity. The destroyer
and regenerator who represents time and procre-
ation. The most important god in Nepal, he's often
represented by a *lingam*, his *shakti* is Pahrvati, his
animal is the bull Nandi and his common symbols
are the trident and drum. His home is Mt Kailash in
Tibet. He is supposed to have thousands of forms.
Mahhahdev, the Great God, is also a manifestation of
Shiva, and so is Natarahj the god of cosmic dancing.
He's supposed to smoke hashish.

Tara   *tah*·rah   तारा
represents the principle of 'femaleness' for both
Hindus and Buddhists, and takes various forms,
(Green Tara and White Tara are among them).

Vishnu   *vish*·ṇu   विष्णु
third member of the Hindu trinity; the Preserver. He
appeared on earth in nine incarnations, including the
Buddha and Krishna, with the tenth yet to come. His
vehicle is the Garuda, a mythical bird.

(See pages 181 to 183 for more religious terms.)

FESTIVALS

चाडबाडहरू

Hundreds of festivals, celebrating the many gods and religious deities, are held every year within Nepal. The official state religion is Hinduism, but it mingles harmoniously with Buddhism, and many religious festivals are celebrated together by Hindus and Buddhists. Festivals are held according to the ancient lunar calendar and fall on the days of full or new moons, so the date and month in which they fall changes each year.

ba·sant *pān*·ca·mi   बसन्त पञ्चमि
   January/February – celebration of spring; in honour of Saraswati, the goddess of learning

shi·va·*rah*·tri   शिवरात्रि
   February – Shiva's birthday

ho·li   होली
   February/March – Festival of Colours

lo·sahr   लोसार
   February/March – two-week festival for Tibetan New Year

cait da·*saī*   चैत दशें
   March/April – festival dedicated to Durga (the wrathful form of Pahrvati), six months before the biggest festival Dasain

bis·kat *jah*·trah   बिस्कत जात्रा
   April – feast of the death of the Snake Demons; part of the Nepalese New Year

bud·dha *ja*·yan·ti   बुद्ध जयन्ती
   April/May – Buddha's birthday

rah·to ma·*chen*·dra·nahth *jah*·trah   रातो मछेन्द्रनाथ जात्रा
   April/May – Festival of Red Machendranahth, also known as Bhota Jahtrah (Festival of the Sacred Vest)

ku·mahr·*sah*·sthi   कुमारसास्थी
   May/June – birthday of Kahttikayah, god of war, son of Shiva

nahg *pān*·ca·mi   नाग पँन्चमि
July/August – day of the Snake Gods, who are rain-givers and guardians of water. Snakes are honoured.

ra·chah·*ban*·dhan   रक्षाबन्दन
August – yellow thread is given out by Hindu priests and worn for good luck up until Tihahr or for at least a week. Unlike sacred thread, it's available to women and non-Hindus.

gū·lah   गुँला
August/September – month of Newar Buddhist ceremonies

krish·na ja·*yan*·ti   कृष्ण जयन्ती
August/September – birthday of Krishna, epic hero

tij   तीज
August/September – three-day Festival of Women

in·dra *jah*·trah   इन्द्र जात्रा
September – festival honouring Indra, the rain god

da·*saī* (*dur*·gah *pu*·jah)   दशैं (दुर्गा पूजा)
September/October – Nepal's biggest annual festival. Celebrated in honour of Durga's slaying of the demons. On the eighth day of Dasain, sacrifices and offerings to Durga begin. The ninth day is the main day of sacrifice, on which all Nepalese eat meat. The tenth day is for family celebration.

kaht·tik *pur*·ṇi·mah   कात्तिकया पूर्णिमा
September/October – full moon day of Kartik, marking the end of Dasain and celebrated by gambling

di·*pah*·wa·li   दिपावलि
October/November – the Festival of Lights, on the third and most important day of Tihahr, dedicated to Laxmi

mha *pu*·jah   म्ह पूजा
October/November – Newar New Year; day of selfworship

ti·hahr तिहार
October/November – second-most important Hindu festival
in Nepal (after Dasain), honouring certain animals.

mah·hah·*lax*·mi *pu*·jah महालक्ष्मी पूजा
November – harvest festival

mah·ni rim·du मानी रीमदु
November – three-day Sherpa festival, held at Thyangpoche
monastery in the Solu Khumbu region

Useful Words गुनी शब्द

aū·si	the dark moon	औसी
cahḍ·bahḍ	festival	चाडबाड
cai·tya	lotus-shaped stupa	चैत्य
ci·rahg	ceremonial oil lamp or torch	चीराग
ghaṭ	platform for cremation; riverside steps	घाट
ji·van	life	जीवन
jin·da·gi	lifetime	जिन्दगी
kahl	death	काल
lah·mah	Buddhist spiritual teacher	लामा
mah·ni	stone carved with Buddhist	मानि
maṇ·dap	pavilion	मण्डप
man·tra	prayer; religious incantation	मन्त्र
pahp	sin	पाप
pra·*sahd*	sacred food	प्रसाद
pu·jah	prayer/worship/ceremony	पूजा
pur·ṇi·mah	night of the full moon	पूर्णिमा
rah·*mah*·yahṇ	popular Hindu epic	रामायाण
rath	vehicle of the gods	रथ
sang·gha	community of Buddhists	सङ्घ
stu·pah	Buddhist temple or sanctuary	स्तुपा
va·*hah*·nah	animal of a Hindu god	वहाना
vaj·rah·*cahr*·ya	Newar Buddhist priest	वज्राचार्य
yah·nah	way to Buddhist enlightenment	याना
yo·gi	holy man	योगि

Religious Terms

dhar·ma   धर्म
    religious teaching, law and doctrine defining the path to
    universal harmony via individual morals

gu·ru   गुरु
    spiritual guide who teaches by inspiring people to follow his
    or her example

kar·ma   कर्म
    the law of cause and effect: the cumulative actions of all
    previous lives determine the soul's next rebirth

ling·gam   लीङ्गम
    phallic symbol of Shiva; a symbol of Shiva's creative role

ma·hah·*bhah*·rat   महाभारत
    Hindu epic of the battle between two families

maṇ·da·lah   मण्डला
    mystic circular design used as a meditation device

mokh·sah   मोक्षा
    Hindu equivalent of nir·*bhah*·nah

nir·*bhah*·nah   निर्भाना
    the achievement of a state of enlightenment and spiritual peace
    via the annihilation of individuality and the end of misery and
    pain (caused by desires): the eventual aim of Buddhists

sah·dhu   साधु
    a Hindu ascetic on a spiritual search, usually a follower of
    Shiva, carrying a trident

sam·*sahr*   समसार
    Hindu cycle of transmigration and reincarnation

swas·ti·kah   स्वस्तीका
    for Hindus, a sign of law (*swas*·ti means 'wellbeing'); for
    Buddhists, a symbol of the esoteric doctrine of the Buddha

TIME, DATES &
FESTIVALS

tan·tra   तन्त्र
   psycho-sexual mystic philosophy which leads to enlightenment;
   a major influence on Nepalese Hinduism and Buddhism

ti·kah   तीका
   mark of red *sindur* (vermilion) paste, placed on the forehead

vaj·ra   वज्र
   thunderbolt or diamond, the symbol of Tantric Buddhism;
   represents nir·*bhah*·nah

yo·ni   योनी
   symbol of Pahrvati, representing the female sexual organ

NEVER EVER LEATHER

You may not be allowed inside Hindu temples, but if so,
always remove shoes and any leather items such as belts.
Always walk around Buddhist shrines and stupas clockwise, never anticlockwise. It's customary to present the head
lama with a white scarf, *khata*, as a mark of respect.

BIRTHDAYS   जन्मदिनहरू
When's your ...?   ta·*paī*·ko ... *ka*·hi·le   तपाईंको ... कहिले
                    ho?   हो ?

   birthday   *jan*·ma·din   जन्मदिन
   birthday cake   *jan*·ma·din·ko kek   जन्मदिनको केक
   birthday celebration   *jan*·mot·sab   जन्मोत्सब
   candles   *main*·bat·ti   मैनबत्ती

My ... is on (25 January).
   me·ro ... (pac·*cis*   मेरो ... (पच्चीस
   ja·na·wa·ri)·mah ho   जनवरी)मा हो
Happy Birthday!
   jan·ma·din·ko   जन्मदिनको शुभकामना !
   shu·bha·*kah*·ma·nah!
Blow out the candles!
   main·bat·ti *phuk*·nu·hos!   मैनबत्ती फुक्नुहोस !

WEDDINGS   बिहाहरू

For women, marriage means leaving their families and accepting the authority of their in-laws. Wives may return home to visit their own families, but only with their mother-in-law's permission. Most marriages are still arranged between the two families, although love matches are becoming more common. It's no longer unusual for young Nepalese to have a boyfriend or girlfriend, but these are rarely sexual relationships.

In urban communities the typical marrying age is mid-20s or older, even for women, but it's often younger among rural people. Child marriage still exists.

Best wishes!
  shu·bha·*kah*·ma·nah!   शुभकामना !
Congratulations!
  ba·dhai!   बधाइ !
To the bride and groom!
  du·la·hi ra *du*·la·hah·lai!   दुलही र दुलहालाई !

engagement	*vahg*·dahn	वाग्दान
honeymoon	pra·*mod*·kahl	प्रमोदकाल
rice-feeding ceremony	bhaht khu·*wau*·ne	भात खुवाउने
wedding/marriage	bi·*hah*	बिहा
wedding anniversary	bi·*hah*·ko bahr·si·*kot*·sab	बिहाको बार्षिकोत्सब
wedding cake	bi·*hah*·ko kek	बिहाको केक
wedding guests	*jan*·ta	जन्त
wedding present	bi·*hah*·ko *u*·pa·hahr	बिहाको उपहार

NEWAR TRADITIONAL CULTURE

The Newars are the ethnic group indigenous to the Kathmandu Valley, with a history that goes back at least one millennium. They have a unique language, Newari. Newar life is centred on the family and local community, and the people traditionally live in extended family homes around communal courtyards.

The Newars have a rich cultural, social and spiritual lifestyle. Their traditional occupations are trade and agriculture, and they were originally Buddhist until Hinduism came to Nepal; many follow both philosophies. Ceremonies, feasts and festivals are an important part of everyday life and it's said there's a Newar festival for every day of the year! These are usually organised by community organisations called *guthi* which take care of most communal business.

Newars are famous for their food (see page 128) and the vast number of different dishes. There are a hundred ways to prepare buffalo meat alone! They're also renowned for their art and architecture – woodcarving and pagodas are two Newar specialties.

TIME, DATES & FESTIVALS

TOASTS & CONDOLENCES

शुभकामना र समबेदनाहरू

Bon appetit!	*rahm·ro·sā·ga khah·nu·hos!*	राम्रोसँग खानुहोस !
Bon voyage!	*rahm·ro·sā·ga yah·trah gar·nu·hos!*	राम्रोसँग यात्रा गर्नुहोस !
Get well soon!	*chi·to ni·ko·hu·nu·hos!*	छिटो निकोहुनुहोस !
God protect you!	*bha·ga·bahn·le ra·chah·ga·ros!*	भगबानले रक्षागरोस !
I'm very sorry.	*ma·lai dhe·rai du·khi lahg·yo*	मलाई धेरै दुःखि लाग्यो
My deepest sympathy.	*me·ro sa·hah·nu·bhu·ti li·nu·hos*	मेरो सहानुभूति लिनुहोस

Good luck!	*sa*·phal·hos!	सफलहोस !
Good luck in your travels!	*yah*·trah *sa*·phal·hos!	यात्रा सफलहोस !
Blessing!	bhah·gya·*mah*·ni!	भाग्यमानी !
Hope it goes well!	*ah*·shah cha *rahm*·ro hos!	आशा छ राम्रो होस !
What bad luck!	*kas*·to a·*bhah*·gi!	कस्तो अभागी !
Never mind.	*bhai*·go	भैगो
Long life!	dir·*ghah*·yu!	दीर्घायु !

NUMBERS & AMOUNTS

The Nepalese counting system measures quantities using different base units to those used in English. For example, 'one million' in Nepali is das lahkh (दस लाख), '10 hundred thousand'. The pattern is a little irregular. If you're unsure of the correct form for a number, say the larger number followed by 'and', ra (र), and then the smaller number, for example, tis ra pāhc (तीस र पाँच), '30 and 5' to mean '35', paĩtis (पैंतीस).

CARDINAL NUMBERS

सङ्ख्याहरू

0	*sun·ya*	शून्य
1	ek	एक
2	*du·i*	दुइ
3	tin	तीन
4	cahr	चार
5	pāhc	पाँच
6	cha	छ
7	saht	सात
8	ahṭh	आठ
9	nau	नौ
10	das	दस
11	e·*ghah*·ra	एघार
12	*bah*·hra	बाह्र
13	te·hra	तेह्र
14	*cau*·dha	चौध
15	*pan*·dhra	पन्ध्र
16	so·hra	सोह्र
17	*sa*·tra	सत्र
18	a·*ṭhah*·ra	अठार
19	un·*nais*	उन्नाईस
20	bis	बीस
21	ek·*kais*	एककाईस
22	bais	बाईस

23	teis	तेईस
24	*cau*·bis	चौबीस
25	pac·*cis*	पच्चीस
26	*chab*·bis	छब्बीस
27	sat·*tais*	सत्ताईस
28	aṭ·*thais*	अट्ठाईस
29	u·*nan*·tis	उनन्तीस
30	tis	तीस
40	*cah*·lis	चालीस
50	pa·*cahs*	पचास
60	*sah*·ṭhi	साठी
70	*sat*·ta·ri	सत्तरी
80	*a*·si	असी
90	*nab*·be	नब्बे
100	ek say	एक सय
1000	ek ha·*jahr*	एक हजार
10,000	das ha·*jahr*	दस हजार
100,000	ek lahkh	एक लाख
200,000	*du*·i lahkh	दुइ लाख
one million	das lahkh	दस लाख
ten million	ek *ka*·roḍ	एक करोड्
one billion	ek *a*·rab	एक अरब

ORDINAL NUMBERS   क्रमसूचक सङ्ख्याहरू

Ordinal numbers are formed by adding the suffix -aũ to the relevant cardinal number. The first four are irregular, however, and should be learnt individually:

1st	*pa*·hi·lah	पहिला
2nd	*dos*·rah	दोस्रा
3rd	*tes*·rah	तेस्रा
4th	*caũ*·ṭho	चौँठो
5th	*pāh*·caũ	पाँचौँ
10th	*da*·saũ	दसौँ
20th	*bi*·saũ	बीसौँ

FRACTIONS भागहरू

a quarter	*cau*·thai	चौथाइ
a third	*ti*·hai	तीहाइ
a half	*ah*·dhah	आधा
three-quarters	*pau*·ne	पौने
one-and-a-half	*ḍe*·ḍha	डेढ
two-and-a-half	*a*·ḍhai	अढाई

COUNTERS जना र वटा

When counting people or objects in Nepali, remember to use a counter (or classifier) after the number and before the noun. The counter for objects is *wa*·ṭah (वटा) and for people *ja*·nah (जना), but informally *wa*·ṭah is also used for people. It's a bit like saying 'two *sheets* of paper' or 'two *slices* of bread'. The system is regular after the number three, but the first three should be learnt individually:

one	ek	एक
one (thing)	*eu*·ṭah	एउटा
one (person)	*ek*·ja·nah	एकजना
two	*du*·i	दुइ
two (things)	*du*·i·ṭah	दुइटा
two (people)	*du*·i·ja·nah	दुइजना
three	tin	तीन
three (things)	*tin*·ṭah	तीनटा
three (people)	*tin*·ja·nah	तीनजना
five	pāhc	पाँच
five (things)	pāhc *wa*·ṭah	पाँच वटा
five (people)	pāhc *ja*·nah	पाँच जना
ten	das	दस
ten (things)	das *wa*·ṭah	दस वटा
ten (people)	das *ja*·nah	दस जना

How many? (things)		
ka·ti *wa*·ṭah?	कति वटा ?	
How many? (people)		
ka·ti *ja*·nah?	कति जना ?	

apple	syau	स्याउ
two apples	*du*·i·ṭah syau	दुइटा स्याउ
sister	*ba*·hi·ni	बहिनी
three sisters	tin *ja*·nah *ba*·hi·ni	तीन जना बहिनी
tiger	bahgh	बाघ
five tigers	pãhc *wa*·ṭah bahgh	पाँच वटा बाघ

To make a multiple, place *pal*·ṭa (पल्ट) after the number:

| two times | *du*·i *pal*·ṭa | दुइ पल्ट |
| three times | tin *pal*·ṭa | तीन पल्ट |

USEFUL AMOUNTS   गुनी परिमाणहरू

How much?	*ka*·ti?	कति ?
Please give me ...	*ma*·lai ... *di*·nu·hos	मलाई ... दिनुहोस
I need ...	*ma*·lai ... *cah*·hi·yo	मलाई ... चाहियो
double	*do*·bar	दोबर
a dozen	ek *dar*·jan	एक दर्जन
enough	pra·*shas*·ta	प्रशस्त
many/much/a lot	*thup*·rai	थुप्रै
a pair	ek jor	एक जोर
a bottle of ...	ek *si*·si ...	एक सिसी ...
half a kg of ...	*ah*·dhah *ki*·lo ...	आधा किलो ...
half a dozen	*ah*·dhah *dar*·jan	आधा दर्जन
100 grams	ek say grahm	एक सय ग्राम
a cup of ...	ek kap ...	एक कप ...
a glass of ...	ek gi·*lahs* ...	एक गिलास ...
a jar	su·*rah*·hi	सुराही
a kg	ek *ki*·lo	एक किलो
a packet of ...	ek *po*·ko ...	एक पोको ...
a slice of ...	ek *ṭuk*·rah ...	एक टुका ...
a tin	ṭin	टिन

NUMBERS & AMOUNTS

Nepal is still a relatively safe place to travel, although petty theft from rooms or bags (especially when they're on top of buses) is not uncommon. In main centres, there are special tourist police to help out or, in cases of serious difficulty, you can go to Police Headquarters in Kathmandu. Also take the time to register with your embassy or consulate.

Help!	gu·*hahr*!	गुहार !
Stop!	rok!	रोक !
Go away!	jau!	जाउ !
Thief!	cor!	चोर !
Fire!	*ah*·go!	आगो !
Watch out!	*he*·ra!	हेर !

It's an emergency.
   ah·pat *bha*·yo   आपत् भयो

There's been an accident.
   dur·*gha*·ṭa·nah bha·yo   दुर्घटना भयो

Could you help me please?
   ma·lai *mad*·dat *gar*·na   मलाई मद्दत गर्न
   sak·nu·hun·cha?   सक्नुहुन्छ ?

Could I please use the telephone?
   ma phon *gar*·na sa·kin·cha?   म फोन गर्न सकिन्छ ?

I'm lost.
   ma ha·*rah*·yē   म हरायें

Where's the toilet?
   shau·*cah*·la·ya *ka*·hāh cha?   शौचालय कहाँ छ ?

EMERGENCIES

POLICE

प्रहरी

It's a good idea to get the name and position of the person you're speaking with, asking politely at the beginning. Give your own name first, and show some identification. Nepal has plenty of lawyers, but if you need extra help, it's probably best to contact your embassy or consulate first.

Call the police!
pra·*ha*·ri·lai bo·*lau*·nu·hos!   प्रहरीलाई बोलाउनुहोस !

Where's the police station?
thah·nah *ka*·hāh cha?   ठाना कहाँ छ ?

We want to report an offence.
hah·mi·lai dos ni·*be*·dan   हामिलाई दोष निबेदन
rahkh·nu·par·yo   राख्नुपर्यो

I've been raped.
ma·lai ba·*laht*·kahr *gar*·yo   मलाई बलात्कार गर्यो

I've been robbed.
cor·le *ma*·lai *lut*·yo   चोरले मलाई लुट्यो

They stole my ...	*us*·le *me*·ro ... *cor*·yo	उसले मेरो ... चोर्यो
I've lost my ...	*me*·ro ... ha·*rah*·yo	मेरो ... हरायो
bag/backpack	*jho*·lah	झोला
bags	*jho*·lah·ha·ru	झोलाहरू
camera	*kyah*·me·rah	क्यामेरा
handbag	byahg	ब्याग
money	*pai*·sah	पैसा
papers	*kah*·gaj·pa·tra	कागजपत्र
passport	rah·ha·*dah*·ni	राहदानी
travellers cheques	*trah*·bhlar cek	ट्राभ्लर चेक
wallet	*thai*·li	थैली

My possessions are insured.
me·ro *sah*·mahn·ko *bi*·mah cha   मेरो सामानको बिमा छ

EMERGENCIES

I'm sorry./I apologise.
ma·lai maph gar·nu·hos
मलाई माफ गर्नुहोस
I didn't realise I was doing
something wrong.
ma·lai thah·hah bha·ya·na
मलाई थाहा भयन
me·ro gal·ti bha·yo
मेरो गल्ती भयो
I didn't do it.
mai·le ga·ri·nā
मैले गरिनँ
We're innocent.
hah·mi nir·pa·rahdh chaū
हामि निरपराध छौं
We're foreigners.
hah·mi bi·de·shi chaū
हामि बिदेशी छौं
I want to contact my
embassy/consulate.
ma rahj·du·tah·vahs·mah
म राजदूतावासमा
sam·par·ka gar·nu·par·yo
सम्पर्क गर्नुपर्यो

Can I call someone?
ma·lai ko·hi bo·lai
मलाई कोही बोलाइ
di·nu·hun·cha?
दिनुहुन्छ ?
Can I have a lawyer who speaks English?
ma·lai ang·gre·ji bol·ne
मलाई अङ्ग्रेजी बोल्ने
wa·kil pain·cha?
वकील पाइन्छ ?
Is there a fine we can pay to clear this?
yo bin·ti ca·ḍhau·na·lai,
यो बिन्ती चढाउनलाई,
hah·mi·lai ja·ri·mah·nah
हामिलाई जरिमाना
tir·nu·hun·cha?
तिर्नुहुन्छ ?
Can we pay an on-the-spot fine?
hah·mi·le ja·ri·mah·nah
हामिले जरिमाना
tu·run·ta tir·nu·par·cha?
तुरून्त तिर्नुपर्छ ?

EMERGENCIES

I understand.
  ma *bujh*·chu   म बुझ्छु
I don't understand.
  mai·le bu·*jhi*·na   मैले बुझीन
I know my rights.
  me·ro *a*·dhi·kahr·ko *bah*·re   मेरो अधिकारको बारे
  ma·lai *thah*·hah cha   मलाई थाहा छ
What am I accused of?
  ma·lai *ke*·ko dos la·*gah*·yo?   मलाई केको दोष लगायो ?

You'll be charged with ...	ta·*paī*·lai ....ko dos la·*gaun*·cha ho·*lah*	तपाईंलाई ...को दोष लगाउन्छ होला
He'll/She'll be charged with ...	wa·*hāh*·lai ....ko dos la·*gaun*·cha ho·*lah*	वहाँलाई ...को दोष लगाउन्छ होला
anti-government activity	sar·*kahr*·ko bi·*rodh* ta·ra·khar	सरकारको बिरोध तरखर
assault	ba·*laht*·kahr	बलात्कार
disturbing the peace	a·*shahn*·ti *gar*·ne	अशान्ति गर्ने
illegal entry	*ni*·yam·bi·rodh pra·*besh*	नियमबिरोध प्रबेश
murder	*hat*·yah	हत्या
not having a visa	*bhi*·sah·bi·*nah*	भिसाबिना
overstaying your visa	*bhi*·sah·bhan·dah *dhe*·rai *bas*·ne	भिसाभन्दा धेरै बस्ने
possession (of illegal substances)	(*ni*·yam·bi·rodh *sahr*·ko) *a*·dhi·kahr *pau*·ne	(नियमबिरोध सारको) अधिकार पाउने
rape	ba·*laht*·kahr	बलात्कार
robbery/theft	*cor*·ne	चोर्ने
shoplifting	*mahl*·cor·ne	मालचोर्ने
a traffic violation	ah·wat·*jah*·wat·ko *ul*·lang·ghan	आवतजावतको उल्लङ्घन
working without a permit	*a*·nu·ma·ti·pa·tra·bi·*nah* kahm *gar*·ne	अनुमतिपत्रबिना काम गर्ने

EMERGENCIES

arrested	hi·*rah*·sat·mah *rahkh*·yo	हिरासतमा राख्यो
cell	khor	खोर
consulate	*rahj*·du·tah·vahs	राजदूतावास
embassy	*rahj*·du·tah·vahs	राजदूतावास
fine (payment)	ja·ri·*mah*·nah	जरिमाना
guilty	a·pa·*rah*·dhi	अपराधी
lawyer	*wa*·kil	वकील
not guilty	a·pa·*rah*·dhi *hoi*·na	अपराधी होइन
police officer	pra·*ha*·ri/pu·*lis*	प्रहरी/पुलिस
police station	*thah*·nah	ठाना
prison	*jhyahl*·khah·nah	इयालखाना
trial	*mud*·dah	मुद्दा

HEALTH स्वास्थ्य

On the trekking circuits, there are small hospitals in Jiri, Phaplu and Khunde (near Namche Bazaar), while the Himalayan Rescue Association (HRA) has a medical facility in Pheriche, on the Everest Trek, and the Edmund Hilary Hospital is at Khumjung. On the Annapurna Circuit, go to the HRA aid post at Manang.

Please call a doctor!
dahk·tar·lai bo·*lau*·nu·hos! डाक्टरलाई बोलाउनुहोस !
Please call an ambulance!
em·bu·lens bo·*lau*·nu·hos! एम्बुलेन्स बोलाउनुहोस !
Please call a helicopter!
he·li·kep·tar bo·*lau*·nu·hos! हेलिकेप्टर बोलाउनुहोस !
I'm ill.
ma bi·*rah*·mi chu म बिरामी छु
My friend is ill.
me·ro *sah*·thi bi·*rah*·mi cha मेरो साथी बिरामी छ

EMERGENCIES

I have altitude sickness.
ma·lai uc·*cai*·le bi·*rah*·mi
lahg·yo

मलाई उच्चाइले बिरामी
लाग्यो

He/She has altitude sickness.
wa·hāh·lai uc·*cai*·le bi·*rah*·mi
lahg·yo

वहाँलाई उच्चाइले बिरामी
लाग्यो

I have medical insurance.
me·ro ḍahk·ṭa·ri *bi*·mah cha

मेरो डाक्टरी बिमा छ

We need transport.
hah·mi·lai *yah*·tah·yaht *cah*·hi·yo

हामिलाई यातायात चाहियो

In this dictionary, the following notation applies in regard to parts of speech:

Nouns are not indicated unless they can be mistaken as adjectives, in which case they're followed by (n). Likewise, adjectives are only followed by (adj) when their use can be mistaken for a noun. Verbs are preceded by 'to'. This serves to distinguish a verb from its noun counterpart, eg, 'to book' versus 'book'.

A

to be able (can)	*sak·nu*	सक्नु
abortion	*gar·bha·paht*	गर्भपात
about	*-bah·re*	-बारे
above	*-mah·thi*	-माथि
abroad	*bi·desh*	बिदेश
to accept (agree to)	*mahn·nu*	मान्नु

Do you accept/agree?
ta·paī mahn·nu·hun·cha?   तपाई मान्नुहुन्छ ?
I accept/agree.
ma mahn·chu   म मान्छु

accident	*dur·gha·ṭa·nah*	दुर्घटना
accommodation (rented)	*ḍe·rah*	डेरा
to ache	*dukh·nu*	दुख्नु
across	*-pah·ri*	-पारि
activist	*kahr·ya·kahr*	कार्यकार
actor	*a·bhi·ne·tah/ a·bhi·ne·tri* (m/f)	अभिनेता/ अभिनेत्री
addict	*lat bha·ya·ko mahn·che*	लत भयको मान्छे
addiction	*lat*	लत
address	*ṭhe·gah·nah*	ठेगाना
administration	*pra·shah·san*	प्रशासन
to admire	*tah·riph gar·nu*	तारिफ गर्नु
admission (to enter)	*bhar·nah*	भर्ना
to admit	*swi·kahr gar·nu*	स्वीकार गर्नु
adult (n)	*ba·yask*	बयस्क
advice	*sal·lah·ha*	सल्लाह
to advise	*sal·lah·ha di·nu*	सल्लाह दिनु
aerogram	*ha·wai·pa·tra*	हवाईपत्र
aeroplane	*ha·wai·ja·hahj*	हवाईजहाज
to be afraid	*ḍa·rau·nu*	डराउनु
after	*-pa·chi*	-पछि
(in the) afternoon	*diū·so*	दिउँसो
again	*phe·ri*	फेरि
against	*bi·rodh*	बिरोध
age	*u·mer*	उमेर

aggressive	*nir·da·yi*	निर्दयी
ago	*a·ghi*	अघि
to agree to	*mahn·nu*	मान्नु

> I don't agree.
> ma *mahn·di·na* म मान्दिन
> Agreed!
> *man·jur bha·yo!* मन्जुर भयो !

agriculture	*khe·ti·pah·ti*	खेतीपाती
ahead	*a·ghi*	अघि
aid	*sa·ha·yog*	सहयोग
air	*hah·wah*	हावा
air-conditioned	*bah·tah·nu·ku·lit*	बातानुकुलीत
airmail	*ha·wai·ḍahk*	हवाईडाक
airport	*bi·mahn·stal*	विमानस्थल
airport tax	*bi·mahn·stal·ko kar*	विमानस्थलको कर
alarm clock	*ghaṇ·ṭi gha·ḍi*	घण्टी घडी
alcohol	*rak·si*	रक्सी
all	*sa·bai*	सबै
all day	*din·bha·ri*	दिनभरि
allergy	*a·lahr·ji*	अलार्जि
to allow	*a·nu·ma·ti di·nu*	अनुमति दिनु

> It's allowed.
> *a·nu·ma·ti cha* अनुमति छ
> It's not allowed.
> *a·nu·ma·ti chai·na* अनुमति छैन

almost	*jhan·ḍai*	झान्डै
alone	*ek·lai*	एक्लै
along	*-bha·ri · -hun·dai*	-भरि · -हुन्दै
already	*a·ghi*	अघि
also	*pa·ni*	पनि
altitude	*uc·cai*	उच्चाइ
always	*sa·dhaī*	सधैं
amateur	*la·ha·ḍi*	लहडी
ambassador	*rahj·dut*	राजदूत
among	*ma·dhye*	मध्ये
anaesthetic	*nish·ce·tak*	निश्चेतक
ancient	*prah·cin*	प्राचीन
and	*ra*	र
and then/so	*a·ni*	अनि
anger	*ris*	रिस
to get angry	*ri·sau·nu*	रिसाउनु
animal	*ja·nah·war*	जनावर
ankle	*go·li·gāh·ṭho*	गोलीगाँठो
annoyed	*dik·ka*	दिक्क
annual	*bahr·sik*	बार्षिक

B

to answer	*ut*·tar *di*·nu	उत्तर दिनु
ant	ka·*mi*·lah	कमिला
antibiotics	ahn·ṭi·bi·*yo*·ṭik	आन्टीबीयोटीक
antique (n)	pu·*rah*·no *bas*·tu	पुरानो बस्तु
any	ke·hi	केही
anyone	ko·hi	कोही
anything	ke·hi	केही
anywhere	ja·häh	जहाँ
apartment	ḍe·rah	डेरा
appendix	a·*pen*·ḍiks	अपेण्डीक्स
apple	syau	स्याउ
appointment	bheṭ *gar*·ne sa·*ma*·ya	भेट गर्ने समय
approximately	*lag*·bhag	लगभग
archaeological	pu·rah·*tat*·wi·ya	पुरातत्वीय
architecture	*vahs*·tu·ka·lah	वास्तुकला
to argue	ba·has *gar*·nu	बहस गर्नु
argument	ba·has	बहस
arm	pah·khu·rah	पाखुरा
to arrive	pug·nu	पुग्नु
art	ka·*lah*	कला
art gallery	ka·*lah*·ko ghar	कलाको घर
arthritis	bahth	बाथ
artist	ka·*lah*·kahr	कलाकार
artwork	ka·*lah* kahm	कला काम
ashtray	ahsh·ṭre	आश्ट्रे
to ask	sodh·nu	सोध्नु
to ask for	mahg·nu	माग्नु
aspirin	ais·pi·rin	आईस्पिरिन्
asthma	dam·ko *bya*·thah	दमको ब्यथा
asthmatic	dam *bya*·thah·ko *ro*·gi	दम ब्यथाको रोगी
at	-mah	-मा
atmosphere	bah·yu·*maṇ*·ḍal	बायुमण्डल
autorickshaw	*tyahm*·pu	ट्याम्पु
available	*pain*·cha	पाइन्छ
awful	bi·*rak*·ta·lahg·do	बिरक्तलाग्दो

B

baby	bac·cah	बच्चा
baby bottle	dudh khu·*wau*·ne *si*·si	दूध खुबाउने सिसी
baby food	bac·cah·ko *khah*·nah	बच्चाको खाना
babysitter	bac·cah *her*·ne *mahn*·che	बच्चा हेर्ने मान्छे
back	pi·ṭhū	पिठु
backbone	ḍhaḍ	ढाड
backpack	jho·lah	झोला
at the back (behind)	pa·*chah*·ḍi	पछाडि

D I C T I O N A R Y

B

bad	kha·*rahb*	खराब
bag	*jho*·lah	झोला
baggage	*mahl*·sah·mahn	मालसामान
baggage claim	*mahl*·sah·mahn *li*·ne thaŭ	मालसामान लिने ठाउँ
balcony	*bahr*·da·li	बार्दली
ball	*bha*·kun·ḍo	भकुन्डो
band	bahnḍ	बाण्ड
bandage	*paṭ*·ṭi	पट्टी
bank	baïk	बैंक
banknote	*baïk*·noṭ	बैंकनोट
bar	bahr	बार्
barber	ha·*jahm*	हजाम
to bargain	*mol*·tol *gar*·nu	मोलतोल गर्नु
barley	jau	जौ
basil	*tul*·si	तुलसी
basket	ṭo·ka·ri	टोकरी
bat	ca·me·ro	चमेरो
to bathe	nu·*hau*·nu	नुहाउनु
bathroom	snahn *kak*·sha •	स्नान कक्ष •
	bahṭh·rum	बाथरूम
battery	*ma*·sa·lah	मसला
to be	*hu*·nu	हुनु
beach	ba·*lau*·ṭe ki·*nahr*	बलौटे किनार
bean	*si*·mi	सिमी
bear	*bhah*·lu	भालु
beard	*dah*·hri	दाही
beautiful	*sun*·dar	सुन्दर
because	*ki*·na·bha·ne	किनभने
bed	khaṭ	खाट
bedbug	u·*dus*	उडुस
bedding	bi·*chyau*·nah	बिछ्यौना
bedroom	*khaṭ*·ko ko·ṭhah	खाटको कोठा
bee	*mau*·ri	मौरी
beef	*gai*·ko *mah*·su	गाईको मासु
beer	*bi*·yar	बियर
beer (rice)	chyahng	छ्याङ
beer (millet)	*tum*·bah	तुम्बा
before	*a*·ghi	अघि
beggar	*mahg*·ne	माग्ने
to begin	*su*·ru *gar*·nu	सुरु गर्नु
behind	pa·*chah*·ḍi	पछाडि
belief	bi·*shwahs*	बिश्वास
to believe	bi·*shwahs gar*·nu	बिश्वास गर्नु
below	*ta*·la	तल
belt	*pe*·ṭi	पेटी
beside	*cheu*·mah	छेउमा

best	*sab·bhan·dah rahm·ro*	सबभन्दा राम्रो
bet	*bah·ji*	बाजी
better	*jhan rahm·ro*	झन् राम्रो
between	*bic·mah*	बीचमा
bicycle	*sai·kal*	साइकल
big	*thu·lo*	ठूलो
bill	*bil*	बिल
binoculars	*dur·bin*	दूरबीन
biography	*ji·va·ni*	जीवनी
bird	*ca·rah*	चरा
birth certificate	*jan·ma pra·mahn·pa·tra*	जन्म प्रमाणपत्र
birthday (official)	*ja·yan·ti*	जयन्ती
birthday (personal)	*jan·ma·din*	जन्मदिन
biscuit	*bis·kut*	बिस्कुट
to bite	*tok·nu*	टोक्नु
to bite (snake only)	*das·nu*	डस्नु
bitter	*ti·to*	तीतो
black	*kah·lo*	कालो
B&W (film)	*kah·lo se·to (ril)*	कालो सेतो (रील)
blanket	*kam·mal*	कम्मल
to bleed	*ra·gat au·nu*	रगत आउनु
to bless	*ah·shir·bahd di·nu*	आशीर्बाद दिनु
blessing	*ah·shir·bahd*	आशीर्बाद
blind (adj)	*an·dho*	अन्धो
blizzard	*hiü·ko āh·dhi*	हिउँको आँधी
blood	*ra·gat*	रगत
blood group	*ra·gat sa·mu·ha*	रगत समूह
blood pressure	*rak·ta·cahp*	रक्तचाप
low/high blood	*gha·te·ko/bha·de·ko*	घटेको/भडेको
pressure	*rak·ta·cahp*	रक्ताचाप
blood test	*ra·gat·ko jāhc*	रगतको जाँच
blouse	*co·lo*	चोलो
blue	*ni·lo*	निलो
to board	*cadh·nu*	चढ्नु
boat	*dung·gah*	डुङ्गा
body	*ji·u*	जीउ
boiled water	*u·mah·le·ko pah·ni*	उमालेको पानी
bomb	*go·lah*	गोला
bone	*hahd*	हाड
book	*ki·tahb*	किताब
to book	*sany·cit gar·nu*	सञ्चित गर्नु
bookshop	*ki·tahb pa·sal*	किताब पसल
boots	*but*	बुट
border	*si·mah·nah*	सिमाना
boring	*wahk·ka hu·ne*	वाक्क हुने
to borrow	*sah·pat li·nu*	सापट लिनु

boss	*mah·lik*	मालिक
both	*du·bai*	दुबै
bottle	*si·si*	सिसी
bottle opener	*si·si khol·ne*	सिसी खोल्ने
(at the) bottom	*pĩd(·mah)*	पींद(मा)
box	*bah·kas*	बाकस
boy	*ke·ṭah*	केटा
boyfriend	*pre·mi*	प्रेमि
brain	*gi·di*	गिदी
branch	*hãh·gah*	हाँगा
brassware	*pi·tal·ko sah·mahn*	पितलको सामान
brave	*ba·hah·dur*	बहादुर
bread	*ro·ṭi*	रोटी
bread (flat)	*ca·pah·ṭi*	चपाती
bread (deep fried)	*pu·ri*	पुरी
bread (loaf of)	*pau·ro·ṭi*	पाउरोटी
to break	*phuṭ·nu • bhãhc·nu*	फुट्नु • भाँच्नु
breakfast	*bi·hah·na·ko khah·nah*	बिहानको खाना
breast	*stan*	स्तन
to breathe	*sahs pher·nu*	सास फेर्नु
bribe	*ghus*	घूस
to bribe	*ghus di·nu*	घूस दिनु
bridge	*pul*	पुल
bright	*u·jyah·lo*	उज्यालो
to bring	*lyau·nu*	ल्याउनु
broken	*phuṭ·yo*	फुट्यो
brother (elder)	*dai*	दाइ
brother (younger)	*bhai*	भाइ
brothers	*dah·ju·bhai*	दाजुभाइ
brown	*khai·ro*	खैरो
bruise	*coṭ*	चोट
brush	*bu·rus*	बुरुस
to brush (hair)	*ka·pahl kor·nu*	कपाल कोर्नु
to brush (teeth)	*dãht mahjh·nu*	दांत माझ्नु
bucket	*bahl·ṭin*	बाल्टिन
Buddhism	*bud·dha dhar·ma*	बुद्ध धर्म
bug (insect)	*ki·rah*	कीरा
buff meat	*rãh·gah·ko mah·su*	राँगाको मासु
buffalo	*rãh·gah/bhai·si (m/f)*	राँगा/भैसी
to build	*u·bhyau·nu*	उभ्याउनु
building	*bha·wan*	भवन
to burn	*pol·nu*	पोल्नु
bus	*bas*	बस
bush (shrub)	*boṭ*	बोट
business	*be·pahr*	बेपार
businessperson	*be·pah·ri*	बेपारी

busy	*bes*·ta	बेस्त
but	*ta*·ra	तर
butter	*ma*·khan	मखन
butterfly	*pu*·ta·li	पुतली
button	țāhk	टाँक
to buy	*kin*·nu	किन्नु

> I'd like to buy ...
> *ma*·lai ... *kin*·na man *lahg*·yo   मलाई ... किन्न मन लाग्यो
> Where can I buy a ticket?
> *ți*·kaț *ka*·hāh *kin*·na *sa*·kin·cha?   टिकट कहाँ किन्न सकिन्छ ?

| by | -le | -ले |

C

cabbage	ban·dah·*ko*·bi	बन्दाकोबि
cafe	*kyah*·phe	क्याफे
calendar	*sam*·bat	साम्बत
to call	bo·*lau*·nu	बोलाउनु
camera	*kyah*·me·rah	क्यामेरा
camera shop	*kyah*·me·rah *pa*·sal	क्यामेरा पसल
to camp	*shi*·bir *gar*·nu	शिबिर गर्नु

> Can we camp here?
> *hah*·mi *ya*·hāh *shi*·bir *gar*·nu·hun·cha?   हामि यहाँ शिबिर गर्नुहुन्छ ?

camping	*shi*·bir	शिबिर
camp site	*shi*·bir *gar*·ne țhaū	शिबिर गर्ने ठाउँ
can (to be able)	*sak*·nu	सक्नु

> We can do it.
> *hah*·mi *gar*·na *sak*·chaū   हामि गर्न सक्छौं
> I can't do it.
> ma *gar*·na *sak*·di·na   म गर्न सक्दिन

can	țin	टिन
can opener	țin *khol*·ne	टिन खोल्ने
to cancel	*rad*·da *gar*·nu	रद्द गर्नु
candle	*main*·bat·ti	मैनबत्ती
cap	*țo*·pi	टोपी
capital city	*rahj*·dhah·ni	राजधानी
capitalism	*pū*·ji·bahd	पूँजीबाद
car	*mo*·țar	मोटर
cardamom (black)	a·*laī*·ci	अलैंची
cardamom (green)	su·ku·*mel*	सुकुमेल
cards	tahs	तास
to care (about)	*pyah*·ro *gar*·nu	प्यारो गर्नु
to be careful	hos *gar*·nu	होस गर्नु

> Be careful!
> hos *gar*·nu·hos!   होस गर्नुहोस !

to take care of	*ja·tan gar·nu*	जतन गर्नु
carpet	*ga·lai·cah*	गलैंचा
carrot	*gah·jar*	गाजर
to carry	*bok·nu*	बोक्नु
carry basket	*ḍo·ko*	डोको
cashew	*kah·ju*	काजु
cashier	*kha·jahny·ci*	खजाञ्ची
cassette	*ṭep*टेप	
castle	*ma·hal*	महल
cat	*bi·rah·lo*	बिरालो
cauliflower	*kau·li*	काउली
cave	*gu·phah*	गुफा
to celebrate	*ma·nau·nu*	मनाउनु
cemetery	*ci·hahn*	चिहान
centre	*bic*	बीच
century	*sha·tahb·di*	शताब्दि
ceramics	*mah·ṭah·kah*	माटाका
	bhāh·ḍah·kū·ḍah	भाँडाकुँडा
cereal	*an·na*	अन्न
certain	*pak·kah • nish·cit*	पक्का • निश्चित

Are you certain?
ta·pai·lai nish·cit cha? तपाईलाई निश्चित छ ?
I'm certain.
ma·lai nish·cit cha मलाई निश्चित छ

certificate	*pra·mahn·pa·tra*	प्रमाणपत्र
chain	*si·kri*	सिक्री
chair	*mec*	मेच
championship	*sar·ba·bi·je·tah*	सर्वबिजेता
chance	*dau*	दाउ
to change (money)	*saht·nu*	साट्नु
small change	*khu·drah pai·sah*	खुद्रा पैसा
charming	*ra·mai·lo*	रमाइलो
cheap	*sas·to*	सस्तो

Cheat!
thag! ठग !

to check	*jāh·cau·nu*	जाँचाउनु
cheek	*gah·lah*	गाला
cheese	*cij*	चीज
chemist	*au·sa·dhi pa·sal*	औषधी पसल
chess	*bud·dhi·cahl*	बुद्धिचाल
chest	*chah·ti*	छाती
chicken	*ku·khu·rah*	कुखुरा
chicken meat	*ku·khu·rah·ko mah·su*	कुखुराको मासु
child	*bac·cah*	बच्चा
childminding	*bac·cah her·ne*	बच्चा हेर्ने

children (own)	cho·rah·cho·ri	छोराछोरी
children (general)	ke·tah·ke·ti	केटाकेटी
chilli pepper	khur·sah·ni	खुर्सानी
chocolate	cak·let	चक्लेट
choko squash	is·kus	ईस्कुस
cholera	hai·jah	हैजा
to choose	chahn·nu	छान्नु
Christian	i·sai	इसाई
Christianity	i·sai dhar·ma	इसाई धर्म
church	gir·jah·ghar	गिर्जाघर
cigarette	cu·rot	चुरोट
cigarette paper	cu·rot kah·gaj	चुरोट कागज
cinema	si·ne·mah	सिनेमा
cinnamon	dahl·ci·ni	दाल्चिनी
circus	ta·mah·sah	तमासा
citizen	nah·ga·rik	नागरिक
city	sha·har	शहर
city centre	sha·har·ko bic	शहरको बीच
city wall	sha·har·ko par·khahl	शहरको पर्खाल
class (social)	bar·ga	बर्ग
class system	bar·ga·ko thi·ti	बर्गको थिति
to clean	sa·phah gar·nu	सफा गर्नु
clerk	ba·hi·dahr	बहिदार
clever	ca·lahkh	चलाख
cliff	bhir	भीर
to climb	cadh·nu	चढ्नु
clinic	ci·kit·sah·la·ya	चिकित्सालय
clock	bhit·te gha·di	भित्ते घडी
to close	ban·da gar·nu	बन्द गर्नु
closed	ban·da	बन्द
cloth	ka·pa·dah	कपडा
clothing	lu·gah	लुगा
clothing store	lu·gah pa·sal	लुगा पसल
cloud	bah·dal	बादल
cloudy	bad·li	बदली
cloves	lwahng	ल्वाङ्ग
coast	ki·nahr	किनार
coat	kot	कोट
cobbler	sahr·ki	सार्की
cockroach	sähng·glo	साँङ्ग्लो
coconut	na·ri·wal	नरिवल
coffee	ka·phi	कफी
coin	mu·drah	मुद्रा
cold (weather)	jah·do	जाडो
cold (to the touch)	ci·so	चिसो

| It's cold. | |
| jah·do/ci·so cha | जाडो/चिसो छ |

cold water	*ci·*so *pah·*ni	चिसो पानी
cold (viral infection)	*ru·*ghah	रुघा
to have a cold	*ru·*ghah *lahg·*nu	रुघा लाग्नु
colleague	*så·*gi	सँगी
to collect	ja·*mau·*nu	जमाउनु
college	ma·hah·bi·*dyah·*la·ya	महाविद्यालय
colour	rang	रङ्ग
comb	*kåi·*yo	काँइयो
to come	*au·*nu	आउनु
comedy	hah·sya·pur·ṇa *ra·ca·*nah	हास्यपूर्ण रचना
comfortable	*ah·*rahm	आराम
communism	sohm·ya·bahd	साम्यबाद
communist	sohm·ya·bah·di	साम्यबादी
companion	sah·thi	साथी
company	kam·pa·ni	कम्पनी
compass	di·shah·su·cak *yan·*tra	दिशासूचक यन्त्र
compassion	ka·*ru·*nah	करुणा
concert	kan·sarṭ	कन्सर्ट
condom	ḍhahl	ढाल
to confirm	pak·kah *gar·*nu	पक्का गर्नु

conservative	pu·rah·tan·*bah·*di	पुरातनबादी
to be constipated	*di·*sah *kas·*nu	दिसा कस्नु
constipation	*di·*sah *ka·se·*ko	दिसा कसेको
consulate	rahj·du·tah·vahs	राजदूतावास
contaminated	*ju·*tho	जुठो
contraception	gar·bha·ni·rodh	गर्भनिरोध
contraceptive device	*pa·ri·*bahr ni·*yo·*jan·ko	परिवार नियोजनको
	sah·dhan	साधन
contract	ṭhek·kah	ठेक्का
convent	ahsh·ram	आश्रम
conversation	ku·rah·*kah·*ni	कुराकानी
cook	bhahn·se	भान्से
to cook	pa·*kau·*nu	पकाउनु
cool (adj)	*shi·*tal	शीतल

cooperative (n)	sah·jhah	साझा
coriander (dried)	dha·ni·yåh	धनियाँ
coriander (fresh)	ha·ri·yo dha·ni·yåh	हरियो धनियाँ
corn	*ma·*kai	मकै
corner	*ku·*nah	कुना

C

corrupt	*bhras·ta*	भ्रष्ट
corruption	*bhras·tah·cahr*	भ्रष्टाचार
to cost	*lahg·nu*	लाग्नु

How much does it cost to go to ...?
... jah·na·lai ka·ti pai·sah lahg·cha? ... जानलाई कति पैसा लाग्छ ?

cotton	*su·ti*	सुती
cough	*kho·ki*	खोकी
to count	*gan·nu*	गन्नु
country	*desh*	देश
countryside	*sha·har bah·hi·ra·ko bheg*	शहर बाहिरको भेग
coupon	*ku·pan*	कुपन
court (legal)	*a·dah·lat*	अदालत
courtyard	*cok*	चोक
cow	*gai*	गाई
cowshed	*goth*	गोठ
craft	*ka·lah*	कला
cramp	*baū·dyai*	बौडघाइ
crazy	*bau·lah·hah*	बौलाहा
cream	*tar*	तर
credit	*u·dhah·ro*	उधारो
credit card	*kre·dit kahrd*	केडीट कार्ड

Can I pay by credit card?
kre·dit kahrd·le tir·nu·hun·cha? केडीट कार्डले तिर्नुहुन्छ ?

creek	*kho·lah*	खोला
cremation	*dah·ha·sā·skahr*	दाहसंस्कार
crocodile	*go·hi*	गोही
crop	*bah·li*	बाली
cross-country trail	*go·re·to bah·to*	गोरेटो बाटो
crow	*kahg*	काग
crowd	*hul*	हूल
cucumber	*kāh·kro*	काँक्रो
to cuddle	*kahkh·mah cyahp·nu*	काखमा च्याप्नु
to cultivate	*khan·jot gar·nu*	खनजोत गर्नु
cultural show	*sāh·skri·tik pra·dar·shan*	सांस्कृतिक प्रदर्शन
culture	*sā·skri·ti*	संस्कृति
cumin	*ji·rah*	जीरा
cup	*kap*	कप
cupboard	*da·rahj*	दराज
curd (yogurt)	*da·hi*	दही
current affairs	*tah·jah kah·ro·bahr*	ताजा कारोबार
curtain	*par·dah*	पर्दा
customs	*bhan·sahr*	भन्सार
cut (n)	*ghau*	घाउ
to cut	*kaht·nu*	काट्नु

DICTIONARY

207

CV (resume)	*bai·yo·dah·tah*	बाइयोडाटा
to cycle	*sai·kal ca·lau·nu*	साइकल चलाउनु
cycling	*sai·kal ca·lau·ne*	साइकल चलाउने
cyclist	*sai·kal ca·lau·ne mahn·che*	साइकल चलाउने मान्छे

D

dad	bah	बा
daily	*din·hū*	दिनहुँ
dairy	*dug·dha·shah·lah*	दूधशाला
dairy products	*dudh·ko khah·nah*	दूधको खाना
damp	*o·si·lo*	ओसिलो
to dance	*nahc·nu*	नाच्नु
dancer	*nar·ta·ki*	नर्तकी
dangerous	*kha·ta·rah*	खतरा
dark	*ã·dhyah·ro*	अँध्यारो
date (appointment)	*bhet gar·ne sa·ma·ya*	भेट गर्ने समय
date *(Bikram* calendar)	*ga·te*	गते
date (Gregorian calendar)	*tah·rikh*	तारिख
dates (fruit)	*cho·ha·rah*	छोहरा
daughter	*cho·ri*	छोरी
dawn	*bi·hahn*	बिहान्
day	din	दिन
in (six) days	*(cha) din pa·chi*	(छ) दिन पछि
day after tomorrow	*par·si*	पर्सि
day before yesterday	*as·ti*	अस्ति
dead	*ma·re·ko*	मरेको
deaf	*ba·hi·ro*	बहिरो
death	*mri·tyu*	मृत्यु
to decide	*nir·na·ya gar·nu*	निर्णय गर्नु
deck of cards	tahs	तास
deep	*ga·hi·ro*	गहिरो
deer	*mri·ga · ha·riṇ*	मृग · हरिण
to defecate	*di·sah gar·nu*	दिसा गर्नु
deforestation	*ban·bi·nahs*	बनबिनास
degree (extent)	*u·pah·dhi*	उपाधि
delayed (late)	*a·be·lah*	अबेला
delicious	*mi·tho*	मीठो
delirium	*mur·chah*	मुर्छा
democracy	*pra·jah·tan·tra*	प्रजातन्त्र
demonstration	*ju·lus*	जुलूस
dentist	*dãht·ko ḍahk·tar*	दातको डाक्टर
to deny	*na·mahn·nu*	नमान्नु
to depart	*pras·thahn gar·nu*	प्रस्थान गर्नु
departure	*pras·thahn*	प्रस्थान
descendant	*san·tahn*	सन्तान

English	Transliteration	Nepali
design	*na·mu·nah*	नमुना
destination	*la·cha • u·de·shya*	लक्ष • उद्देश्य
to destroy	*nahsh gar·nu*	नाश गर्नु
development	*bi·kahs*	विकास
diabetes	*ma·dhu·me·ha*	मधुमेह
diabetic	*ma·dhu·me·ha ro·gi*	मधुमेह रोगी
diaper	*bac·cah·ko ṭah·lo*	बच्चाको टालो
diarrhoea	*jhah·ḍah • pa·khah·lah*	झाडा • पखाला
diary	*din·car·yah*	दिनचर्या
dice/die	*go·ṭi*	गोटी
dictatorship	*tah·nah·shah·hi*	तानाशाही
dictionary	*shab·da·kosh*	शब्दकोश
to die	*mar·nu*	मर्नु
different	*pha·rak*	फरक
difficult	*gah·hro*	गाह्रो
dinner	*bhaht*	भात
direct (from a to b)	*si·dhah*	सिधा
direct (manner)	*si·dhah*	सिधा
direction	*di·shah*	दिशा
director	*ḍai·rek·ṭar*	डाईरेक्टर
dirty	*pho·hor*	फोहोर
disabled	*a·pahng·ga*	अपाङ्ग
disadvantage	*be·phai·dah*	बेफाइदा
discount	*chuṭ*	छुट
to discount	*gha·ṭau·nu*	घटाउनु
to discover	*pat·tah lau·nu*	पत्ता लाउनु
discrimination	*po·cha·paht*	पक्षपात
disease	*rog*	रोग
dish (container)	*bhāh·ḍah*	भाँडा
dish (food)	*pa·ri·kahr*	परिकार
disinfectant	*ji·vah·ṇu·ra·hit*	जीवाणुरहित
distance (eg, 3 km)	*kos*	कोस
dizzy	*ring·ga·ṭah*	रिङ्गटा
to do	*gar·nu*	गर्नु

> **What are you doing?**
> *ta·paī ke gar·nu·hun·cha?* तपाई के गर्नुहुन्छ ?
> **I didn't do it.**
> *mai·le ga·ri·nā* मैले गरिनँ

English	Transliteration	Nepali
doctor	*ḍahk·ṭar*	डाक्टर
dog	*ku·kur*	कुकुर
doll	*pu·ta·li*	पुतली
dome	*stu·pah*	स्तुपा
donkey	*ga·dhah*	गधा
door	*ḍho·kah*	ढोका
double	*do·bar*	दोबर

double bed	du·i·ja·nah·ko khaṭ	दुइजनाको खाट
double room	du·i·ja·nah·ko ko·ṭhah	दुइजनाको कोठा
down	ta·la	तल
downhill	o·rah·lo	ओरालो
downward	ta·la·ti·ra	तलतिर
dozen	dar·jan	दर्जन
drama (play)	nah·ṭak	नाटक
dramatic	nah·ṭa·ki·ya	नाटकीय
dream	sa·pa·nah	सपना
to dream	sa·pa·nah dekh·nu	सपना देख्नु
dress	jah·mah	जामा
to dress	lu·gah la·gau·nu	लुगा लगाउनु
drink	pahn	पान्
to drink	pi·u·nu	पिउनु
drinking water	khah·ne pah·ni	खाने पानी
to drive	hāhk·nu	हाँक्नु
drowsy	ung	उङ
drug (illegal)	na·sah·lu au·sa·dhi	नसालु औषधी
drug (legal)	o·kha·ti	ओखती
drug addiction	o·kha·ti·ko lat	ओखतीको लत
drums	da·mah·hah • ḍhol	दमाहा • ढोल
to be drunk	rak·si lahg·nu	रक्सी लाग्नु
dry	suk·khah	सुक्खा
to dry (clothes)	(lu·gah) su·kau·nu	(लुगा) सुकाउनु
duck	hāhs	हाँस
during	a·ba·dhi	अबधि
dusk	san·dhyah·kahl	सन्ध्याकाल
dust	dhu·lo	धूलो
dysentery	ra·gat·mah·si	रगतमासी

E

each	ha·rek	हरेक
eagle	cil	चील
ear	kahn	कान
early	sa·be·rai	सबेरै

It's early.
sa·be·rai ho — सबेरै हो

to earn	ka·mau·nu	कमाउनु
earring	ṭap	टप
Earth	pri·thi·bi	पृथिबी
earth (soil)	mah·to	माटो
earthquake	bhuī·cah·lo	भुईंचालो
east	pur·ba	पूर्व
easy	sa·ji·lo	सजिलो

to eat	*khah·nu*	खानु
economical	*kam·khar·chi·lo*	कमखर्चिलो
economy	*ar·tha bya·bas·thah*	अर्थ व्यवस्था
education	*shi·chah*	शिक्षा
eel	*bahm*	बाम
egg	*phul · aṇ·dah*	फुल · अण्डा
eggplant	*bhahṇ·tah*	भाण्टा
elbow	*ku·hi·no*	कुहिनो
election	*cu·nahb*	चुनाव
electricity	*bi·ju·li*	बिजुली
elephant	*haht·ti*	हात्ती
else	*a·ru*	अरु
email	*i·mel*	ईमेल
embarrassed	*laj·jit*	लज्जित
embarrassment	*lahj*	लाज
embassy	*rahj·du·tah·vahs*	राजदूतावास
embroidery	*buṭ·ṭah*	बुट्टा
emergency	*ah·pat*	आपत्
employee	*jah·gi·re*	जागिरे
employer	*mah·lik/mah·lik·ni* (m/f)	मालिक / मालिकनी
empty	*khah·li*	खाली
end	*an·ta*	अन्त
to end	*an·ta hu·nu*	अन्त हुनु
endangered species	*kha·ta·rah·mah*	खतरामा
	par·ne bar·ga	पर्ने बर्ग
energy	*shak·ti*	शक्ति
engagement	*vahg·dahn*	वाग्दान
engine	*in·jin*	इन्जिन
engineer	*in·ji·ni·yar*	इन्जिनियर
English	*ang gre·ji*	अङ्ग्रेजी
to enjoy	*maj·jah lahg·nu*	मज्जा लाग्नु
enough	*pra·shas·ta*	प्रशस्त
to be enough	*pug·nu*	पुग्नु

| Enough! | |
| *bha·yo !* | भयो ! |

| to enter | *pas·nu* | पस्नु |

| Do not enter. | |
| *pra·besh ni·sedh* | प्रवेश निषेध |

entertaining	*maj·jah lahg·ne*	मज्जा लाग्ने
envelope	*khahm*	खाम
environment	*bah·tah·ba·raṇ*	बातावरण
epilepsy	*chah·re rog*	छारे रोग
equal	*ba·rah·bar*	बराबर
equality	*sa·mahn·tah · ba·rah·ba·ri*	समानता · बराबरी
equipment	*sah·mahn*	सामान

evening	*be·lu·kah*	बेलुका
event	*gha·ṭa·nah*	घटना
Everest (Mount)	*sa·gar·mah·thah*	सगरमाथा
every	*ha·rek*	हरेक
every day	*ha·rek din*	हरेक दिन
exact(ly)	*ṭhik*	ठीक
example	*u·dah·ha·raṇ*	उदाहरण
excellent	*ut·tam*	उत्तम
exchange	*sah·ṭo*	साटो
to exchange	*sahṭ·nu*	साटनु
exchange rate	*sahṭ·ne reṭ*	साटने रेट
excluded	*bah·hek*	बाहेक

Excuse me.
ma·lai mahph gar·nu·hos   मलाई माफ गर्नुहोस

exercise book	*kah·pi*	कापि
exhibition	*pra·dar·sha·ni*	प्रदर्शनी
exile	*desh ni·kah·lah*	देश निकाला
exit	*ni·kahs*	निकास
exotic	*bi·ci·tra*	विचित्र
to expect	*a·pe·chah gar·nu*	अपेक्षा गर्नु
expensive	*ma·hã·go*	महँगो
experience	*a·nu·bhab*	अनुभव
to experience	*a·nu·bhab gar·nu*	अनुभव गर्नु
exploitation	*sho·saṇ*	शोषण
export	*nir·yaht*	निर्यात
to export	*nir·yaht gar·nu*	निर्यात गर्नु
to extend	*thap·nu*	थप्नु
eye	*ãh·khah*	आँखा

F

face	*a·nu·hahr*	अनुहार
factory	*kahr·khah·nah*	कारखाना
factory worker	*kahr·khah·nah·ko maj·dur*	कारखानाका मजदूर
faeces	*di·sah*	दिसा
fair (festival)	*me·lah*	मेला
faith	*bi·shwahs*	विश्वास
falcon	*bahj*	बाज
fall (autumn)	*sha·rad ri·tu*	शरद ऋतु
to fall	*khas·nu*	खस्नु
false	*jhu·ṭo*	झूटो
family	*pa·ri·bahr*	परिवार
famous	*pra·sid·dha*	प्रसिद्ध
fan (cooling)	*pã·khah*	पंखा
far	*ṭah·ḍhah*	टाढा
farm	*khet·bah·ri*	खेतबारी

farmer	ki·*sahn*	किसान
fast (adj)	*chi*·to	छिटो
fast (n)	*bar*·ta	बर्त
fat	*mo*·to	मोटो
father	*bu*·wah	बुवा
father-in-law	*sa*·su·rah	ससुरा
fault	*ka*·sur	कसुर
faulty	kahm na·*gar*·ne	काम नगर्ने
fear	ḍar	डर
to fear	*ḍar*·nu	डर्नु
feast	bhoj	भोज
fee	*shul*·ka	शुल्क
to feed	khu·*wau*·nu	खुवाउनु
to feel	*lahg*·nu	लाग्नु
to feel like	man *lahg*·nu	मन लाग्नु
feelings	*cit*·ta	चित्त
female (animal)	*po*·thi	पोथी
female (person)	stri	स्री
fence	bahr	बार
fennel	soph	सोफ
fenugreek	*me*·ṭhi	मेठी
festival	*cahḍ*·bahḍ • *jah*·trah	चाडबाड • जात्रा
fever	*ja*·ro	जरो
(a) few	*tho*·rai	थोरै
fiction	*kal*·pit *ka*·thah	कल्पित कथा
field	khet	खेत
fig	*an*·jir	अन्जीर
fight	*jha*·ga·ḍah	झगडा
to fight	*laḍ*·nu	लड्नु
to fill	*bhar*·nu	भर्नु
film (cinema)	philm • cal·*ci*·tra	फिल्म • चलचित्र
film (photographic)		
colour film	*rang*·gin ril	रँगीन रील
B&W film	*kah*·lo *se*·to ril	कालो सेतो रील
filter	*cahl*·ni	चाल्नी
filtered	*chah*·ne·ko	छानेको
filtered water	*phil*·tar *pah*·ni	फिल्टर पानी
to find	*pau*·nu	पाउनु
fine (n)	ja·ri·*mah*·nah	जरिमाना
finger	*aū*·lah	औंला
fingernail	nang	नङ
fire	*ah*·go	आगो
firewood	*dau*·rah	दाउरा
first	*pa*·hi·lah	पहिला
fish	*mah*·chah	माछा
fish shop	*mah*·chah *pa*·sal	माछा पसल

flag	*jhan·ḍah*	झण्डा
flashlight (torch)	ṭarc	टर्च
flat (adj)	*cyahp·to*	च्याप्टो
flea	u·*pi·yāh*	उपियाँ
flight	u·ḍahn	उडान
floor (of house)	bhu·ī	भुईं
floor (storey)	ghar·ko ta·lah	घरको तला
flour	pi·ṭho	पीठो
flower	phul	फूल
flu	ru·ghah·kho·ki·ko ja·ro	रुघाखोकीको जरो
fly	jhī·gah	झिंगा
fog	ku·i·ro	कुइरो
to follow	pa·chyau·nu	पछ्याउनु
food	khah·nah	खाना
food poisoning	khah·nah kha·rahb	खाना खराब
foot	khuṭ·ṭah	खुट्टा
on foot	hi·ḍe·ra	हिंडेर
football (soccer)	laht·te bha·kun·ḍo	लात्ते भकुन्डो
footpath	go·re·ṭo	गोरेटो
for	-ko lah·gi	-को लागि
foreign(er)	bi·de·shi	बिदेशी
forest	ban	बन
forever	sa·dhaī	सधैं
to forget	bir·sa·nu	बिर्संनु

I forget.
ma *bir*·san·chu   म बिर्संन्छु
Forget it! (Don't worry!)
bhai·go !   भैगो !

to forgive	maph gar·nu	माफ गर्नु
fork	kāh·ṭah	कांटा
fortnight	pan·dhra din	पन्ध्र दिन
fox	phyau·ro	फ्याउरो
free (at liberty)	swa·tan·tra	स्वतन्त्र
free (of charge)	sit·taī	सित्तैं
freedom	swa·tan·tra·tah	स्वतन्त्रता
to freeze	jam·nu	जम्नु
fresh	tah·jah	ताजा
fried	bhu·ṭe·ko	भुटेको
friend	sah·thi	साथी
friendly	mi·lan·sahr	मिलनसार
to frighten	ḍa·rau·nu	डरउनु
frog	bhyah·gu·to	भ्यागुतो
from (place)	-bah·ṭa	-बाट
from (time)	-de·khi	-देखि
in front of	-a·gah·ḍi	-अगाडि
frost	tu·sah·ro	तुसारो

frostbite	tu·*sah*·ro·le *khah*·ya·ko	तुसारोले खायको
fruit	*phal*·phul	फलफूल
fruit picking	*phal*·phul *ṭip*·ne	फलफूल टिप्ने
full	*bha*·ri	भरि
fun	*maj*·jah	मज्जा
to have fun	*maj*·jah *lahg*·nu	मज्जा लाग्नु
to make fun of	*hãh*·so u·*ḍau*·nu	हाँसो उडाउनु
funeral	ma·*lahm*	मलाम
future (n)	bha·*bi*·sya	भविष्य

G

game (sport)	khel	खेल
garage	*gyah*·rej	ग्यारेज
garbage	*mai*·lah	मैला
garden	ba·*gai*·cah	बगैंचा
gardening	*mah*·li·ko kahm	मालीको काम
garlic	*la*·sun	लसुन
gas	gyāhs	ग्याँस
gas cylinder	gyāhs *si*·lin·ḍar	ग्याँस सिलीन्डर
gate	*ḍho*·kah	ढोका
gay man	sa·ma·*ling*·ga	समलिङ्ग
	sam·*bho*·gi *pu*·rus	सम्भोगी पुरुष
gem	ju·*hah*·raht	जुहारात

Get lost!		
bhahg !		भाग !

to get off (bus)	or·*la*·nu	ओर्लनु
to get up	*uṭh*·nu	उठ्नु
ghat	ghaṭ	घाट
ghee	ghi·*u*	घिउ
gift	u·pa·*hahr*	उपहार
ginger	a·du·*wah*	अदुवा
girl	ke·*ṭi*	केटी
girlfriend	pre·mi·*kah*	प्रेमिका
to give	*di*·nu	दिनु

Please give me ...		
ma·*lai* ... *di*·nu·hos		मलाई ... दिनुहोस

glass	gi·*lahs*	गिलास
to go	*jah*·nu	जानु

Let's go.		
jaũ		जाऊँ
We'd like to go to ...		
hah·mi·lai ...*mah jah*·na man *lahg*·yo		हामीलाई ...मा जान मन लाग्यो
Go straight ahead.		
si·dhah *jah*·nu·hos		सिधा जानुहोस

to go on foot	hi·*de*·ra *jah*·nu	हिंडेर जानु
goal	gol	गोल्
goalkeeper	*gol*·ki	गोल्की
goat	*bahkh*·ro	बाख्रो
goatmeat	kha·si·ko *mah*·su	खसीको मासु
god	*de*·va·tah	देवता
God	*bha*·ga·bahn	भगबान
goddess	*de*·va·tah	देवता
gold (n)	sun	सुन
gold (adj)	*sun*·ko	सुनको
good	*rahm*·ro	राम्रो
goodbye	na·ma·*ste*	नमस्ते
goodnight	shu·bha·*rah*·tri	शुभरात्री
goods	*sah*·mahn	सामान
government	sar·*kahr*	सरकार
gram	grahm	ग्राम
grandchildren	nah·ti·*nah*·ti·ni	नातिनातिनी
grandfather	*bah*·je	बाजे
grandmother	ba·*jyai*	बज्यै
grape	*ā*·gur	अँगुर
grapefruit	*bho*·ga·te	भोगटे
grass	ghāhs	घाँस
grateful	gun *mahn*·ne	गुन मान्ने
great (powerful)	bi·*shahl*	विशाल

Great!
kha·ta·rah! खतरा !

greedy	*lo*·bhi	लोभी
green	ha·*ri*·yo	हरियो
Gregorian calendar	*is*·vi sam·bat	इस्वी सम्बत्
grey	*khai*·ro	खैरो
to grow (crop)	ub·*jau*·nu	उब्जाउनु
to grow (in size)	*badh*·nu	बढ्नु
guava	*am*·bah	अम्बा
to guess	*an*·dahj *gar*·nu	अन्दाज गर्नु
guest	*pah*·hu·nah	पाहुना
guesthouse	*pah*·hu·nah ghar	पाहुना घर
guide	*bah*·to de·*khau*·ne *mahn*·che	बाटो देखाउने मान्छे
guidebook	nir·*de*·shan·ko ki·*tahb*	निर्देशनको किताब
guilty	a·pa·*rah*·dhi	अपराधी
not guilty	a·pa·*rah*·dhi hoi·na	अपराधी होइन
guitar	gi·*tahr*	गितार
gym	byah·*yahm*·shah·lah	ब्यायामशाला
gymnastics	byah·*yahm*	ब्यायाम

H

hair	ka·*pahl*	कपाल
hairbrush	ka·*pahl kor*·ne bu·*rus*	कपाल कोर्ने बुरुस
hairpin	*käh*·țah	काँटा
half	*ah*·dhah	आधा
half a litre	*ah*·dhah *li*·țar	आधा लिटर
hallucination	bhram	भ्रम
hammer	ghan	घन
hand	haht	हात
handbag	byahg	ब्याग
handicraft	*has*·ta·ka·lah	हस्तकला
handkerchief	ru·*mahl*	रुमाल
handmade	*haht*·le *ba*·ne·ko	हातले बनेको
handsome	*sun*·dar	सुन्दर
happy	*khu*·si	खुसी

Happy Birthday!
jan·ma·din·ko shu·bha·*kah*·ma·nah!   जन्मदिनको शुभकामना !

hard (difficult)	*gah*·hro	गाह्रो
hard (not soft)	ka··ḍah	कडा
harness	sahj	साज
hashish	ca·res	चरेस
hat	țop	टोप
to have	cha	छ

Do you have ...?
ta·*paī* ... cha?   तपाई ... छ ?
I have ...
ma ... cha   म ... छ

he (pol)	wa·*hāh*	वहाँ
he (inf)	u·ni · tyo · yo	ऊनी • त्यो • यो
head	țau·ko	टाउको
headache	țau·ko dukh·yo	टाउको दुख्यो
headstrap	nahm·lo	नाम्लो
health	swahs·thya	स्वास्थ्य
health post	ci·kit·*sah*·la·ya	चिकित्सालय
to hear	sun·nu	सुन्नु
heart	mu·țu	मुटु
heat	rahp	राप
heater (electric)	hi·țar	हिटर
heaven	swar·ga	स्वर्ग
heavy	ga·hraū	गह्रौं
hell	na·rak	नरक
hello	na·ma·ste	नमस्ते

Hello? (answering a call)
ha·*jur*?   हजुर ?

| helmet | pha·lah·me to·pi | फलामे टोपी |
| to help | mad·dat gar·nu | मद्दत गर्नु |

| Help! | | |
| gu·hahr! | | गुहार ! |

hemp	pa·tu·wah	पटुवा
hemp powder	bhahng	भाङ्ग
hen	ku·khu·ri	कुखुरी
herb	ja·di·bu·ti	जडीबूटी
here	ya·hāh	यहाँ
high	u·co	उचो
to hike	pai·dal gar·nu	पैदल गर्नु
hiking	pai·dal yah·trah	पैदल यात्रा
hiking route	pai·dal·ko bah·to	पैदल बाटो
hill	dāh·dah	डाँडा
hillperson	pa·hah·di	पहाडी
Hindu	hin·du	हिन्दु
Hindu calendar	bik·ram sam·bat	विक्रम सम्बत्
Hinduism	hin·du dhar·ma	हिन्दू धर्म
hip (n)	cahk	चाक
to hire	bhah·dah·mah li·nu	भाडामा लिनु

| I want to hire ... | | |
| ma ... bhah·dah·mah li·nu par·yo | | म ... भाडामा लिनु पर्यो |

hobby	cahkh	चाख
hole	pwahl	प्वाल
holiday	bi·dah	विदा
holy	pa·bi·tra	पवित्र
home	ghar	घर
homeless	su·kum·bah·si	सुकुम्बासी
honest	i·mahn·dahr	इमानदार
honey	ma·ha	मह
honeymoon	pra·mod·kahl	प्रमोदकाल
hookah	huk·kah	हुक्का
horrible	ghin·lahg·do	घिनलाग्दो
horse	gho·dah	घोडा
horseriding	gho·dah cadh·na	घोडा चढ्न
hospital	as·pa·tahl	अस्पताल
hospitality	bya·ba·hahr	ब्यवहार
hot (to the touch)	tah·to	तातो
hot (weather)	gar·mi	गर्मी

| It's hot. | | |
| gar·mi cha | | गर्मी छ |

hot water	tah·to pah·ni	तातो पानी
to be hot	gar·mi/tah·to lahg·nu	गर्मी/तातो लाग्नु
hotel	ho·tel	होटेल
hour	ghan·tah	घण्टा
house	ghar	घर

housework	ba·dhahr·*kū*·dhahr	बढार्कुँढार
how (quality)	*kas*·to	कस्तो
how (means)	*ka*·sa·ri	कसरी

How do I get to ...?
...mah *ka*·sa·ri *jah*·ne? ...मा कसरी जाने ?
How do you say ...?
...lai ke *bhan*·cha? ...लाई के भान्छ ?

how much/many	*ka*·ti	कति
hug	*ā*·*gah*·lo	अँगालो
human (n)	*mah*·nis	मानिस
human rights	mah·nab·*a*·dhi·kahr	मानवअधिकार
humid	*bahs*·pi·ya	बाष्पीय
(one) hundred	(ek) say	(एक) सय
hungry	bhok	भोक

Are you hungry?
ta·*paī*·lai bhok *lahg*·yo? तपाईंलाई भोक लाग्यो ?
I'm hungry.
ma·lai bhok *lahg*·yo मलाई भोक लाग्यो

to hurry	ha·*tahr gar*·nu	हतार गर्नु
(in a) hurry	ha·*tahr*	हतार
hurt	cot	चोट
to hurt (ache)	*dukh*·nu	दुख्नु
to hurt (cause someone pain)	du·*khau*·nu	दुखाउनु
husband (own)	*log*·ne	लोग्ने
husband (someone else's)	*sri*·mahn	श्रीमान
hut	*jhu*·pro	झुप्रो

I

I	ma	म
ice	*ba*·raph	बरफ
ice axe	*gaī*·ti	गैती
ice cream	*khu*·wah *ba*·raph	खुवा बरफ
ice peak	hi·*mahl*	हिमाल
idea	bi·*cahr*	बिचार
identity card	pa·ri·ca·ya pa·tra	परिचय पत्र
idol	*mur*·ti	मूर्ति
if	*ya*·di • *bha*·ne	यदि • भने
ill	bi·*rah*·mi	बिरामी
illegal	*ni*·yam·bi·rodh	नियमबिरोध
illness	rog	रोग
imagination	*kal*·pa·nah	कल्पना
imitation (fake)	*nak*·kal	नक्कल
immediately	tu·*run*·tai • *a*·hil·yai	तुरुन्तै • अहिल्यै
immigration	a·*dhyah*·ga·man	अध्यागमन
import	*ah*·yaht	आयात

to import	*ah*·yaht *gar*·nu	आयात गर्नु
important	ma·*hat*·twa·pur·na	महत्त्वपूर्ण

It's important.
ma·*hat*·twa·pur·na cha — महत्त्वपूर्ण छ
It's not important.
ma·*hat*·twa·pur·na*chai*·na — महत्त्वपूर्ण छैन

impossible	a·*sam*·bhab	असम्भव
imprisonment	kah·rah·*bahs*	काराबास
in	-mah	-मा
in front of	-a·*gah*·di	-अगाडि
incense burner	dhup *dah*·ni	धूप दानि
including	sa·met	समेत
incomprehensible	na·*bu*·jhi·ne	नबुझिने
inconvenient	a·*su*·bi·dhah	असुबिधा
India	*bhah*·rat	भारत
indigestion	a·pac	अपच
industry	u·dyog	उद्योग
inflammation	sun·ni·ye·ko a·bas·thah	सुन्नीयेको अबस्था
influenza	ru·ghah·*kho*·ki·ko ja·ro	रुघाखोकीको जरो
informal	a·nau·pa·*cah*·rik	अनौपचारिक
information	jahn·*kah*·ri	जानकारी
to inject	*bhi*·tra pa·*sau*·nu	भित्र पसाउनु
injection	su·i	सूई
injury	cot	चोट
ink	*ma*·si	मसी
insect	*ki*·rah	कीरा
inside	*bhi*·tra	भित्र
instructor	*shi*·chak • a·*dhyah*·pak	शिक्षक • अध्यापक
insurance	*bi*·mah	बिमा
interesting	cahkh *lahg*·do	चाख लाग्दो
intermission	*bish*·rahm	बिश्राम
international	an·tar·*rah*·stri·ya	अन्तर्राष्ट्रिय
interview	an·tar·*bahr*·tah	अन्तर्बार्ता
to invite	*nim*·tah *gar*·nu	निम्ता गर्नु
iodine	ai·din	आईडीन्
Islam	is·*lahm dhar*·ma	इस्लाम धर्म
island	*tah*·pu • dwip	टापु • द्वीप
it	tyo · yo	त्यो • यो
to itch	ci·*lau*·nu	चिलाउनु

J

jackal	syahl	स्याल
jail	*jhyahl*·khah·nah	इयालखाना
jar	su·*rah*·hi	सुराही
jealous	*dah*·hah	डाहा

jeans	*jin*·paint	जीनपाइन्ट
Jew/Jewish	*ya*·hu·di	यहुदी
jewel	ju·*hah*·raht	जुहारात
jewellery	*ga*·ha·nah	गहना
job	kahm	काम
job advertisement	*kahm*·ko pra·*cahr*	कामको प्रचार
joke	khyahl • *that*·tah	ख्याल • ठट्टा

I'm joking.
mai·le khyahl *ga*·re·ko   मैले ख्याल गरेको

journalist	pa·tra·*kahr*	पत्रकार
journey	*yah*·trah	यात्रा
Judaism	ya·*hu*·di *dhar*·ma	यहुदी धर्म
judge	nyah·*yah*·dhish	न्यायाधीश
jug	su·*rah*·hi	सुराही
juice	ras	रस
to jump	u·*phra*·nu	उफ्रनु
jumper (sweater)	*swi*·tar	स्विटर
jungle	ban	बन
justice	*nyah*·ya	न्याय

K

keen (to ...)	... *gar*·ne *ut*·suk	... गर्ने उत्सुक
kerosene	ma·*ti*·tel	मटितेल
key	*sāh*·co	साँचो
to kick	*laht*·ta·le hir·*kau*·nu	लात्तले हिर्काउनु
kidney	mir·*gau*·lah	मिर्गौला
to kill	*mahr*·nu	मार्नु
kilogram	*ki*·lo	किलो
kilometre	*ki*·lo	किलो
kind (type)	*ki*·sim	किसिम
kindergarten	*nar*·sa·ri	नर्सरी
kindness	*da*·yah	दया
king	*rah*·jah	राजा
kiss	mwāi	म्वाई
to kiss	mwāi *khah*·nu	म्वाई खानु
kitchen	*bhahn*·chah	भान्छा
kitten	bi·*rah*·lah·ko *chau*·ro	बिरालाको छाउरो
knee	*ghũ*·dah	घुँडा
knife	*cak*·ku • *khu*·ku·ri	चक्कु • खुकुरी
to know (person)	*cin*·nu	चिन्नु
to know (something)	*thah*·ha *hu*·nu	थाह हुनु

I don't know.
ma·lai·*thah*·ha *chai*·na   मलाई थाह छैन

knowledge	*thah*·ha	थाह

L

lace (shoe)	*phit·tah*	फित्ता
lake	tahl	ताल
lamp	*bat·ti*	बत्ती
lamp (ceremonial)	*ci·rahg*	चीराग
lamp (made of sacred butter)	dip	दिप
land	*jag·gah*	जग्गा
landslide	*pa·hi·ro*	पहिरो
language	*bhah·sah*	भाषा
large	*ṭhu·lo*	ठूलो
last	*an·tim • ga·ya·ko*	अन्तिम • गयको
last month	*ga·ya·ko ma·hi·nah*	गयको महीना
last night	*hi·jo rah·ti*	हिजो राति
last week	*ga·ya·ko hap·tah*	गयको हप्ता
last year	*ga·ya·ko bar·sa*	गयको बर्ष
late	*ḍhi·lo*	ढिलो

It's late.
ḍhi·lo cha   ढिलो छ

to laugh	*hāhs·nu*	हाँस्नु
to launder	*dhu·nu*	धुनु
laundry	*lu·gah·dhu·ne ṭhaū*	लुगाधुने ठाउँ
law	*kah·nun*	कानुन
lawyer	*wa·kil*	वकील
laxative	*ju·lahph*	जुलाफ
lazy	*al·chi*	अल्छी
leader	*ne·tah*	नेता
leaf	paht	पात
to learn	*sik·nu*	सिक्नु
leather	*chah·lah*	छ्याला
leathergoods	*chah·lah·ko sah·mahn*	छ्यालाको सामान
to leave	*choḍ·nu*	छोड्नु
ledge	cheu	छेउ
leech	*ju·kah*	जुका
left	*bah·yāh*	बायाँ
leg	*go·ḍah*	गोडा
legal	*kah·nu·ni*	कानूनी
to legalise	*kah·nu·ni ah·dhahr di·nu*	कानूनी आधार दिनु
lemon	*kah·ga·ti*	कागती
lens	*ai·nah*	ऐना
lentils	dahl	दाल
black lentils	*kah·lo dahl*	कालो दाल
brown lentils	*khai·ro dahl*	खैरो दाल
red lentils	*mu·sur dahl*	मुसुर दाल
leopard	*ci·tu·wah*	चितुवा
leper	*kus·ṭhi*	कुष्ठी
leprosy	*kus·ṭa·rog*	कुष्ठरोग

lesbian	stri *sam*·bho·gi *ai*·mai	स्त्री सम्भोगी आइमाई
less	kam	कम
letter	*ci*·thi	चिठी
liar	dhāht	ढाँट
library	pus·ta·*kah*·la·ya	पुस्तकालय
lice/louse	*jum*·rah	जुम्रा
to lie (down)	*lad*·nu	लड्नु
to lie (dishonest)	*dhāht*·nu	ढाँट्नु
life	*ji*·van • *jin*·da·gi	जीवन • जिन्दगी
light (n)	*bat*·ti	बत्ती
light (colour)	*phi*·kah	फिका
lightbulb	cim	चिम
lightning	*bi*·ju·li *cam*·kai	बिजुली चम्काई
lightweight	ha·*lu*·kah	हलुका
like	*jas*·to	जस्तो
to like	man *par*·nu	मन पर्नु
line	*re*·khah	रेखा
lion	*si*·ha	सिंह
lips	oth	ओठ
to listen	*sun*·nu	सुन्नु
little (small)	*sah*·no	सानो
a little (bit)	a·li a·li • a·li·ka·ti	अलि अलि • अलिकति
to live (life)	*bāhc*·nu	बाँच्नु
to live (somewhere)	*bas*·nu	बस्नु

Long live ...!	
ja·ya ...!	जय ...!

liver	ka·le·jo	कलेजो
lizard	che·*pah*·ro	छेपारो
load	*bhah*·ri	भारी
local	*sthah*·ni·ya	स्थानीय
location	thaũ	ठाउँ
lock	*tahl*·cah	ताल्चा
to lock	*tahl*·cah *gar*·nu	ताल्चा गर्नु
lodge	laj	लज
long	*lah*·mo	लामो
to look	*her*·nu	हेर्नु
to look after	*her*·bi·cahr *gar*·nu	हेरविचार गर्नु
to look for	*khoj*·nu	खोज्नु
loose	*khu*·ku·lo	खुकुलो
to lose	ha·*rau*·nu	हराउनु
loss	*nok*·sahn	नोक्सान
lost	ha·*rau*·na	हराउन
a lot	*dhe*·rai	धेरै
loud	*uc*·ca	उच्च
love (general)	*mah*·yah	माया
love (romantic)	prem	प्रेम

I love you.		
ma ta·*paī*·lai *mah*·yah *gar*·chu		म तपाईलाई माया गर्छु
low	*ho*·co	होचो
to lower	gha·*tau*·nu	घटाउनु
luck	*bhah*·gya	भाग्य
lucky	bhah·gya·*mah*·ni	भाग्यमानी
luggage	*mahl*·sah·mahn	मालसामान
lump	*dal*·lo	डल्लो
lunch	*ca*·me·nah	चमेना
lunchtime	*ca*·me·nah·ko *be*·lah	चमेनाको बेला
lung	*phok*·so	फोस्सो
luxury	bi·*lahs*	बिलास

M

machine	kal	कल
made of	-le *ba*·ne·ko	-ले बनेको
magazine	*pa*·tri·kah	पत्रिका
magician	*jah*·du·gar	जादुगर
mail	dâhk	डाँक
mailbox	pa·tra·*many*·ju·sah	पत्रमञ्जुषा
main road	pra·*mukh bah*·to	प्रमुख बाटो
main square	pra·*mukh* cok	प्रमुख चोक
majority	dhe·rai·*ja*·so	धेरैजसो
to make	ba·*nau*·nu	बनाउनु
malaria	*au*·lo	औलो
male (animal)	*bhah*·le	भाले
male (person)	nar	नर
male & female (adj)	nar·*nah*·ri	नरनारी
man & woman (n)	nar·*nah*·ri	नरनारी
man (formal)	pu·*rus*	पुरुष
man (husband)	*log*·ne·mahn·che	लोग्नेमान्छे
man (old)	*bu*·dho	बूढो
man (young)	*ke*·tah	केटा
mankind	*mah*·nab	मानब
manager	*hah*·kim	हाकिम
mandarin	*sun*·ta·lah	सुन्तला
mango	âhp	आँप
many	*dhe*·rai	धेरै
map	*nak*·sah	नक्सा

Please show me on the map.		
nak·sah·mah *ma*·lai de·*khau*·nu·hos		नक्सामा मलाई देखाउनुहोस
marijuana	*gâh*·jah	गाँजा
market	ba·*jahr*	बजार
weekly market	haht ba·*jahr*	हात बजार
marriage	bi·*hah*	बिहा

to marry	bi·*hah* gar·nu	बिहा गर्नु
mask	ma·*kun*·ḍo	मकुण्डो
massage	*mah*·lis	मालिस
mat	gun·dri	गुन्द्री
matches	sa·lai	सलाइ
mattress	ḍa·sa·nah	डसना
maybe	shah·yad	शायद
me	ma·lai	मलाई
meal	khah·nah	खाना
to measure	nahp·nu	नाप्नु
measurement	nahp	नाप
meat	mah·su	मासु
mechanic	mi·stri	मिस्त्री
medal	tak·mah	तक्मा
medicine	au·sa·dhi	औषधी
meditation	dhyahn	ध्यान
to meet	bhet·nu	भेट्नु

I'll meet you.
ma ta·*paī*·lai *bhet*·chu
म तपाईंलाई भेट्छु

melon	tar·bu·jah	तरबुजा
to melt	pa·*gahl*·nu	पगाल्नु
member	sa·*das*·ya	सदस्य
meningitis	me·ni·*jai*·tis	मेनिंजाइटीस
menstruation	ma·hi·nah·bah·ri	महीनाबारी
menu	men·yu	मेन्यु
message	kha·bar	खबर
metal	dhah·tu	धातु
middle	bic	बीच
midnight	ma·*dhya*·raht	मध्यरात
military service	sai·nik se·bah	सैनिक सेवा
milk	dudh	दूध
millet	ko·do	कोदो
million	das lahkh	दस लाख
mind	man	मन
mine	me·ro	मेरो
minute	mi·nat	मिनट

Just a minute.
ek·chin
एकछिन

mirror	ai·nah	ऐना
miscarriage	rak·ta·paht	रक्तपात
to miss (bus)	chal·nu	छल्नु
mistake	gal·ti	गल्ती
to mix	mi·*sau*·nu	मिसाउनु
modern	ah·*dhu*·nik	आधुनिक
moisturiser	mukh·mah la·*gau*·ne krim	मुखमा लगाउने क्रीम
moment	ek·chin	एकछिन

monastery	*gum·*bah · bi·*hahr* · ba·*hahl*	गुम्बा · बिहार · बहाल
money	*pai·*sah	पैसा
mongoose	*nyau·*ri *mu·*sah	न्याउरी मूसा
monk (Buddhist)	*bhi·*chu · *lah·*mah	भिक्षु · लामा
monkey	*bāh·*dar	बाँदर
monsoon	*bar·*khah	बर्खा
month	*ma·*hi·nah	महीना
this month	yo *ma·*hi·nah	यो महीना
monument	*smah·*rak	स्मारक
moon	*can·*dra·mah	चन्द्रमा
moon (dark)	*aū·*si	औसी
moon (full)	*pur·*ṇi·mah	पूर्णिमा
more	*a·*ru	अरू
morning	bi·*hah·*na	बिहान
mosque	*mas·*jid	मस्जिद
mosquito	lahm·*khuṭ·*ṭe	लामखुट्टे
mosquito net	*jhul	झुल
mother	*ah·*mah	आमा
mother-in-law	*sah·*su	सासू
motorcycle	*mo·*ṭar *sai·*kal	मोटर साइकल
mountain	pa·*hahḍ	पहाड
mountain bike	*maun·*ṭen baik	माउन्टेन बाइक
mountain climbing	pa·*hahḍ caḍh·*nu	पहाड चढ्ने
mountain hut	pa·*hah·ḍi jhu·*pro	पहाडी झुप्रो
mountain path	pa·*hah·ḍi bah·*to	पहाडी बाटो
high mountain path	hi·*mahl·*ko bah·*to	हिमालको बाटो
mountain range	*shre·*ṇi	श्रेणी
mountaineer	par·ba·*tah·*ro·hi	पर्वतारोही
mouse	*mu·*sah	मूसा
moustache	*jū·*gah	जुँगा
mouth	*mukh	मुख
to move	ca·*lau·*nu	चलाउनु
movie	*philm	फिल्म
much	*dhe·*rai	धेरै
mucus	*kaph	कफ
mud	*hi·*lo	हिलो
multicoloured	*rang·*gin	रंगीन
mum	*ah·*mai	आमै
muscle	*māh·*sha·pe·shi	मांशपेशी
museum	sā·gra·*hah·*la·ya	संग्रहालय
mushroom	*cyau	च्याउ
music	*sang·*git	सङ्गीत
musician	*sang·*git·kahr	सङ्गीतकार
Muslim	*mu·*sal·mahn	मुसलमान
mute	*lah·*to	लाटो
mutton	*bhē·*ḍah·ko *mah·*su	भेंडाको मासु
my	*me·*ro	मेरो

name	nahm	नाम
napkin	ru·*mahl*	रुमाल
narcotic	*lah*·gu *au*·sa·dhi	लागु औषधी
narrow	*säh*·ghu·ro	साँघुरो
nationality	rah·stri·ya·tah	राष्ट्रियता
nature	pra·kri·ti	प्रकृति
nausea	wahk·wah·ki	बाकबाकि
near	na·jik	नजीक
nearby	na·ji·kai	नजिकै
necessary	ah·ba·shyak	आवश्यक
neck	ghäh·ti	घाँटी
necklace	mah·lah	माला
needle (sewing)	si·yo	सियो
needle (syringe)	si·rinj	सिरिन्ज
Nepalese knife	khu·ku·ri	खुकुरी
net	jahl	जाल
never	ka·hi·le *hoi*·na	कहिले होइन
new	na·yäh	नयाँ
news	sa·mah·cahr	समाचार
newspaper	a·kha·bahr	अखबार
next	ar·ko · *au*·ne	अर्को · आउने
next month	ar·ko ma·hi·nah	अर्को महीना
next week	ar·ko hap·tah	अर्को हप्ता
next year	ar·ko bar·sa	अर्को बर्ष
next to	na·jik	नजीक
nice	rahm·ro	राम्रो
nickname	u·pa·nahm	उपनाम
night	raht	रात
no (definition)	hoi·na	होइन
no (location)	chai·na	छैन
no (permission)	hun·dai·na	हुन्दैन
noise	ah·wahj	आवाज
noisy	hal·lah	हल्ला
none	ke·hi pa·ni	केही पनि
noon	ma·dhyahn·ha	मध्यानह
no one	ko·hi (pa·ni)	कोही (पनि)
north	ut·tar	उत्तर
nose	nahk	नाक
notebook	kah·pi	कापी
nothing	ke·hi (pa·ni)	केही (पनि)
novel	u·pan·yahs	उपन्यास
now	a·hi·le	अहिले
nowadays	hi·jo·ah·ja	हिजोआज
number	sang·khyah	सङ्ख्या
nurse	nars	नर्स

O

English	Transliteration	Nepali
oats	*jai*	जइ
obvious	*spas*·ta	स्पष्ट
ocean	*ma*·hah·sah·gar	महासागर
o'clock	*ba*·jyo	बज्यो
occupation	*pe*·shah	पेशा
of	-ko	-को
offence	dos	दोष
to offend	*a*·pa·mahn *gar*·nu	अपमान गर्नु
to offer	*di*·nu	दिनु
office	kahr·*yah*·la·ya	कार्यालय
office worker	kar·ma·*cah*·ri	कर्मचारी
often	*ak*·sar	अक्सर

Oh!
oho! • e! — ओहो ! • ऎ !

English	Transliteration	Nepali
oil	tel	तेल
ointment	*ma*·la·ham	मलहम
OK	*thik* cha • *hun*·cha • has	ठीक छ • हुन्छ • हस
old (man/woman)	bu·*dho*/bu·*dhi*	बूढो/बूढी
old (thing)	pu·*rah*·no	पुरानो
old city	pu·*rah*·no *sha*·har	पुरानो शहर
on	-mah	-मा
on foot	hĩ·*de*·ra	हिँडेर
on time	*thik* sa·*ma*·ya·ko	ठीक समयको
once	ek·co·*ti*	एकचोटी
onion	pyahj	प्याज
only	*mah*·trai	मात्रै
open	kho·le·ko	खोलेको
to open	*khol*·nu	खोल्नु
opening	ud·*ghah*·*tan*	उद्घाटन
opera	*sang*·git·ma·ya *nah*·tak	सङ्गीतमय नाटक
opinion	*rah*·ya	राय
opportunity	*mau*·kah	मौका
opposite (point of view)	*bi*·pa·rit	विपरीत
opposite (side)	*ul*·to	उल्टो
or	ki	कि
oral	*mau*·khik	मौखिक
orange (adj)	*sun*·ta·lah rang	सुन्तला रङ्ग
orange (n)	*sun*·ta·lah	सुन्तला
order	ah·desh	आदेश
to order	ah·*desh di*·nu	आदेश दिनु
ordinary	sah·*dhah*·ran	साधारण
organisation	*sang*·gha	सङ्घ
to organise	*ban*·do·bas·ta mi·*lau*·nu	बन्दोबस्त मिलाउनु
original	*mau*·lik	मौलिक
ornament	*ga*·ha·nah	गहना

P

other	ar·ko • a·ru	अर्को • अरु
otherwise	na·tra	नत्र
out(side)	bah·hi·ra	बाहिर
over	-mah·thi	-माथि
overnight	raht·bha·ri	रातभरि
overseas	bi·desh(·mah)	बिदेश(मा)
to owe	riṇ lahg·nu	ऋण लाग्नु

I owe you.
mai·le ta·paī·lai riṇ lahg·yo — मैले तपाईलाई ऋण लाग्यो
You owe me.
ta·paī·le ma·lai riṇ lahg·yo — तपाईले मलाई ऋण लाग्यो

owl	ul·lu	उल्लु
own	ahph·no	आफ्नो
to own	ahph·no ba·nau·nu	आफ्नो बनाउनु
owner	sah·hu·ji/sah·hu·ni (m/f)	साहुजी/साहुनी
ox	go·ru	गोरु
oxygen	prahṇ·bah·yu	प्राणबायु

P

package	po·ko • baṭ·ṭah	पोको • बट्टा
packet	po·ko • baṭ·ṭah	पोको • बट्टा
padlock	tahl·cah	ताल्चा
page	pan·nah	पन्ना
pagoda	ga·jur	गजुर
pain	du·khai	दुःखाई
painful	du·khad	दुःखद
to paint	ci·tra ba·nau·nu	चित्र बनाउनु
painter	ci·tra·kahr	चित्रकार
painting	ci·tra · thahng·kah	चित्र · थाङ्का
painting (art)	ci·tra·ka·lah	चित्रकला
pair (n)	jor	जोर
palace	dar·bahr	दरबार
pale	phi·kah	फिका
pan (cooking)	bah·ṭah	बाटा
pan (frying)	tahp·ke	ताप्के
pan (wok)	ka·rah·hi	कराही
paper	kah·gaj	कागज
parcel	pu·lin·dah	पुलिन्दा
parents	ah·mah bu·wah	आमा बुबा

Pardon?
ha·jur? — हजुर ?

park	u·dyahn	उद्यान
to park	gah·ḍi rok·nu	गाडि रोक्नु
parliament (building)	sā·sad (bha·wan)	संसद (भवन)
parrot	su·gah	सुगा
part	khaṇ·ḍa	खण्ड

to participate	bhahg *li*·nu	भाग लिनु
particular	bi·*shes*	विशेष
party (feast)	bhoj	भोज
party (political)	dal	दल
pass (n)	*bhan*·jyahng	भन्ज्याङ
passive	nis·kri·ya	निष्क्रिय
passenger	*yah*·tri	यात्री
passport	rah·ha·*dah*·ni	राहदानी
passport number	rah·ha·*dah*·ni·ko sang·*khyah*	राहदानीको सङ्ख्या
past (time)	*bhut*·kahl	भूतकाल
pasture	khar·ka	खर्क
path	bah·*to*	बाटो
patient (adj)	sa·ha·ne • dhai·*rya*·shil	सहने • धैर्यशील
to pay	*tir*·nu	तिर्नु
payment	bhuk·*tah*·ni	भुक्तानी
peace	*shahn*·ti	शान्ति
peach	*ah*·ru	आरु
peacock	ma·*yur*	मयुर
peak	cu·*cu*·ro	चुचुरो
peanut	ba·dahm	बदाम
pear	nahs·pah·ti	नास्पाती
peas	ke·rau	केराउ
pedestrian	pai·dal yah·tri	पैदल यात्री
pen	ka·lam	कलम
pencil	si·sah·ka·lam	सिसाकलम
penis	ling·ga	लिङ्ग
penknife	cak·ku	चक्कु
people	mahn·che·ha·ru • ja·na·tah	मान्छेहरू • जनता
pepper	ma·ric	मरिच
green pepper	bhé·dah khur·*sah*·ni	भेंडा खुर्सानी
per cent	pra·ti·shat	प्रतिशत
perfect	a·*tyut*·tam	अत्युत्तम
performance	nah·tak	नाटक
period pain	ma·hi·nah·bah·ri·ko du·*khai*	महिनाबारीको दुःखाई
permanent	sthah·yi	स्थायी
permanent collection	sthah·yi sang·gra·ha	स्थायी सङ्ग्रह
permission	a·nu·ma·ti	अनुमति
permit	a·nu·ma·ti·pa·tra	अनुमतिपत्र
to permit	a·nu·ma·ti *di*·nu	अनुमति दिनु
persecution	a·*tyah*·cahr	अत्याचार
person	mahn·che	मान्छे
personal	byak·ti·gat	व्यक्तिगत
personality	byak·ti·twa	व्यक्तित्व
to perspire	pa·*si*·nah *au*·nu	पसिना आउनु

pet	*pahl*·tu ja·*nah*·war	पाल्तु जनावर
petition	*bin*·ti·pa·tra	बिन्तीपत्र
petroleum	*kha*·nij tel	खनिज तेल
pharmacy	au·sa·dhi pa·sal	औषधी पसल
pheasant	*kah*·lij	कालिज
to phone	phon *gar*·nu	फोन गर्नु
phone book	*phon*·ko ki·*tahb*	फोनको किताब
photo	*tas*·bir	तस्विर

Can I take a photo?
tas·bir *khic*·nu·hun·cha?　　　　तस्विर खिच्नुहुन्छ ?

photographer	*tas*·bir *khic*·ne ka·*lah*·kahr	तस्विर खिच्ने कलाकार
photography	*tas*·bir *khic*·ne ka·*lah*	तस्विर खिच्ने कला
pick(axe)	*gai*·ti	गैती
to pick up	*li*·na *au*·nu	लिन आउनु
pickle (relish)	a·*cahr*	अचार
piece	*ṭuk*·rah	टुका
pig	*sū*·gur	सुँगुर
pigeon	pa·re·wah	परेवा
pill	*go*·li	गोली
the Pill	pa·ri·bahr ni·*yo*·jan·ko au·sa·dhi	परिवार नियोजनको औषधी
pillow	si·*rah*·ni	सिरानी
pillowcase	si·*rah*·ni·ko khol	सिरानीको खोल
pine tree	*sal*·lah·ko rukh	सल्लाको रूख
pineapple	*bhuī*·ka·ṭa·har	भुईंकटहर
pink	gu·*lah*·phi	गुलाफी
pipe	*cu*·roṭ paip	चुरोट पाईप
place	*ṭhaū*	ठाउँ
plains	ma·*desh* · ta·*rai*	मदेश · तराई
plains dweller	ma·*de*·si	मदेसी
plane	ha·wai·ja·hahj	हवाईजहाज
planet	*sā*·sahr · *gra*·ha	संसार · ग्रह
plant	*bi*·ru·wah	बिरूवा
to plant	*rop*·nu	रोप्नु
plate	thahl	थाल
plateau	sa·ma·tal *ṭah*·ku·ro	समतल टाकुरो
platform (cremation)	*ghaṭ*	घाट
platform (stage)	u·*ṭhah*·ya·ko *ṭhaū*	उठायको ठाउँ
play (theatre)	*li*·lah	लीला
to play cards	tash *khel*·nu	तास खेल्नु
to play (game)	*khel*·nu	खेल्नु
to play (music)	ba·*jau*·nu	बजाउनु
to play sport	*khel*·kud *khel*·nu	खेलकद खेल्नु
player	khe·*lah*·ḍi	खेलाडि
playing cards	tash	तास
to plug	*bu*·jo *lau*·nu	बुजो लाउनु

plum	ah·ru·*ba*·kha·ḍah	आरुबखडा
pocket	*khal*·ti	खल्ती
poetry	*ka*·bi·tah	कबिता
to point (out)	de·*khau*·nu	देखाउनु
poker (fire)	su·*i*·ro	सुइरो
police	pra·*ha*·ri	प्रहरी
politician	rahj·*ni*·ti·gyā	राजनीतिज्ञ
politics	rahj·ni·ti	राजनीति
pollen	pa·*rahg*	पराग
pollution	du·sit	दुषित
pomegranate	a·*nahr*	अनार
pond	po·kha·ri	पोखरी
poor	ga·rib	गरिब
popular	lok·*pri*·ya	लोकप्रिय
pork	sū·gur·ko *mah*·su	सुँगुरको मासु
porter	bha·ri·yah	भरिया
portrait	ah·kri·ti·ci·tra	आकृतिचित्र
possible	sam·bhab	सम्भव

It's (not) possible.
sam·bhab cha (*chai*·na)   सम्भव छ (छैन)

postage	ḍāhk·khar·ca	डाँकखर्च
postcard	*post*·kahrḍ	पोस्टकार्ड
postcode	*post*·koḍ	पोस्टकोड
poster	par·cah	पर्चा
post office	hu·lahk aḍ·ḍah	हुलाक अड्डा
potato	ah·lu	आलु
pot (ceramic)	bhāh·ḍo	भाँडो
pottery	mah·ṭah·kah bhāh·ḍah	माटाका भाँडा
poverty	da·ri·dra·tah	दरिद्रता
power	shak·ti	शक्ति
prayer	man·tra · prahr·tha·nah	मन्त्र · प्रार्थना
to prefer	bes lahg·nu	बेस लाग्नु
pregnant	gar·bha·va·ti	गर्भवती
present (gift)	u·pa·hahr	उपहार
present (time)	bar·ta·mahn	बर्तमान
president	rah·stra·pa·ti	राष्ट्रपति
pressure	thi·cai	थिचाइ
pretty	rahm·ro	राम्रो
to prevent	rok·nu	रोक्नु
price	mol	मोल
pride	gar·ba	गर्ब
priest	pu·*jah*·ri	पूजारी
prime minister	pra·*dhahn man*·tri	प्रधान मन्त्री
print (artwork)	cha·pai	छपाइ
prison	jhyahl·khah·nah	इयालखाना
prisoner	kai·di	कैदी
private	ni·ji	निजी

Q

English	Transliteration	Nepali
problem	sa·*mas*·yah	समस्या
process	*kahm*·ko *bi*·dhi	कामको विधि
to process	*pra*·kri·yah ca·*lau*·nu	प्रक्रिया चलाउनु
procession (march)	ju·*lus*	जुलूस
procession (wedding)	*jan*·ti	जन्ति
produce	ut·*pah*·dan	उत्पादन
to produce	ut·*pah*·dan *gar*·nu	उत्पादन गर्नु
producer	ut·*pah*·dak	उत्पादक
profession	pe·shah	पेशा
professional	khahs pe·shah bi·*gyá*	खास पेशा बिज्ञ
profit	*nah*·phah	नाफा
programme	*kah*·rya·kram	कार्यक्रम
projector	*pra*·che·pak	प्रक्षेपक
promise	ba·can	बचन
to promise	ba·can *di*·nu	बचन दिनु
proposal	*pras*·tahb	प्रस्ताब
proprietor	*sah*·hu·ji/*sah*·hu·ni (m/f)	साहुनी / साहुजी
prostitute	be·shyah	बेश्या
to protect	ba·*cau*·nu	बचाउनु
protected forest	ba·*cah*·ye·ko ban	बचायेको बन
protected species	ba·*cah*·ye·ko *bar*·ga	बचायेको बर्ग
protest	bi·*rodh*	बिरोध
to protest	bi·*rodh gar*·nu	बिरोध गर्नु
protest march	ju·*lus*	जुलूस
public (adj)	*sahr*·ba·ja·nik	सार्बजनिक
public (n)	*ja*·na·tah	जनता
public toilet	shau·*cah*·la·ya	शौचालय
to pull	*tahn*·nu	तान्नु
pump	pamp	पम्प
puncture	pwahl	प्वाल
to punish	*dan*·da *di*·nu	दण्ड दिनु
puppy	*ku*·kur·ko*chau*·ro	कुकुरको छाउरो
pure	co·kho	चोखो
purple	pyah·ji	प्याजी
to push	gha·*ced*·nu	घचेड्नु
to put (down)	*rahkh*·nu	राख्नु
to put in	*hahl*·nu	हाल्नु

Q

English	Transliteration	Nepali
qualifications	*yog*·ya·tah	योग्यता
quality	gun	गुन
queen	*rah*·ni	रानी
question	*prash*·na	प्रश्न
quick(ly)	*chi*·to	छिटो
quiet	*shahn*·ta	शान्त
quietly	bi·*stah*·rai	बिस्तारै
quilt	*si*·rak	सिरक

R

rabbit	kha·*rah*·yo	खरायो
race (culture)	*jah*·ti	जाति
race (sport)	dauḍ	दौड
racing bike	re·sing baik	रेसिङ बाइक
racism	*jah*·ti·bahd	जातिबाद
radio	re·ḍi·yo	रेडियो
radish	*mu*·lah	मुला
to rain	pah·ni par·nu	पानी पर्नु

It's raining.
pah·ni par·cha पानी पर्छ

rainy season	bar·saht	बर्सात
raisin	dahkh	दाख
rally	ja·*maht*	जमात
to rape	ba·*laht*·kahr gar·nu	बलात्कार गर्नु
rare	dur·labh	दुर्लभ
rash	sujh	सुझ
rat	*mu*·sah	मूसा
raw	kāh·co	काँचो
razorblade	pat·ti	पत्ती
to read	padh·nu	पढ्नु
ready	ta·yahr	तयार
to realise	bodh gar·na sak·nu	बोध गर्न सक्नु
reason	kah·raṇ	कारण
receipt	bil	बिल
to receive	prahp·ta gar·nu	प्राप्त गर्नु
recent	hahl·sahl·ko	हालसालको
recently	hahl·sah·lai	हालसालै
to recognise	cin·nu	चिन्नु
to recommend	si·*phah*·ris gar·nu	सिफारिस गर्नु
to recover	ni·ko·hu·nu	निकोहुनु
recyclable	ri·*sai*·kal gar·na sa·ki·ne	रीसाइक्ल गर्न सकिने
recycling	ri·*sai*·kal	रीसाइक्ल
red	rah·to	रातो
referee	ma·*dhyas*·tha	मध्यस्थ
reference	pra·*mahṇ*·pa·tra	प्रमाणपत्र
refugee	sha·ra·*ṇahr*·thi	शरणार्थी
to refund	phar·*kau*·nu	फर्काउनु
to refuse	a·*swi*·kahr gar·nu	अस्वीकार गर्नु
region	che·tra	क्षेत्र
regional	prah·*de*·shik	प्रादेशिक
regulation	ni·yam	नियम
relationship	mi·lahp	मिलाप
to relax	ah·rahm gar·nu	आराम गर्नु
religion	dhar·ma	धर्म

religious	*dhahr·*mik	धार्मिक
remaining	*bāh·*ki	बाँकी
to remember	sam·*jha·*nu	सम्झानु
remote	*dur·*gam	दुर्गम
rent	*bhah·*dah	भाडा
to rent	*bhah·*dah·mah *li·*nu	भाडा लिनु
to repair	*mar·*mat *gar·*nu	मर्मत गर्नु
to repeat	do·ha·*rau·*nu	दोहराउनु
republic	gan·*rah·*jya	गणराज्य
request	a·nu·rodh	अनुरोध
reservation	*sany·*cit	सञ्चित
to reserve	*sany·*cit *gar·*nu	सञ्चित गर्नु
resignation	rah·ji·*nah·*mah	राजीनामा
to respect	*mahn·*nu	मान्नु
responsibility	jim·me·*dah·*ri	जिम्मेदारी
to rest	*ah·*rahm *li·*nu	आराम लिनु
restaurant	bho·ja·*nah·*la·ya	भोजनालय
resting place (tree)	cau·*tah·*rah	चौतारा
resume (CV)	*bai·*yo·dah·tah	बाइयोडाटा
retired	a·wa·*kahsh *li·*ya·ko	अवकाश लियको
to return	*phar·*ka·nu	फर्कनु
return ticket	jah·ne·au·ne *ţi·*kaţ	जानेआउने टिकट
review	sa·*mah·*lo·ca·nah	समालोचना
revolution (people's)	*krahn·*ti	क्रान्ति
rhinoceros	*gaí·*dah	गैंडा
rhododendron	lah·li·*gu·*rāhs	लालीगुराँस
rhythm	*la·*ya • tahl	लय • ताल
rib	*ka·*rang	करङ
rice (beaten)	*cyu·*rah	च्यूरा
rice (cooked)	bhaht	भात
rice (uncooked)	*cah·*mal	चामल
rice (unhusked)	dhahn	धान
rich	*dha·*ni	धनी
rickshaw	*rik·*shah	रीक्सा
to ride (a horse)	*cadh·*nu	चढ्नु
right (correct)	ţhik	ठीक
right (not left)	dah·*yāh	दायाँ
to be right (correct)	*mil·*nu	मिल्नु

You're right.

ta·*paī·*le ţhik *bhan·*nu *bha·*yo	तपाईंले ठीक भन्नु भयो

right now	a·hil·*yai	अहिल्यै
rights	a·dhi·*kahr	अधिकार
human rights	mah·nab·a·dhi·kahr	मानवअधिकार
ring (of phone)	*ghaņ·*ţi	घण्टी
ring (on finger)	*aū·*ţhi	औंठी

R

D
I
C
T
I
O
N
A
R
Y

to ring (bell)	*baj*·nu	बज्नु

I'll give you a ring. ma ta·*paī*·lai phon *gar*·chu		म तपाईलाई फोन गर्छु

to rip off	*thag*·nu	ठग्नु
ripe	*pah*·ke·ko	पाकेको
risk	*kha*·ta·rah	खतरा
river	*na*·di	नदी
road (route)	*bah*·to	बाटो
road (paved)	*sa*·dak	सडक
road map	*bah*·to·ko *nak*·sah	बाटोको नक्सा
to rob	*cor*·nu	चोर्नु
rock	*pa*·ha·ro	पहरो
to roll (up)	*ber*·nu	बेर्नु
to roll (move)	*gud*·nu	गुड्नु
romance	*mi*·tho·pan • *pre*·mah·lahp	मीठोपन • प्रेमालाप
room	*ko*·thah	कोठा
room number	*ko*·thah·ko *nam*·bar	कोठाको नम्बर
rooster	*bhah*·le *ku*·khu·rah	भाले कुखुरा
rope	*do*·ri	डोरी
rough	*khas*·ro	खस्रो
round	*go*·lo	गोलो
to row (a boat)	(*dung*·gah) ca·*lau*·nu	(डुङ्गा) चलाउनु
to rub	*dal*·nu	दल्नु
rubbish	*pho*·hor	फोहोर
rug	*sah*·no ga·*laī*·cah	सानो गलैंचा
ruins	bhag·*nah*·ba·shes	भग्नावशेष
rule (regulation)	*ni*·yam	नियम
to run (away)	da·*gur*·nu	दगुर्नु
rupees	ru·*pi*·yāh	रुपियाँ

S

sad	*du*·khi	दुःखी
safe (adj)	su·*ra*·chit	सुरक्षित
safe (n)	su·*ra*·chit thaū	सुरक्षित ठाउँ
safety pin	huk	हुक
saffron	*ke*·shar	केशर
saint (Hindu)	ma·*haht*·mah	महात्मा
saint (Muslim)	pir	पीर
salary	*ta*·lab	तलब
sale	*bi*·kri	बिक्री
salt	nun	नुन
salty	nu·*ni*·lo	नुनिलो
same	u·*hi*	उही
sand	*bah*·lu·wah	बालुवा
sandal	*cap*·pal	चप्पल
sari	*sah*·di	साडी

S

to save	ba·*cau*·nu	बचाउनु
to say	*bhan*·nu	भन्नु
to scale	*cadh*·nu	चढ्नु
scared	*ḍar*·lahg·do	डरलाग्दो
scarf	do·*paṭ*·ṭah	दोपट्टा
scenery	*dri*·shya	दृश्य
school	bi·*dyah*·la·ya	बिद्यालय
science	bi·*gyahn*	बिज्ञान
scientist	bai·*gyah*·nik	बैज्ञानिक
scissors	*kaĩ*·ci	कैंची
to score	*prahp*·ta gar·nu	प्राप्त गर्नु
sculpture	*mur*·ti·ka·lah	मूर्तिकला
sea	sa·*mu*·dra	समुद्र
seaside	sa·*mu*·dra·ko ki·*nahr*	समुद्रको किनार
seat	*ṭhaũ*	ठाउँ
to be seated	ba·si *rahkh*·nu	बसी राख्नु
second (adj)	*dos*·rah	दोस्रा
second (n)	se·*keṇḍ*	सेकेण्ड
secret (adj)	*gop*·ya	गोप्य
secretary	sa·*cib*	सचिब
to see (look at)	*her*·nu	हेर्नु
to see (observe)	*dekh*·nu	देख्नु

> We'll see!
> he·*raũ!* हेरौं !
> I see. (understand)
> *bujh*·yo बुझ्यो
> See you later.
> *phe*·ri *bhe*·ṭaũ·lah! फेरी भेटौंला !
> See you tomorrow.
> *bho*·li *bhe*·ṭaũ·lah! भोलि भेटौंला !

seed	bi·*u*	बीउ
selfish	*swahr*·thi	स्वार्थी
to sell	*bec*·nu	बेच्नु
to send	pa·*ṭhau*·nu	पठाउनु
sensible	bi·*be*·ki	विवेकी
sentence (prison)	*nir*·ṇa·ya	निर्णय
sentence (words)	*bah*·kya	बाक्य
to separate	chu·*ṭyau*·nu	छुट्याउनु
serious	*gam*·bhir	गम्भीर
servant	*no*·kar	नोकर
to serve	*se*·bah gar·nu	सेवा गर्नु
service	*se*·bah	सेवा
sesame seed	*til*·ko bi·*u*	तिलको बिउ
several	a·*nek*	अनेक
to sew	si·*u*·nu	सिउनु
sex (gender)	*ling*·ga	लिङ्ग
sex (intercourse)	*sam*·bhog	संभोग

D I C T I O N A R Y

to have sex	*sam·bhog gar·nu*	संभोग गर्नु
sexism	*ai·mai·pra·ti·ko ghri·nah*	आइमाईप्रतिको घृणा
sexy	*sam·bho·gi*	सम्भोगी
shade	*shi·tal*	शीतल
shadow	*chah·yāh*	छायाँ
shampoo	*dhu·lai*	धुलाइ
shape	*ah·kahr*	आकार
to share	*bāhd·nu*	बाँड्नु
to shave	*khau·ra·nu*	खौरनु
shawl	*odh·ne*	ओढ्ने
she (inf)	*u·ni • tyo • yo*	ऊनी • त्यो • यो
she (pol)	*wa·hāh*	वहाँ
sheep	*bhé·dah*	भेंडा
sheet (bed)	*tan·nah*	तन्ना
sheet (paper)	*tau*	ताउ
shelter	*bahs*	बास
shelves	*da·rahj*	दराज
ship	*pah·ni·ja·hahj*	पानीजहाज
shirt	*ka·mij*	कमिज
to shiver	*kahm·nu*	काम्नु
shoe(s)	*jut·tah*	जुत्ता
shoe shop	*jut·tah·pa·sal*	जुत्ता पसल
to shoot	*hahn·nu*	हान्नु
shop	*pa·sal*	पसल
shopkeeper	*pa·sa·le • sah·hu*	पसले • साहु
to go shopping	*kin·mel jah·nu*	किनमेल जानु
short (height)	*pudh·ko*	पुड्को
short (length)	*cho·to*	छोटो
shortage	*ka·mi*	कमी
shorts	*kat·tu*	कट्टु
shoulder	*kāhdh*	काँध
to shout	*ka·rau·nu*	कराउनु
show	*khel·bahd*	खेलबाड
to show	*de·khau·nu*	देखाउनु
shower	*snahn*	स्नान
to shower	*nu·hau·nu*	नुहाउनु
shrine	*de·wal*	देवल
to shut	*ban·da gar·nu*	बन्द गर्नु
shyness	*lahj*	लाज
sick	*bi·rah·mi*	बिरामी
sickness	*rog*	रोग
side	*cheu*	छेउ
this side	*wah·ri*	वारी
that side	*pah·ri*	पारी
to sign	*sa·hi gar·nu*	सही गर्नु
signature	*sa·hi*	सही
signpost	*sang·ket·cin·ha*	सङ्केतचिन्ह
silence	*maun·tah*	मौनता

silk	*re·sham*	रेशम
silver (adj)	*cāh·di·ko*	चाँदीको
silver (n)	*cāh·di*	चाँदी
similar	*us·tai*	उस्तै
simple	*sa·ral*	सरल
sin	*pahp*	पाप
since (May)	*(mai)·de·khi*	(माइ)देखि
to sing	*gau·nu*	गाउनु
singer	*gah·yak/gah·yi·kah* (m/f)	गायक/गायिका
single (unique)	*ek·lo*	एक्लो
single (unmarried)	*ek·lai*	एक्लै
single man	*ku·mahr*	कुमार
single room	*ek·ja·nah·ko ko·thah*	एकजनाको कोठा
single woman	*ku·mah·ri*	कुमारी
singlet	*gan·ji*	गन्जी
sister (elder)	*di·di*	दिदी
sister (younger)	*ba·hi·ni*	बहिनी
sisters	*di·di·ba·hi·ni*	दिदीबहिनी
sitting posture	*ah·san*	आसन
situation	*a·bas·thah*	अवस्था
size	*saij*	साइज
to ski	*is·ki khel·nu*	इस्की खेल्नु
skiing	*is·ki khel·na*	इस्की खेल्न
skin	*chah·lah*	छाला
sky	*ah·kahsh*	आकाश
to sleep	*sut·nu*	सुल्नु
sleeping bag	*sut·ne jho·lah*	सुल्ले झोला
sleeping pills	*su·tau·ne au·sa·dhi*	सुताउने औषधी
sleepy	*ni·drah*	निद्रा
slow	*dhi·lo*	ढिलो
slowly	*bi·stah·rai*	बिस्तारै
small	*sah·no*	सानो
smell	*bahs*	बास
to smell (create a scent)	*ga·nhau·nu*	गन्हाउनु
to smell (with nose)	*sügh·nu*	सुँघ्नु
to smile	*hāhs·nu*	हाँस्नु
to smoke (cigarettes)	*dhum·ra·pahn gar·nu*	धूम्रपान गर्नु
smoking	*dhum·ra·pahn*	धूम्रपान
snack	*khah·jah*	खाजा
snake	*sar·pa*	सर्प
snow	*hiū*	हिउँ
snow peak	*hi·mahl*	हिमाल
soap	*sah·bun*	साबुन
socialist	*sa·mahj·bah·di*	समाजबादी
sock	*mo·jah*	मोजा
soil	*mah·to*	माटो
soldier	*si·pah·hi*	सिपाही
solid	*thos*	ठोस

some	*ke·hi · ku·nai*	केही · कुनै
someone	*ko·hi*	कोही
something	*ke·hi*	केही
sometimes	ka·hi·le·*kah·hī*	कहिलेकाहीं
son	*cho·rah*	छोरा
song	git	गीत
soon	*cāh·ḍai*	चाँडै
sore	*du·khe·ko*	दुखेको
sorry (condolence)	*da·yah*	दया
sorry (regret)	*duh·khit*	दुःखित

I'm sorry. (apology)
mahph *gar·nu·hos*   माफ गर्नुहोस

soul (spirit)	*aht·mah*	आत्मा
sound	*ah·wahj*	आवाज
soup	*su·ru·wah*	सुरबा
sour	*a·mi·lo*	अमीलो
south	*da·chiṇ*	दक्षिण
souvenir	*ci·no*	चिनो
souvenir shop	*ci·no pa·sal*	चिनो पसल
to sow	*rop·nu*	रोप्नु
soybeans	*bhaṭ·mahs*	भटमास
space (outer space)	an·ta·*ri·*cha	अन्तरिक्ष
space (room to move)	ṭhaū	ठाउँ
to speak	*bol·nu*	बोल्नु
special	bi·*shes*	विशेष
specialist	bi·she·*sa·gyā*	विशेषज्ञ
speed	*ga·ti · beg*	गति · बेग
to spend	*khar·ca gar·nu*	खर्च गर्नु
spice	*ma·sa·lah*	मसला
spicy	*pi·ro*	पिरो
spider	*mah·ku·rah*	माकुरा
spinach	pah·*lung·go*	पालुङ्गो
spirit (soul)	*aht·mah*	आत्मा
spoon	*cam·cah*	चम्चा
sport	*khel·kud*	खेलकुद
sprain	*mar·kai*	मर्काई
spring (coil)	spring	स्प्रिङ
spring (season)	*ba·san·ta ri·tu*	बसन्त ऋतु
square (shape)	*bar·ga·che·tra*	वर्गक्षेत्र
square (town centre)	cok	चोक
squirrel	*lo·khar·ke*	लोखर्के
stage (n)	*rang·ga manyc*	रङ्गमञ्च
stairs	bha·*ryahng*	भर्याङ्ग
stale	*bah·si*	बासी
stamp (postage)	*ṭi·kaṭ*	टिकट
to stand	u·*bhi·nu*	उभिनु
standard	star	स्तर

star(s)	*tah·rah*	तारा
to start	*su·ru gar·nu*	सुरु गर्नु
stationer	*ci·thi·pa·tra pa·sal*	चिठीपत्र पसल
statue	*mur·ti*	मूर्ति
to stay (remain)	*ra·ha·nu*	रहनु
to stay (sit)	*bas·nu*	बस्नु
to steal	*cor·nu*	चोर्नु
steam	*bahph*	बाफ़
steep downhill	*bhi·rah·lo*	भिरालो
steep uphill	*thah·do*	ठाडो
step	*khud·ki·lo*	खुड्किलो
stick	*lath·thi*	लठ्ठी
stomach	*pet*	पेट
stomachache	*pet du·khe·ko*	पेट दुखेको
stone	*dhung·gah*	ढुङ्गा
stop (bus)	*bas bi·sau·ni*	बस बिसौनी
to stop	*rok·nu*	रोक्नु

| Stop! (pol) *rok·nu·hos!* | रोक्नुहोस ! |
| Stop! (inf) *rok!* | रोक ! |

stork	*dha·nesh • nil·ca·rah*	धनेश • नीलचरा
storm	*hu·ri*	हुरी
story	*ka·thah*	कथा
stove (electric)	*hi·tar*	हिटर
stove (kerosene/gas)	*stobh*	स्टोभ
stove (wood)	*cu·lo*	चूलो
straight	*si·dhah*	सिधा
strange	*a·nau·tho*	अनौठो
stranger	*a·pa·ri·cit byak·ti*	अपरिचित व्यक्ति
stream	*kho·lah*	खोला
street	*sa·dak*	सडक
strength	*bal*	बल
strike	*had·tahl*	हडताल
string	*do·ri*	डोरी
to stroll	*ghum·nu*	घुम्नु
strong	*ba·li·yo*	बलियो
stubborn	*a·ter*	अटेर
student	*bi·dyahr·thi*	बिद्यार्थी
studio	*ci·tra·shah·lah*	चित्रशाला
stupid	*mur·kha*	मूर्ख
style	*dhāh·cah • shai·li*	ढाँचा • शैली
suburb	*kāhth*	काँठ
suburbs of ...	*...ko kāhth*	...को काँठ
success	*sa·phal·tah*	सफलता
suddenly	*a·cah·nak*	अचानक
to suffer	*du·kha pau·nu*	दुःख पाउनु

T

sugar	*ci·*ni	चिनी
sugar cane	*u·*khu	उखु
suitcase	*bah·*kas	बाकस
summer	*gar·*mi *mau·*sam	गर्मी मौसम
sun	*sur·*ya	सूर्य
sunny	*gha·mai·*lo	घमाईलो
sunrise	*sur·yo·da·*ya	सूर्योदय
sunset	*sur·yahs·*ta	सूर्यास्त

Sure.		
*pak·*kah		पक्का

surface mail	*gah·ḍi·bah·ta* post	गाडीबाट पोस्ट
surname	thar	थर
surprise	*a·cam·*ma	अचम्म
to survive	*bāhc·*nu	बाँच्नु
sweater (jumper)	*swi·*tar	स्विटर
sweet	*gu·li·*yo	गुलियो
to swim	*pau·*ḍi *khel·*nu	पौडी खेल्नु
swimming	*pau·*ḍi	पौडी
sword	*tar·*bahr	तरबार
sympathy	*sa·hah·nu·bhu·*ti	सहानुभूति
synthetic	*kri·*trim *bas·tu·bah·*ta	कृत्रिम बस्तुबाट
	*ba·nah·ya·kah ku·*rah	बनायका कुरा
syringe	*si·*rinj	सिरिन्ज

T

table	*ṭe·*bul	टेबुल
tail	*puc·*char	पुच्छर
tailor	*su·ci·*kahr	सूचिकार
to take	*li·*nu	लिनु
to take away	*lag·*nu	लग्नु
to take a photo	*tas·*bir *khic·*nu	तस्विर खिच्नु
to talk	*ku·*rah *gar·*nu	कुरा गर्नु
tall	*a·*glo	अग्लो
tasty	*mi·*tho	मीठो
tax	kar	कर
taxi	*ṭyahk·*si	टयाक्सी
tea	*ci·*yah	चिया
teacher	*shi·*chak	शिक्षक
teaching	*shi·*chaṇ	शिक्षण
team	*ṭo·*li	टोली
technique	*ta·ri·*kah	तरिका
telegram	tahr	तार
telephone	phon	फोन
telephone centre	phon *aḍ·*ḍah	फोन अड्डा
to telephone	phon *gar·*nu	फोन गर्नु
telescope	*dur·*bin	दूरबीन

television	*ṭe·li·bhi·jan*	टेलिभिजन
to tell	*bhan·nu*	भन्नु
temperature (fever)	*ja·ro*	जरो
temperature (weather)	*tahp·kram*	तापक्रम
temple (Buddhist)	*stu·pah*	स्तूपा
temple (Hindu)	*man·dir*	मन्दिर
temporary	*a·sthah·yi*	अस्थायी
tent	*pahl*	पाल
tenth	*da·saũ*	दसौं
terrible	*ḍar·lahg·do*	डरलाग्दो
test	*jãhc*	जाँच
tetanus	*dha·nu·rog*	धनुरोग
than	*-bhan·dah*	-भन्दा
to thank	*dhan·ya·bahd di·nu*	धन्यबाद दिनु

Thank you.
dhan·ya·bahd   धन्यबाद

that	*tyo*	त्यो
theatre	*a·bhi·na·ya*	अभिनय
there	*tya·hãh*	त्यहाँ
these	*yi*	यी
they (informal)	*u·ni·ha·ru*	उनीहरू
they (formal)	*wa·hãh·ha·ru*	वहाँहरू
thick	*bahk·lo*	बाक्लो
thief	*cor*	चोर
thin (animal/person)	*du·blo*	दुब्लो
thin (thing)	*pah·ta·lo*	पातलो
thing (abstract)	*ku·rah*	कुरा
thing (material)	*cij • bas·tu*	चीज • वस्तु
things	*cij·bij*	चीजबीज
to think	*bi·cahr gar·nu*	बिचार गर्नु
third (3rd)	*tes·rah*	तेस्रा
thirst	*tir·khah*	तिर्खा
this	*yo*	यो
those	*ti*	ती
thought	*bi·cahr*	बिचार
thread	*dhah·go*	धागो
throat (inside)	*ga·lah*	गला
throat (outside)	*ghãh·ṭi*	घाँटी
thunder	*gar·jan*	गर्जन
thunderstorm	*megh·gar·jan*	मेघगर्जन
	ta·thah bar·sah	तथा बर्षा
Tibetan dress	*cu·bah*	चुबा
tick	*kir·no*	किर्नो
ticket	*ṭi·kaṭ*	टिकट
ticket office	*ṭi·kaṭ aḍ·ḍah*	टिकट अड्डा
tiger	*bahgh*	बाघ
to be tight	*ka·si·nu*	कसिनु

to tighten	*kas*·nu	कस्नु
time	sa·*ma*·ya	समय
time (instance)	*pa*·tak	पटक
timetable	sa·*ma*·ya *tah*·li·kah	समय तालिका
tin (can)	ṭin	टिन
tin opener	ṭin *khol*·ne	टिन खोल्ने
tip (money)	*ba*·kas	बकस
to be tired	*thahk*·nu	थाक्नु
tired	*tha*·kai	थकाइ
to	-mah • -lai	-मा • -लाई
tobacco	*sur*·ti	सुर्ती
today	*ah*·ja	आज
together	sahth·*sah*·thai	साथसाथै
toilet (flushing)	*bahth*·rum	बाठरुम
toilet (pit)	*car*·pi	चर्पी
toilet (public)	shau·*cah*·la·ya	शौचालय
toilet paper	*ṭwai*·leṭ *pe*·par	ट्वाईलेट पेपर
tomato	gol·*bhě*·ḍah	गोलभेंडा
tomorrow	*bho*·li	भोलि
tomorrow afternoon	*bho*·li *diü*·so	भोलि दिउँसो
tomorrow evening	*bho*·li *be*·lu·kah	भोलि बेलुका
tomorrow morning	*bho*·li bi·*hah*·na	भोलि बिहान
tongue	*ji*·bro	जिब्रो
tonight	*ah*·ja *rah*·ti	आज राति
too (also)	*pa*·ni	पनि
too (much)	*dhe*·rai • *sah*·hrai	धेरै • साहै
too expensive	*dhe*·rai ma·*hă*·go	धेरै महँगो
tooth	dâht	दाँत
toothache	dâht *du*·khe·ko	दाँत दुखेको
toothbrush	dâht *mahjh*·ne *bu*·rus	दाँत माझ्ने बुरुस
toothpaste	*many*·jan	मञ्जन
torch (flashlight)	ṭarc	टर्च
to touch	*chu*·nu	छुनु
tour (journey)	*bhra*·maṇ	भ्रमण
to tour	*ghum*·nu	घुम्नु
tourism	par·*ya*·ṭan	पर्यटन
tourist	par·*ya*·ṭak	पर्यटक
tourist information office	par·*ya*·ṭan kahr·*yah*·la·ya	पर्यटन कार्यालय
towards	-*ti*·ra	-तिर
towel	ru·*mahl*	रुमाल
tower	a·*glo* *bha*·wan	अग्लो भवन
town	*na*·gar	नगर
track (footprints)	*hĭ*·ḍe·ko chahp	हिंडेको छाप
track (path)	*go*·re·ṭo	गोरेटो
trade union	*kahm*·ko sa·*mi*·ti	कामको समिति
trader	*sah*·hu	साहु
traffic	ah·wat·*jah*·wat	आवतजावत
	gar·ne *bas*·tu	गर्ने बस्तु

trail	go·re·to • sah·no bah·to	गोरेटो • सानो बाटो
train	rel·gah·ḍi	रेलगाडी
to translate	ul·thah gar·nu	उल्था गर्नु
to travel	yah·trah gar·nu	यात्रा गर्नु
travel office	yah·trah·ko ṭi·kaṭ aḍ·ḍah	यात्राको टिकट अड्डा
travel sickness	gah·ḍi·mah lahg·ne wahk·wahk	गाडीमा लाग्ने वाकवाक
traveller	yah·tri	यात्री
travellers cheque	ṭrah·bhlar cek	ट्राभ्लर चेक
tree	rukh	रूख
trekking	pai·dal yah·trah	पैदल यात्रा
trip	yah·trah	यात्रा
trousers	su·ru·wahl	सुरुवाल
truck	ṭrak • la·ri	ट्रक • लरी
true	sa·hi	सही

It's true.
sa·tya ho　　　　　　　　　　सत्य हो

trust	bi·shwahs	विश्वास
to trust	bi·shwahs gar·nu	विश्वास गर्नु
truth	sa·tya	सत्य
to try	ko·sis gar·nu	कोसिस गर्नु
to try on	la·gai her·nu	लगाइ हेर्नु
T-shirt	gan·ji	गन्जी
tuberculosis	cha·ya·rog	क्षयरोग
tune	tahn	तान
tunic	dau·rah	दौरा
turmeric	be·sahr	बेसार
to turn	moḍ·nu	मोड्नु

Turn left/right.
bah·yāh/dah·yāh moḍ·nu·hos　　बायाँ/दायाँ मोड्नुहोस

twice	du·i pa·ṭak	दुइ पटक
twins	jam·lyah·hah	जम्ल्याहा
type	ki·sim	किसिम
to type	ṭaip gar·nu	टाइप गर्नु
typhoid	ṭai·phaiḍ	टाइफाइड
typical	na·mu·nah hu·ne	नमुना हुने
tyre	ṭah·yar·cak·kah	टायरचक्का

U

umbrella	chah·tah	छाता
uncomfortable	a·sa·ji·lo	असजिलो
under	-mu·ni	-मुनि
underpants	kaṭ·ṭu	कट्टु
to understand	bujh·nu	बुइन
to undress	phu·kahl·nu	फुकाल्नु
unemployed	be·kahr	बेकार

unemployment	be·*kah*·ri	बेकारी
union	sa·*mi*·ti	समिति
universe	*bi*·shwa	विश्व
university	bi·shwa·bi·*dyah*·la·ya	विश्वविद्यालय
unripe	*kāh*·co	काँचो
unsafe	a·*su*·ra·chit	असुरक्षित
until (June)	(*jun*)·sam·ma	(जुन)सम्म
unusual	a·*nau*·tho	अनौठो
up	*mah*·thi	माथि
up there	u *mah*·thi	उ माथि
uphill	u·*kah*·lo	उकालो
upward	*mahs*·ti·ra	मास्तिर
urgent	ja·*ru*·ri	जरुरी
to urinate	*pi*·sahb *gar*·nu	पिसाब गर्नु
urine	*pi*·sahb	पिसाब
useful	*kahm*·lahg·ne • *gu*·ni	कामलाग्ने • गुनी
useless	*bi*·nah·kahm·ko • *rad*·di	बिनाकामको • रद्दी
usually	*ak*·sar	अक्सर
utensil	*bhā*·ḍah	भाँडा

V

vacant	*khah*·li	खाली
vacation (holiday)	*bi*·dah	बिदा
vaccination	khop	खोप
valley	u·*pa*·tya·kah	उपत्यका
valuable	*dah*·mi • a·*mul*·ya	दामी • अमूल्य
value	bhau • mol • *mul*·ya	भाउ • मोल • मूल्य
van	*mahl*·gah·ḍi	मालगाडी
vegetables	tar·*kah*·ri	तरकारी
vegetarian	sah·kah·*hah*·ri	साकाहारी

I'm vegetarian.
ma sah·kah·*hah*·ri hū म साकाहारी हुँ

vegetation	ba·nas·pa·ti	बनस्पति
vehicle	*gah*·ḍi	गाडी
vein	*na*·sah	नसा
venereal disease	bhi·*rī*·gi	भिरिंगि
venue	sthahn	स्थान
very	*dhe*·rai • *ek*·dam	धेर • एकदम
vest	*is*·ṭa·koṭ	इस्टकोट्
view	*dri*·shya	दृश्य
village	gaū	गाउँ
vine	*la*·ha·rah	लहरा
vineyard	ang·*gur*·ko ba·*gaī*·cah	अङ्गुरको बगैंचा
visa	*bhi*·sah	भिसा
to visit	*bheṭ*·na *jah*·nu	भेट्न जानु
vitamin	*bhi*·ṭah·min	भिटामिन

voice	*swar*	स्वर
to vomit	*bahn·tah gar·nu*	बान्ता गर्नु
to vote	*mat kha·sahl·nu*	मत खसाल्नु
vulture	*gid·dha*	गिद्ध

W

to wait	*par·kha·nu*	पर्खनु

Wait!
par·kha·nu·hos! पर्खनुहोस !

waiter	*be·rah*	बेरा
to walk	*hiḍ·nu*	हिंड्नु
wall (boundary)	*par·khahl*	पर्खाल
wall (inner)	*bhit·tah*	भित्ता
wall (outer)	*gah·ro · sāhdh*	गारो • साँध
to want	*cah·ha·nu*	चाहनु

I want ...
ma·lai ... cah·hi·yo मलाई ... चाहियो
Do you want ...?
ta·paī·lai ... cah·hi·yo? तपाईलाई ... चाहियो ?

war	*la·ḍaī*	लडाई
wardrobe	*da·rahj*	दराज
warm	*nyah·no*	न्यानो
to warn	*ce·tah·wa·ni di·nu*	चेताबनी दिनु
to wash (dishes)	*mahjh·nu*	माझनु
to wash (people)	*nu·hau·nu*	नुहाउनु
to wash (things/ face/hands/feet)	*dhu·nu*	धुनु
watch	*gha·ḍi*	घडी
to watch	*her·nu*	हेर्नु
water	*pah·ni*	पानी
water (boiled)	*u·mah·le·ko pah·ni*	उमालेको पानी
water (drinking)	*khah·ne pah·ni*	खाने पानी
water (mineral)	*mi·na·ral wah·ṭar*	मिनरल बाटर
water bottle	*pah·ni·ko bo·tal*	पानीको बोतल
waterfall	*jhar·nah*	झर्ना
wave	*chahl*	छाल
way	*bah·ṭo*	बाटो

Please tell me the way to ...
... jah·ne kun bah·ṭo ho? ... जाने कुन बाटो हो ?
Which way?
kun bah·ṭo? कुन बाटो ?
Way Out
ni·kahs निकास

we	*hah·mi(·ha·ru)*	हामि(हरू)
weak	*kam·jor*	कमजोर

wealthy	*dha*·ni	धनी
to wear	la·*gau*·nu	लगाउनु
weather	*mau*·sam	मौसम
wedding	bi·*hah*	बिहा
wedding cake	bi·*hah*·ko kek	बिहाको केक
wedding present	bi·*hah*·ko u·pa·hahr	बिहाको उपहार
week	*hap*·tah	हप्ता
this week	yo *hap*·tah	यो हप्ता
to weigh	*jokh*·nu	जोख्नु
weight	jo·*khai*	जोखाइ
welcome (n)	*swah*·ga·tam	स्वागतम
to welcome	*swah*·gat gar·nu	स्वागत गर्नु
welfare	*bha*·lai	भलाइ
well (adj)	san·*cai*	सन्चै
west	*pash*·cim	पश्चिम
wet	*bhi*·je·ko	भिजेको
what	ke	के

What's he/she saying?
wa·*hāh* ke *bhan*·nu·hun·cha?   वहाँ के भन्नुहुन्छ ?
What time is it?
ka·ti ba·*jyo*?   कति बज्यो ?

wheat	*ga*·hū	गहुँ
wheel	*cak*·kah	चक्का
wheelchair	*pahng*·grah	पाङ्ग्रा
	bha·ya·ko mec	भयको मेच
when	*ka*·hi·le	कहिले

When does it leave?
ka·ti ba·je choḍ·cha?   कति बजे छोड्छ ?

where	ka·*hāh*	कहाँ

Where's the bank?
baik ka·*hāh* cha?   बैंक कहाँ छ ?

which	kun	कुन
white	se·to	सेतो
who	ko	को

Who is it?
ko ho?   को हो ?
Who are they?
wa·*hāh*·ha·ru ko ho?   वहाँहरू को हो ?

whole	*sing*·gai	सिङ्गै
whose	kas·ko	कस्को
why	*ki*·na	किन

Why is the museum closed?
sā·gra·*hah*·la·ya *ki*·na ban·da ho?   संग्रहालय किन बन्द हो ?

wide	pha·rah·*ki*·lo	फराकिलो
wife (own)	*swahs*·ni	स्वास्नी
wife (someone else's)	sri·*ma*·ti	श्रीमती

wild animal	*jang*·ga·li ja·*nah*·war	जङ्गली जनावर
to win	*jit*·nu	जित्नु
wind	*hah*·wah	हावा
window	jhyahl	झ्याल
windblown	*hah*·wah	हावा
windy	*hah*·wah *lahg*·ne	हावा लाग्ने
wing(s)	pa·khe·*tah*	पखेटा
winner	bi·*je*·tah	बिजेता
winter	*jah*·do ma·*hi*·nah	जाडो महिना
wire	tahr	तार
wise	*bud*·dhi·mahn	बुद्धिमान्
to wish	*ic*·chah *gar*·nu	इच्छा गर्नु
with	-sã·ga • -*si*·ta • -le	-सँग •-सित • -ले
within	-*bhi*·tra	-भित्र
within an hour	ek *ghan*·tah·bhi·tra	एक घण्टाभित्र
without	-*bi*·nah	-बिना
without filter	*cahl*·ni·bi·nah	चाल्नीबिना
wok (pan)	ka·*rah*·hi	कराही
woman (inf)	*ai*·mai	आइमाई
woman (pol)	*ma*·hi·lah	महिला
woman (old)	*bu*·dhi	बूढी
woman (wife)	*swahs*·ni·mahn·che	स्वास्नीमान्छे
woman (young)	ke·*ṭi*	केटी
wonderful	a·*cam*·ma *rahm*·ro	अचम्म राम्रो
wood	kahṭh	काठ
wooden article	*kahṭh*·bah·ṭa *ba*·ne·ko	काठबाट बनेको
	bas·tu	बस्तु
wool	un	ऊन
word	*shab*·da	शब्द
work	kahm	काम
to work	kahm *gar*·nu	काम गर्नु
work permit	*kahm*·ko *a*·nu·ma·ti *pa*·tra	कामको अनुमतिपत्र
worker	*maj*·dur • *kahm*·dahr	मजदुर • कामदार
worker (office)	kar·ma·*cah*·ri	कर्मचारी
workplace	kahr·*yah*·la·ya	कार्यालय
workshop	kahr·ya·shah·lah	कार्यशाला
world	sã·*sahr*	संसार
World Cup	warlḍ kap	वर्ल्ड कप
worm (animal)	*ki*·rah	कीरा
worms (intestinal)	*ju*·kah	जुका
worried	pir	पीर
to worry	pir *gar*·nu	पीर गर्नु
worse	jhan *na*·rahm·ro	झन नराम्रो
worship	*pu*·jah	पूजा
worth	bhau • mol • *mul*·ya	भाउ • मोल • मूल्य
wound	ghau	घाउ
to write	*lekh*·nu	लेख्नु
writer	le·*khak*	लेखक

writing paper	*lekh*·ne *kah*·pi	लेख्ने कापी
wrong (amiss)	be·*thik*	बेठीक
wrong (incorrect)	*ga*·lat	गलत
wrong (injustice)	an·*yah*·ya	अन्याय

I'm wrong. (not right)
ma *ga*·lat *chū* म गलत छुँ

I'm wrong. (my fault)
ma *ga*·lat *hū* म गलत हुँ

Y

yak	*caū*·ri·gai	चौरीगाई
yak meat	*caū*·ri·gai·ko *mah*·su	चौरीगाईको मासु
yam	*ta*·rul	तरुल
year	*bar*·sa • sahl	बर्ष • साल
this year	yo *bar*·sa	यो बर्ष
yellow	pa·*hē*·lo	पहेंलो
yes	ha·*jur*	हजुर
yesterday	*hi*·jo	हिजो
yesterday afternoon	*hi*·jo diū·so	हिजो दिउँसो
yesterday evening	*hi*·jo be·lu·kah	हिजो बेलुका
yesterday morning	*hi*·jo bi·*hah*·na	हिजो बिहान
yet	a·jha·sam·ma	अझासम्म
yeti	ye·ti	येति
yoga	yo·gah	योगा
yogurt	da·hi	दही
you (sg)	*ti*·mi/ta·*paī* (inf/pol)	तिमी/तपाई
you (pl)	*ti*·mi·ha·ru/ ta·*paī*·ha·ru (inf/pol)	तिमीहरू/ तपाईहरू
young	ja·*wahn*	जवान
youth	*yu*·bak	युबक

Yuck!
chi! छि !

Z

zodiac	*rah*·shi·ca·kra	राशिचक्र
zone	*any*·cal	अञ्चल
zoo	*ci*·ḍi·yah·khah·nah	चिडियाखाना

SUSTAINABLE TRAVEL

As the climate change debate heats up, the matter of sustainability becomes an important part of the travel vernacular. In practical terms, this means assessing our impact on the environment and local cultures and economies – and acting to make that impact as positive as possible. Here are some basic phrases to get you on your way …

COMMUNICATION & CULTURAL DIFFERENCES

I'd like to learn some of your local dialects.

ma·*lah*·i sthah·*ni*·ya bo·li	मलाई स्थानीय बोली
ra *bhah*·shah *sik*·na	र भाषा सिक्न
man·*lah*·gyo	मनलाग्यो

Would you like me to teach you some English?

ma ta·pah·ī·*lah*·i a·li·*ka*·ti	म तपाईंलाई अलिकति
ang·*gre*·ji *bhah*·shah	अङ्ग्रेजी भाषा
si·kah·*i*·di·ū?	सिकाइदिउँ ?

Is this a local or national custom?

| yo sthah·*ni*·ya ki | यो स्थानीय कि |
| desh·bha·*ri*·ko ca·*lan* ho? | देशभरिको चलन हो ? |

I respect your customs.

| ma ta·pah·ī·ha·*ru*·ko | म तपाईंहरुको |
| ca·*lan*·ko *ij*·jat *gar*·chu | चलनको इज्जत गर्छ |

COMMUNITY BENEFIT & INVOLVEMENT

I'd like to volunteer my skills.

ma·*lah*·i ah·*phu*·le	मलाई आफूले
jah·*ne*·ko ku·rah·*ha*·ru	जानेको कुराहरु
si·kah·*u*·na man·*par*·cha	सिकाउन मनपर्छ

Are there any volunteer programs available in the area?

tyas ṭhah·*ū*·mah ku·*nai*	त्यस ठाउँमा कुनै
swa·yam·*se*·bak	स्वयंसेवक
kahr·ya·kram·*ha*·ru chan?	कार्यक्रमहरु छन् ?

What sorts of issues is this community facing?

ya·*hāh*·kah mahn·che·ha·*ru*·le		यहाँका माछ्नेहरुले
kas·to ki·*sim*·ko		कस्तो किसिमको
du·kha·*kash*·ṭa *bhog*·nu		दुख-कष्ट भोग्नु
pa·ri·ra·*he*·ko cha?		परिरहेको छ ?

agriculture	kri·*shi*·ko	कृषिको
problem	sa·*mas*·yah	समस्या
deforestation	ban bi·*nahsh*	वन विनाश
drinking water	*khah*·ne pah·*ni*·ko	खाने पानीको
problem	sa·*mas*·yah	समस्या
electricity	bi·*ju*·li	बिजुली
flood/landslide	bah·*ḍhi* pa·hi·*ro*·ko	बाढी पहिरोको
problem	sa·*mas*·yah	समस्या
lack of education	shi·*chyah*·ko ka·*mi*	शिक्षाको कमी
migration	ba·*sah*·i·sa·*rah*·i·ko	बसाई-सराइको
problem	sa·*mas*·yah	समस्या

ENVIRONMENT

Where can I recycle this?

ma yo *ka*·hāh ri·sah·*i*·kal	म यो कहाँ रिसाइकल
gar·na sak·*chu*?	गर्न सक्छु ?

TRANSPORT

Can we get there by public transport?

hah·*mi* tya·*hāh* bas·*bah*·ṭa	हामी त्यहाँ बसबाट
jah·na sak·*chaū*?	जान सक्छौं ?

Can we get there by bike?

hah·*mi* tya·*hāh*	हामी त्यहाँ
sah·i·*kal*·mah *jah*·na	साइकलमा जान
sak·*chaū*?	सक्छौं ?

I'd prefer to walk there.

ma·*lah*·i tya·*hāh* hī·*ḍe*·ra	मलाई त्यहाँ हिँडेर
jah·na man·*lahg*·cha	जान मनलाग्छ

ACCOMMODATION

I'd like to stay at a locally run hotel.

ma·*lah*·i ya·*bī*·ko	मलाई यहाँको
mahn·*che*·le ca·lah·e·ko	मान्छेले चलाएको
ho·*tel*·mah *bas*·na man·*par*·cha	होटेलमा बस्न मनपर्छ

Can I turn the air conditioning off and open the window?

ma e·*si* ban·*da* ga·*re*·ra	म ए.सी. बन्द गरेर
jhyahl kho·*lū*?	भ्याल खोलूँ ?

There's no need to change my sheets.

me·ro o·*chyahn*·ko	मेरो ओछ्यानको
tan·nah *pher*·nu par·*dai*·na	तन्ना फेर्नु पर्दैन

SHOPPING

Where can I buy locally produced goods/souvenirs?

sthah·*ni*·ya mah·nis·ha·*ru*·le	स्थानीय मानिसहरुले
ta·*yahr* ga·*re*·kah	तयार गरेका
sah·mahn·*ha*·ru ka·*hāh*	सामानहरु कहाँ
kin·na pah·*in*·cha?	किन्न पाइन्छ ?

FOOD

Do you sell locally produced food?

ta·*pah*·ī sthah·*ni*·ya	तपाई स्थानीय
ma·*nis*·le ba·nah·*e*·ko	मानिसले बनाएको
khah·nah *bec*·nu·*hun*·cha?	खाना बेच्नुहुन्छ ?

Do you sell organic produce?

ta·*pah*·ī de·*shi*·mal ra ki·*rah*	तपाई देशीमल र किरा
mahr·ne au·*sha*·dhi	मार्ने औषधी
na·*rah*·khi ut·*pah*·dan	नराखी उत्पादन
ga·*re*·ko *khah*·nah	गरेको खाना
bec·nu·*hun*·cha?	बेच्नुहुन्छ ?

Which Nepali food should I try?

ma kun ne·*pah*·li	म कुन नेपाली
khah·nah *khah*·ū?	खाना खाउँ ?

SIGHTSEEING

Does your company hire local guides?
ta·pah·*ī*·ko kam·pa·*ni*·le
sthah·*ni*·ya ga·hi·ḍha·ru·*lah*·i
bhah·*ḍah*·mah lin·*cha*?

तपाईंको कम्पनीले
स्थानीय गाइडहरुलाई
भाडामा लिन्छ ?

Does your company donate money to charity?
ta·pah·*ī*·ko kam·pa·*ni*·le
dahn·*dhar*·ma gar·*ne*
sās·thah·*lah*·i *can*·dah
din·*cha*?

तपाईंको कम्पनीले
दान-धर्म गर्ने
संस्थालाई चन्दा
दिन्छ ?

Does your company visit local businesses?
ta·pah·*ī*·ko kam·*pa*·ni
sthah·*ni*·ya byah·*pahr*
bya·ba·sah·ya·*ha*·ru
her·na jahn·*cha*?

तपाईंको कम्पनी
स्थानीय व्यापार
व्यवसायहरु
हेर्न जान्छ ?

Are cultural tours available?
sāhs·*kri*·tik bhra·maṇ·*ha*·ru
gar·na pah·*in*·cha?

साँस्कृतिक भ्रमणहरु
गर्न पाइन्छ ?

Does the guide speak local dialects?
gah·*iḍ*·le sthah·*ni*·ya *bo*·li
ra *bhah*·sha bol·*cha*?

गाइडले स्थानीय बोली
र भाषा बोल्छ ?